HOW TO MOTIVATE PEOPLE

FRAN TARKENTON

HOW TO MOTIVATE PEOPLE

The Team Strategy for Success

with TAD TULEJA

1817

HARPER & ROW, PUBLISHERS, New York
Cambridge, Philadelphia, San Francisco,
London, Mexico City, São Paulo, Singapore, Sydney

FIRST EDITION

Designer: C. Linda Dingler

Library of Congress Cataloging-in-Publication Data

Tarkenton, Fran.
  How to motivate people.

  Includes index.
    1. Employee motivation.   I. Tuleja, Tad, 1944–
II. Title.
HF5549.5.M63T37   1986   658.3′14   85–45237
ISBN 0–06–015543–4

86 87 88 89 90 RRD 10 9 8 7 6 5 4 3 2 1

CONTENTS

INTRODUCTION: THE MISSING INGREDIENT IN MANAGEMENT:
WHAT TURNS PEOPLE ON   1

PART I: THE P.R.I.C.E. MOTIVATION SYSTEM

1   PINPOINTING   25
2   RECORDING   43
3   INVOLVEMENT   62
4   CONSEQUENCES   78
5   EVALUATION   100

PART II: TWO ESSENTIAL MOTIVATING SKILLS

6   REFLECTIVE LISTENING   119
7   MOTIVATIONAL ASSERTIVENESS   142

PART III: PUTTING IT ALL TOGETHER

8   BUILDING YOUR TEAM   165
9   CREATIVE PROBLEM SOLVING   187
10   CONFLICT MANAGEMENT   207

CONCLUSION: MOTIVATING TO WIN   226

INDEX   233

HOW TO MOTIVATE PEOPLE

THE MISSING INGREDIENT IN MANAGEMENT: WHAT TURNS PEOPLE ON

> The smartest and most agile player is useless unless he has
> also what I call the great desire, mental heat,
> the old ziperoo.
> —"PAPA BEAR" GEORGE HALAS

In over a quarter of a century of playing football, I had a lot of people—coaches, teammates, friends—try to get me "up" for a particular game or stretch of games. There was one person who did that better than anybody else—Bud Grant. Bud was the head coach of the Minnesota Vikings, for whom I quarterbacked for much of my professional career, and he was successful in getting the best out of his people because he understood one fundamental rule of human nature: If you want somebody to do something for you, the one thing you cannot do, ever, is bullshit him.

Not once in all my years of playing for Bud did I ever see him hand a player a bill of goods. From the very first day that you walked into a Vikings practice, you knew that this man was telling it like it was. You didn't get any phony, rah-rah pep talks and you didn't get any of that "We're number one" garbage, and you didn't get him threatening, or cajoling, or insulting you into better performance. With Bud Grant you knew right off

1

that there were certain things that were going to be expected of you. You knew you'd have to deliver those things if you wanted to stay with the Vikings. And you knew that if you didn't deliver, you'd soon be back picking watermelons in rural Georgia.

I don't mean he said, "Here it is, shape up now or scram." He'd tell you just what he wanted, and if you didn't do it right the first time, he'd work with you, he'd explain what you were doing wrong so you could improve. He was demanding, yes, but never impatient. Bud was a man who knew exactly what he wanted and who knew how to tell you what that was without making you feel used, or intimidated, or had.

He carried the "No bullshit" philosophy into every game we had coming. If we were going up against a team that we could beat with our shoelaces tied together, he'd say so—and he'd tell us exactly what to watch out for so we didn't get too cocky and blow it. If we were going up against a team that was better than we were, he'd tell us *that* too—and what we could do to beat the odds.

I remember one afternoon when Bud told us that the other team was better. "These guys have got more than you do," he said, straight out. "But you can still kick their tails if you play *smarter* than they do. And here's how you're going to do that."

And he proceeded to lay out all the precise, particular things we were going to have to do to play that smarter ball game. This is what I want you to do. One, two, three. And if you do these things, you're going to win the ball game. To a new player in Bud's system, who was used to the usual inspirational stuff about winning one for the Gipper and not letting your family down, it was a revelation. And it got him results.

But Grant's system of getting the best out of his players only began with what he said to us *before* the game. He always followed up afterward—after we had kicked some better team's tail, or blown a sure thing by ignoring his instructions. I might have felt turned on in the middle of a certain second quarter, and overthrown a pass because my mechanics were wrong. Grant would take me aside after the game and say, "Francis, you threw to the right receiver, but you overthrew him because your stride was too long." Those after-the-game lessons were what really counted.

You know the old expression about Nature abhorring a vacuum. It's true of human nature, too. Human nature will not abide an empty promise. And people find out real quick whose promises are empty and whose will carry the freight. You might be able to bullshit me into running through a brick wall once by telling me I "owe it to the team." But once I brush off the brick dust and get my shoulder out of the cast, you'd better be there telling me how I did and thanking me for my participation—or that wall will never be threatened again.

I don't guess that the Viking teams I played on were the best all-round athletes, or the best trained, or the highest paid players of their time. But I'll tell you one thing: we *loved* our work. We were *up* for those games. And, as a result, we performed, we gave our best. For a simple reason. We were responding, from the first game of every season, to Grant's extraordinary combination of clear, crisp directions before the game and clear, crisp feedback afterward.

Like every good coach—and like every good manager of people, no matter what the business—Grant didn't concentrate on making his people stronger or faster or more coordinated. He just enabled them to put their natural strength, and speed, and coordination together better by adding a mental component that, over and over, made all the difference.

For the past twelve years I've run a management consulting company out of Atlanta, advising hundreds of businesses on how to increase their productivity by increasing their people's performance. I've found the same thing true in business as I've found in sports: What's central to quality performance is always the *psychological* component. And the ability to instill that component in a team is what separates great coaches like Bud Grant from the many merely good ones.

How does a good manager do this? How do you get somebody to do what he ordinarily can't (or won't) do? How can you fulfill what John D. Rockefeller said was the primary goal of good management: to show "average people how to do the work of superior people"? In other words, how do you turn people on?

3

What I'm talking about is *motivation*, and every good manager knows it's critical. In the words of one of the greatest people managers, Green Bay Packers coach Vince Lombardi, "Coaches who can outline their plays on a blackboard are a dime a dozen. The ones who win get inside their players and motivate."

Lombardi proved that, and so did Grant. No game is won on the turf alone. It's won inside the head. Without what "Papa Bear" George Halas called the "old ziperoo," the best conditioned player in the world is still going to play below par. I don't care if you do three hundred one-hand pushups every morning and eat roofing nails for breakfast. If you don't have that fire in your belly when the game starts, you're going to get your tail beat by a ninety-pound weakling who does.

This isn't true just in sports. In my past twelve years as a business consultant, I've found the basic lesson of good coaching repeated again and again. If you want the best from the people in your plant, your division, your corporation, you've got to do exactly what all the great coaches have done. You've got to turn your people on.

Of course, teaching management how to turn people on has become a major industry in itself in the past decade. Because of the falling productivity of American businesses in the 1970s, dozens of solutions have been proposed to get that supposedly "lazy" factor of production, the U.S. worker, more *involved* in his work. A lot of these solutions have been presented in gimmicky, fly-by-night programs that went nowhere, although the underlying philosophy of many of the programs—the "productivity through people" approach popularized by Tom Peters and others—is a sound and necessary one.

At my company that philosophy is employed with a very practical twist. We use many of the concepts now being given lip service in the "human management" programs. We even speak about setting up Quality Circles and about what Peter Drucker, years ago, called "Self-Management by Objectives." But we take the lessons of Drucker and others one step beyond where they normally go. We add one "nonphilosophical" element—an element that is seldom discussed effectively by managers attempting to implant the CEO's latest pet program.

That element is motivation.

MOTIVATION: THE KEY TO PERFORMANCE

My experiences in professional sports and in business consulting have, of course, been very different in many ways, but there is a common feature that relates to the productivity tangle. The lesson I've learned both on the field and in the boardroom is this: *People don't change their behavior unless it makes a difference for them to do so.*

It sounds simple, doesn't it? It is simple, but it's constantly being ignored, at all levels of management and in every industry. Managers who are looking at dipping productivity figures expect their people to "shape up," to regain "pride in their work." But they expect them to do this without being given any *reason* for doing so. To put it in psychological terms, they expect their people to change their behavior (so that productivity rises), but they are either unwilling or incapable of providing them with the *motivation* they need to make that necessary change. And without motivation, nothing happens. I firmly believe that the principal reason for the frequent poor showing of "human management" is the neglect, among managers who are in a position to influence people's behavior, of that *impulse toward change* that goes under the name of motivation.

It's not that managers don't *want* to motivate their people. They do. They just don't know how to go about it. And the reason is very simple: They simply do not understand *what it is* that will turn their people on.

In this book, as in our seminars, we focus on this unknown element. We identify what it is that excites people and makes them want to work harder. We show how to use that motivating force to create real behavior change—and to make that changed behavior remain in place not just for the lifetime of some gimmicky program, but for as long as there are *people* to manage. If the day ever comes that people are entirely replaced by robots, we won't have to worry about motivation any more. Until then, it will remain the key element in making "human management" actually *work.*

I've said that motivation, in our productivity system, is the "nonphilosophical" element that sets us apart from most other "human management" programs. That point needs clarifying. I don't have anything against philosophy. But it does seem to me that, in most discussions of motivation, you get a banquet of abstract theorizing and little attention to *results*. Take your standard college-freshman course in psychology—the first and last lesson most people get in "motivation theory."

The conventional "Introduction to Motivation" begins with the observation that nobody really knows "what it is" that motivates human behavior—and then proceeds to define all the "whats" that theorists have come up with over the years as the "root cause" of why we do things. Popular candidates include the "need for achievement," the "fear of failure," the "hunger for affiliation," and "the self-actualization principle." The current favorite seems to be stimulation: motivation geniuses are filling volumes debating whether "homeostasis" or "excitation" is the real, fundamental state of the human psyche.

This is an interesting enough question, but to somebody whose fundamental interest is in motivating people to achieve better performance results, it's about as relevant as the ancient debate over the nature of the human soul. In fact, a lot of the theories you hear about the "ultimate" causes of human action remind me of theologians' arguments about ontology and first causes and free will. It's no accident that, in the early days of psychology, many people were offended by the whole science because they felt it was tampering with "God's domain."

Now, I'm a preacher's son myself, and I'm certainly not suggesting that questions about "ultimate causes" are fruitless. In a way I guess they're the only questions that really matter. But they belong in the classroom and the pulpit, not the boardroom or the factory floor. You can figure out exactly why people perform—and you can dramatically affect their performance—without understanding anything at all about the Soul. Or about its secular equivalent, the Mind.

This heretical notion is not original with me. It was first put forward by the behaviorist school of psychology, founded by John Watson just after World War I and brought to wide public attention throughout the middle years of this century by the Harvard psychologist B. F. Skinner. In this book, as in the sem-

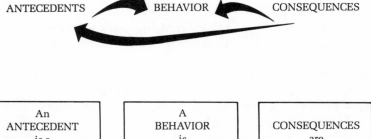

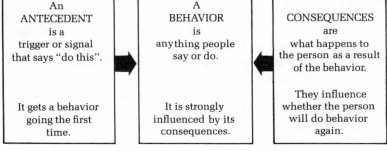

Figure 1

inars we run to improve industrial productivity, I'll be supporting a basically behaviorist position. This means that I'll be talking not about ultimate causes, but about those proximate, immediate causes that you can actually *measure*, and that you can *use* to change people's behavior.

The reason for my behaviorist bias is very practical. I've found, quite simply, that it *works*. This has been true in business no less than on the playing field. And it's just as true in every aspect of daily life.

THE "ABC MODEL": BEYOND "ATTITUDE"

The core of our company's motivational system is what we call the "ABC Model" of human behavior. You can see the ABC Model in diagram form in Figure 1. Notice that it consists of three basic elements: Antecedents, Behavior, and Consequences. Notice, too, that we define a Behavior as anything that people say or do; that Antecedents *precede* Behaviors, or get the Behaviors started; and that Consequences are what happen as a *result* of the Behaviors performed.

In the classic rat experiments of the early behaviorists, this model was very much in evidence. In one of these experiments, Skinner taught a rat to push a lever by providing it with food every time it did so. The original Antecedent here may have been the rat's accidental brushing against the lever, or it may have been the rodent's curiosity. For whatever reason the animal performed the particular Behavior of lever-pushing, though, it was immediately rewarded with food—the Consequence of the Behavior. Once it was rewarded several times, the rat made the connection between lever-pushing and eating, and continued to perform the Behavior, so it would continue to reap the reward. It had learned a previously unknown Behavior because that Behavior made a difference in its life.

Similar cause-and-effect experiments were performed with variations many times, not just on rats, but on various higher species, including humans. The critical variable in all these experiments was the Consequences, and the critical discovery was this: By controlling the Consequences of a Behavior, you could change the Behavior itself. This relates to what I said earlier in the chapter: people don't change their behavior unless it *makes a difference* to them to do so. So, if you want a rat to push a lever, make a difference to him by giving him food when he does. If you want him to stop pushing it, follow the lever-pushing with an electric shock. It may not be elegant, but it works.

This discovery—that you could alter behavior by altering its apparent effects—not only revolutionized psychiatry in the 1930s; it also has had a profound effect on the way motivation is managed, on the playing field, in the work place, indeed everywhere. The shocking lesson of Watson's and Skinner's experiments was that, if you wanted to change (improve) a person's performance in a given area, you didn't have to know the "real" or "ultimate" reason behind his current performance: that is, you didn't have to know *why* he behaved as he did. Without knowing anything at all about "unresolved Oedipal conflicts" or a person's love life, you could alter the Behavior simply by modifying the Consequences.

A lot of people didn't want to hear that. The news pissed off the psychiatrists, for example, since they were accustomed to charging forty bucks a pop for therapy sessions designed specifically to uncover "why" a given set of Behaviors was performed. It didn't tickle the humanists either. They didn't like the idea that humans were merely "talking rats," and they didn't think that psychology should confine itself to mere "manipulation" of its subjects.

We see this resistance to "manipulation" all the time in our seminars. And we see vestiges of the old-fashioned, "searching for the Soul" approach to psychology, too. Only the managers we teach don't talk about Mind or the Soul. They talk about internal make-up or personality. Usually they call it "attitude."

In teaching our system of motivation, we usually begin by asking the group members, "What do you think makes your best workers perform as they do?" and, "What makes the worst ones perform badly?" The answers are always revealing. Almost without exception, the managers focus not on things that *they* could do to influence the behavior of their people (that is, on the Consequences they could introduce for good or bad performance), but on the workers' own *internal* state—the "why" that "makes" them act the way they do.

For example, when asked to define what makes the people on their most productive shift so good, plant managers consistently say things like this: "They've got the right attitude," "They've got pride in their work," "They care about the company," and, "They've just got a lot of initiative." Asked to identify why the slow shift remains slow, they say: "That's just a lazy line," "They don't pay attention to what they're doing," and, "Just a bad attitude all around."

Explaining things by referring to an "attitude" that is impervious to management control is both the most common and the most aggravating "explanation" that managers give for why a certain level of performance is not happening. It's an easy cop-out that shifts responsibility off the manager's shoulders and identifies some tenuous but immovable "force" as the reason his people won't perform. "It's not my fault," the hidden message reads. "These guys are just bad seeds." (In other words, they're just "evil" because they won't learn *on their own* which are the right levers to push.)

Anybody who has ever played on a sports team and has seen the dramatic effect that good coaching can have knows that this is nonsense. In professional sports especially, most teams today are pretty equally matched: there's very little difference in the "talent levels" of the players on a first-ranked team and those on a team in the middle. The difference is in the quality of coaching—which is to say, the quality of "people management." Invariably in high-level sports, the most successful teams are the ones whose coaches are most skilled in "manipulating" their people toward the kind of Behaviors that win games. Exactly the same principle applies in business, and in every other situation where learning creatures (like people), not robots, are involved. So the manager who complains that his people "just won't get cracking" is really saying that *he* doesn't know how to turn them on. And—here's a news flash for you—the one who can't explain why his *best* people are doing so well is in the same boat, or soon will be. If the only clue you have to why your people perform is that will-o'-the-wisp, their "attitude," sooner or later that attitude is going to go "bad." Because it's not something you can control.

Because focusing on internal attitudes always leads to a management dead end, we advise the managers who attend our programs to focus on *externals* instead. Forget about your people's "ultimate causes" and "real" mental states, we say. You can't change those things anyway, no matter how hard you plead or preach. What you can change is their external behavior. And you do that by manipulating Consequences. That's the "ultimate cause" of all good motivation.

MOTIVATE AND DEMOTIVATE

In the rat experiment I talked about above, the manipulation of Consequences was designed to motivate the animal *toward* a particular Behavior. But you can also change the Consequences of a Behavior so that they "demotivate" the person *away* from the Behavior, and toward something more desirable. One famous example is Knute Rockne's supposed "short but sour" speech to the Notre Dame team one afternoon when they had played way below par the first half. Legend has it that, instead of a drawn-out tirade, he just walked into the locker room and said, "Oh, excuse me ladies, I thought this was the Notre Dame locker room." It got him peak performance the second half.

In this situation, Rockne was faced with a fundamental managerial question: How do you reverse a bad trend? How do you turn your people away from negative Behavior? Rockne solved the problem in a subtly behaviorist fashion. Responding to their miserable on-field performance in the first half, he offered his players a clearly demotivating Consequence: in this case, a snide insult. Because they didn't like that Consequence, they were demotivated away from the Behavior that had brought the Consequence about. And they played up to par in the second half.

Now, maybe the team had changed its "attitude" about the game, and maybe not. Maybe the players had adopted a collective "high norm Achievement motive" or a greater need for "psychic homeostasis" or an intensified "approbation-seeking quotient," and it was that changed mental construction that enabled them to win the game. I don't know. And, as somebody concerned with results, I feel about this question the way Rhett Butler felt about Scarlett O'Hara's broken heart: I don't really give a damn. In fact I don't see how anybody can really *know* what's going on in somebody else's mind: you can guess, but you can't really track it. What you can know, and observe, and track about this hypothetical situation is the change in the team's Behavior—and it's logical to assume that this came about

11

as a result of the negative *external* Consequence: the coach's sardonic put-down.

What I'm saying here about motivation and demotivation has been understood for years by behavior scientists. In fact, my terms "motivating Consequence" and "demotivating Consequence" are variants on the old laboratory chestnuts "positive and negative reinforcement." The invaluable lesson that has come out of dozens of studies of reinforcement is that this "manipulation" of an external environment does something that no quick-fix program and no "Come on, boys, let's all pull together" speech ever can do: it makes that critical *difference* to people that enables them to improve their performance.

It also—and this is the funny part—enables them to change the way they evidently *feel* about that performance. There's a wonderful irony here. Attempts to change attitudes directly almost invariably fail, while attempts to change external behavior alone often result not only in external improvement, but in a visibly improved "attitude" as well.

We see this all the time in our business. If you're a sales manager and one of your field representatives is making half as many sales calls as his colleagues, you can yell all you want about him needing to show "greater responsibility" or "more hustle." Maybe he'll respond to this pressure and maybe he won't. But put him on straight commission for a while, and you'll get immediate results: his "attitude" *and* his work will improve. The lesson is the same: Change the Consequences, and you can alter the Behavior.

But, of course, there are Consequences and there are Consequences. One of the great challenges of any manager is being able to "psych out" individuals under his command, so that he delivers the appropriate Consequences to the appropriate people at the appropriate time. What may be music to Roger's ears could be just grating to Harry or Joan, and one of the worst mistakes a manager can make in attempting to improve performance is in assuming that the pat on the back or the snide remark or the "commission only" ploy will work for everybody the same way. In the chapter on Consequences, I'll go into some detail on this point. Now I just want to mention what is probably the single most common problem in getting managers to motivate and demotivate: the resistance on the part of many managers to accept the very concept of Consequences itself.

THE 4:1 SYNDROME—AND THE REVERSE

Many of the folks we advise on Consequences and reinforcement react initially as if we were asking them to learn a new language over the weekend (which, in a sense, we are). Over the years we have heard a variety of "logical" and traditional complaints against concentrating on "externals."

First of all, many managers resist the idea of altering Consequences because, as I said above, it gives them an easy out: it enables them to shift the blame for falling productivity entirely onto the "bad" worker's shoulders. It's the old "pass the buck" routine perfected in military circles, and often (and disastrously) used in many other social circles as well. The general yells at the colonel and the colonel yells at the lieutenant, and the lieutenant, whose squad is responsible for the snafu, doesn't ask himself, "How can I get these guys moving?" Instead he just yells at the private. And nothing changes.

Secondly, as I hinted at before, many managers are uncomfortable about manipulating Consequences because they don't like the idea of "manipulation" itself. It has a real bad press, that word. If you're manipulating somebody, it means you're pulling his strings when he doesn't know it; it means you're putting one over on him. And nobody likes to do that. At least nobody likes to be *thought* of as doing it. In fact, we all manipulate each other all the time. One of the dictionary meanings of "manipulate" is simply "to manage or utilize skillfully." When a line manager increases the productivity of his people by 12 percent with the promise of an end-of-year bonus, isn't he manipulating them? When a coach gets superhuman effort out of a bunch of mere humans by threatening them with two hundred pushups each, isn't that manipulation? Sure it is. It's just not recognized as such. Sometimes I think that, in business, managers are less afraid of *being* manipulative than of carrying around the name.

A final reason that the use of Consequences is rare in business is that many hard-nosed managers are categorically opposed to giving out positive reinforcement because they feel that this will cause their people to lose "respect" for them, or because they feel there's no reason to reward someone for doing something that he's supposed to be doing anyway. This last objection to the idea of changing Consequences is extremely common among managers who have worked their way up the hard way, and think everybody else should, too.

You know the kind of guy I mean. He's got one string on his violin, and it plays "Nobody gave me nothing." He got dumped on for thirty years by people who retired five years ago, and now he's in charge of a bunch of junior managers who weren't even born thirty years ago, and he's going to make them pay for the stupidities of the last generation. No matter how good they are, he got *his* ass kicked, and so will they.

This unwillingness to reward (to positively reinforce) good behavior is probably the single most important reason behind certain managers' inability to effect change in their people. It's also a critical factor in the failure of most "human management" programs to address the real day-to-day problems of operating businesses. I said earlier that what we add to those programs is the critical element of motivation. One of the most innovative, and consistently effective, features of our motivation approach is that we encourage positive reinforcement not just for "superior" work but for so-called "normal" behavior as well. In many firms that's considered a "radical," even dangerous idea.

In our programs we talk about a "4:1 Syndrome." In most business situations, and indeed in most human situations, we feel that, given reasonably clear directions about what they're supposed to be doing, most people will do a good job about four times as frequently as they will do a below-par or simply lousy job. People who screw up their basic tasks more frequently than that just don't last very long, so that it makes sense to assume that, other things being equal, the average person is going to perform his or her work *at least adequately* about 80 percent of the time.

Now, assuming that managers want good rather than bad behavior, assuming they want productivity and performance to remain at least adequate at all times, they should reinforce that 80 percent figure by motivating and demotivating their people in approximately the same proportion as the good and bad Behaviors that they see. It's common sense, isn't it? The person who works well four days out of five ought to be praised four times as often as he's dumped on.

But guess what? That's exactly the opposite of what happens.

In most businesses, reinforcement appears as a pernicious mirror image of behavior, rather than an accurate gauge of its effectiveness. A line supervisor will work well 80 percent of the time, but 80 percent of the comments that his plant manager makes to him will focus on that 20 percent of the time that he is performing *under* par! The 80 percent of the time that he works well will simply go by without comment, because that's what he's "supposed" to be doing.

Back in 1970, when I was quarterbacking for the New York Giants, the team owner, a quiet, contemplative man named Wellington Mara, gave a midseason talk that I will never forget. At that point our record for the season was 0–3, the third loss having been to New Orleans a couple of days before. We had played good ball against them—not great ball, but good ball—and lost because of what films later showed was clearly an official's incorrect call. No matter. We knew we had really won that game, and so did Wellington Mara. He told us that straight off, and then he told us that he knew we were a solid ball club, and that someday—maybe next Sunday against the Philadelphia Eagles—we were going to turn this slow start around and make it to the playoffs.

It was a solid, simple, low-key speech that, in retrospect, typifies for me what motivation ought to be about. Mara wasn't talking to superstars, and he knew it. He was talking to a group of hard-working guys who, in their last time on the field, had performed "at least adequately," and had gotten no strokes at all for it. He gave us those strokes. With the simple confidence he projected, he let us know that the 4:1 performance syndrome was real, and that we were, most of the time, doing our jobs pretty well. No rah-rah. No "Let's do better next time." Just the facts and a quiet thank you.

With Mara's words in our minds, we took the field against Philadelphia the following Sunday and beat them 30–23. It was the first in a string of victories that would get us second place that year in the NFC eastern division with a 9–5 record. No champagne parties. But all in all not a bad showing. And a lot of it due, I'm convinced, to Mara's timely encouragement.

That kind of thing is so rare, in business as well as sports, that it stands out dramatically when it happens. Which is pretty weird when you consider the good effects it can have when it's used.

Now, I don't mean you should praise people for doing nothing, or that you should let lousy performance get by. There's nothing wrong with criticizing a worker's lack of performance, and, in fact, if you don't do that, he's going to screw up even more. But what about the adequate 80 percent? Isn't it illogical to jump on him when he's doing badly and to *ignore* him when he's doing well? Isn't that going to give him the idea that, as long as he doesn't visibly and flagrantly screw up, nobody is going to notice that he's there? And isn't there a possibility that, since we all crave attention of *some* sort, he will actually be *encouraged* to perform badly, because bad performance at least gets him noticed?

I'm not being facetious, although a traditionally trained manager might think so. In our productivity consulting business we continually study the effects of positive reinforcement, negative reinforcement, and *no* reinforcement, and we come continually to the same conclusions. We will speak in some detail about these in the chapter on Consequences, but the basic facts are these:

1. Behavior that is reinforced by *positive* Consequences tends to *continue* or to *increase*. If your child cleans up her room without being asked and you reward her by taking her to Baskin-Robbins, she will clean the room again. If a plant supervisor implements an effective new preventive maintenance system and the vice-president of his division sends him an appreciative letter, that system will be checked and updated.

2. Behavior that is demotivated by *negative* Consequences tends to *decrease*. There are some wrinkles to this basic observation, which we'll iron out in a section on the "Punishment Effect" in another chapter, but the central observation is valid. If the child keeps her room messy for a week and you deprive her of weekend TV privileges until it is clean, the chances are that some picking up will begin before the *Smurfs* show starts on Saturday morning. If the vice-president calls the supervisor on the carpet for having no sound PM policy, he will look to that deficiency in the near future.

3. Good, productive Behaviors that are *not* reinforced in any way tend to *decrease* over time. This is what we call the "Extinction Effect," and it is of enormous importance to anyone who wishes to motivate others. If your child cleans her room and you say nothing because she's "supposed to keep it clean and you don't want to spoil her," don't look for it to be cleaned again next week. If the plant manager's herculean effort is seen by top management as "just part of his job description," expect Hercules to turn into Tom Thumb. The point is infrequently noticed: nobody will continue to perform well unless you reinforce his motivation to do so. You've got to *keep* making that difference.

Because Extinction is lurking around every behavioral corner in human interaction, and because positive reinforcement is the only way to combat its ill effects, I'll speak a great deal in this book about how to achieve effective reinforcement of desirable Behaviors—especially when those Behaviors are thought to be "givens." It has been our experience in a wide range of different industries that today's given, if it is taken for granted, inevitably turns into a forgotten: the doleful results of that process are today everywhere evident in American industry. I firmly believe that one of the American business community's principal challenges in this decade is to overcome the traditional managerial view that "you don't reward somebody for doing what he's supposed to do," and to move toward a management dynamic in which there is just as much energy expended in keeping the up side up as in keeping the down side down.

PRODUCTIVITY THROUGH PEOPLE

This requires a lot more than pretty speeches and midweek seminars on "people matter" topics for select groups of middle management. It requires nothing less than a reorientation of management philosophy and culture away from the old adversarial view and toward a "participative management" or "team concept" approach. And I mean reorientation on all levels, not just a blowsy pep talk by the CEO, a few trial Quality Circles, and back to business as usual.

The real reason most of the "human management" approaches to the productivity problem have failed is not that they are irrelevant to business reality, but that they are *extremely* relevant, and yet have not been *recognized* as such, by the vast majority of managers. They have been force-fed into various management structures without a serious understanding of the *behavioral changes* that are necessary to make them more than philosophy. They have been bandied about in board meetings, but have not really been integrated into actual day-to-day business reality, because it is still widely (though erroneously) believed that, given the opportunity, people want to get away with doing nothing. If you believe that, naturally, you're going to look on the manager's job as indistinguishable from that of a policeman's.

The idea of "productivity through people" has been around now for decades, and in spite of the fact that some businesses have used it to extremely good effect, it has not yet caught on widely in business circles, and that is one major reason why this nation's industrial base is not yet out of the low-productivity woods. The reason is that, to be truly effective, the concept itself has to be *reinforced*, and at every level of a business's operation. Unfortunately, this is still a novel concept in many

American firms, and especially (and ironically) in those smoke-stack industries whose innovation and forthrightness built our economic base in the first place.

There are instructive exceptions. One of the most famous is that of the California computer firm Hewlett-Packard, which has not only endorsed a "people-centered" philosophy for years, but reinforces that philosophy at every level. Any business executive can get up and spout platitudes about how "people matter" and about how "we all have to pull together now." Any business can print up posters about motivation and productivity and paste them up on plant walls. But unless every person in the organization understands that people really *do* matter, unless every employee from CEO to night janitor knows that better Behavior will make a *difference* to them, it's all sound, and fluff, and P.R. (which, with fifty cents, will buy you a cup of coffee).

When William Hewlett, cofounder of Hewlett-Packard, speaks of his company's commitment to "the human side of management," people *do* listen, because they know from experience that it's not just stockholder-report window-dressing. The intimate and frequent contact at H-P between front-office managers, line supervisors, and production workers is seen not as the latest MBA gimmick, but as a matter of business survival. People at Hewlett-Packard understand that management, from the CEO's office on down, do intend to listen to their people, do value individual input, and do see an intimate and constant connection between productivity and people.

At Hewlett-Packard, that connection is reinforced by a company-wide profit-sharing plan that gives yearly, measurable reinforcement to behaviors that improve productivity. Because of the way the plan is structured, every H-P employee understands that if he falls down on the job, his bonus is going to fall, too, and that if he gives it 110 percent, his bankbook is going to show the difference. That's using Consequences well, to create not smarter "rats," but a team of motivated individuals who give a damn where their company is going.

But manipulation of financial rewards is only one motivating factor and—take a tip from someone who played in a six-figure league for eighteen years—it is *never* the most important one.

If higher pay and generous benefit plans were enough to boost performance levels, the General Motors work force would be out-performing Toyota three to one. That just ain't so, because the Consequences that really get folks moving are never just monetary ones. They're all intangibles. Things like a memo of appreciation. Coffee and doughnuts when you don't expect them. Wellington Mara's quiet speech.

I know it sounds corny. But it's true. Pay hikes and bonuses don't hurt, of course, since we all like what money will buy. But like the Beatles used to say, it won't buy you love, and to some curious and maybe immeasurable degree, the most effective motivating Consequences are seen as a kind of love: they're the human touches that make a job worth doing, whatever the level of pay. And this is most important when the person you're trying to motivate is no superstar, but just another "usually adequate" sales rep, or supervisor, or secretary.

Unfortunately, it's precisely these folks that many managers prefer to ignore. They have time to punish the worker whose sloppiness costs the plant thirty-seven minutes of down time. They have time to tack up an "Employee of the Week" award to thank the one worker who really stands out. But that leaves a huge number of people in between, people who are neither "eagles" nor slackers, and who are simply trying to meet their basic obligations by performing "at least adequately" under pressure. One of the principal lessons of this book is that those people need reinforcement, too—and in fact may actually need it more than the Employee of the Week or the slacker.

You do not motivate those people by resorting to uplifting speeches. No pep talk is going to get somebody moving unless it's linked to specific Behaviors and specific Consequences. That is the first and most important lesson of the motivational system I'll be laying out in this book.

Why should you care about that lesson? Because it's a simple matter of survival. I don't care if you're an NFL linebacker, a middle manager in a steel production plant, or somebody who's just landed a job with a huge and supposedly "faceless" corporation. Whatever your situation, you're going to have to deal with people, and you're going to have to get them, one way or another, to perform in ways that are to your advantage and not against it. If you want to survive, that is.

The secret to "getting people to perform" your way is motivation. And the secret to motivation is understanding the differences between what turns people on and what turns them off.

That's what this book is about. In it I've distilled a dozen years of productivity-improvement experience, and almost two decades of NFL leadership experience, into a model of behavior management that can work for you, in your situation, right now. The primary focus here is a business one. In this book I ask the current generation of managers to meet a stimulating challenge. The challenge is in a sense analogous to the challenge faced by the great nineteenth-century entrepreneurs: those up-from-poverty idea jockeys who, with little more than mother wit and a few opportunities, transformed the North American continent into the greatest industrial force the world has ever known. They did that by being willing to take risks, and by taking responsibility for their actions. We have come to a watershed in American business culture where that same sense of risk-taking and accountability is again desperately needed. Whether or not it is met well will depend not just on managerial "will" and "attitude" but on business leaders' ability to apply some time-tested reinforcement principles to every "human management" situation they encounter. You can take this text as a playbook to enable you to do that more effectively.

Obviously what I'm saying here has an application beyond the business community, and I hope that the book may also assist those fathers and mothers, husbands and wives, close friends and casual acquaintances, that have their own "people management" problems, and who would profit by a fuller understanding of how to get others to do things "your way."

Whether you are a business executive wondering how to get a sluggish assembly line to come up to speed, a carpool driver plagued by a consistently late arrival, or a working mother whose husband just "doesn't do dishes," you share a common human dilemma: how to get a "significant other" to behave in a fashion that more closely approximates what you feel is productive or otherwise desirable. The principles outlined in this book will show you how to affect that other person's behavior not in a simply manipulative or rigidly controlling manner, but in a way that ultimately benefits you both. To some extent the root lesson of "participative management" is the root lesson of all human interaction: that a combination of Consequences and cooperation is bound to create better productivity than any mixture of pep talk and command.

My company, the Tarkenton Productivity Group, has put that lesson in place in countless businesses plagued by productivity problems. We do it by teaching both workers and management a few basic behavioral principles, and by showing them how to apply those principles on the job through a coherent, well-structured system. We call it the P.R.I.C.E. Motivation System.

The acronym P.R.I.C.E. stands for "Pinpointing, Recording, Involvement, Consequences, and Evaluation." In the following section I'll be explaining how you can incorporate these elements into your business to turn your people on effectively.

PART I
THE P.R.I.C.E.
MOTIVATION SYSTEM

ONE

PINPOINTING

> We can all be geniuses because one definition of genius is
> the infinite capacity for taking pains. Perfection in details is
> essential. Generalities don't count.
> —KNUTE ROCKNE

Any time you try to change your teammates or coworkers' performance, you face a problem of discrepancy—a difference between what is happening at that moment and what *you want* to have happen in the future. Your aim is to bridge that discrepancy by motivating the person, by turning him or her on. The only way you can do that is to demonstrate to the person that it's going to make a difference to *him* if he changes.

Showing him that is tricky enough in itself, even when you know exactly what's wrong in the situation, and understand exactly what Behavior changes are going to make the difference. A lot of managers never even get that far. They know that *something* is wrong with the performance picture, but they have trouble defining exactly *what*. As a result their attempts at motivation fall flat. Since they can't visualize the distance between "here" and "there" accurately themselves, they don't describe it properly to the person they're trying to motivate, he doesn't understand where it is he's supposed to be going—and nothing changes.

You've probably heard the expression "getting all your ducks in a line." In business it usually means getting all the variables of a complicated deal under control at the same time, so you can solve the problem or make the sale as neatly as the hunter who brings down his birds with no fuss—as if they were lined up in a shooting gallery. Well, trying to get somebody motivated to change without knowing exactly what you want him to do is like hunting ducks with a blindfold on. If the fields are full of the critters, you can pull off a couple of barrels blind, and maybe, just maybe, you'll bring one home for dinner. But it's not likely. As Texas football coach Darrell Royal says about the "breaks" his team's supposed to have gotten from time to time: "You've got to be in a position for luck to happen. Luck doesn't go around looking for a stumblebum."

Not in football, not in duck-hunting, and not in business either. As a manager who needs to get his people up for changing their behavior, unless you know what you're looking for and what steps you need to take to get there, you're just like the blindfolded duck hunter or Coach Royal's stumblebum. *Maybe* the good Lord will look down and say, "Let's help this bozo out." But it's not likely. You want to solve a performance problem, you've got to do just what the old duck hunter does: size up the quarry, and *take aim.*

In my company we use the term "Pinpointing" to mean about the same thing as "taking aim." Pinpointing is the first step in our P.R.I.C.E. motivation system—the first step in the "P.R.I.C.E." you've got to be willing to pay if you want to move from a lousy "here" to a more satisfying "there."

When I talk about the need for Pinpointing in corporate and industrial operations, I use the term both generally and very specifically. Generally it's a synonym for "aiming" or "focusing precisely." Specifically, I use it to highlight the need to focus on:

1. individual *objectives,* either personal or collective, that can feed into company-wide goals

2. individual *Behaviors* done by one or more of the people whose performance concerns you

3. individual *outcomes* which are the result of those Behaviors and which may or may not coincide with the objectives you want

The three are clearly related, and I'll be talking about connections between them throughout this chapter.

PINPOINTING: DEFINITIONS

First, let me clarify the difference between Behaviors and outcomes, since the two are very often confused. A Behavior is simply something that a person says or does. I flick on a light switch, or throw a screen pass, or complain to a friend about the heat. Those are Behaviors. An outcome is what happens as the result of the Behavior. The light goes on, the pass is caught or intercepted, my friend hands me a beer. Those are outcomes. Of course many outcomes (catching the pass, handing the beer) can be Behaviors also—and can lead to further outcomes. But the basic distinction is important to keep in mind, because managers frequently focus *only* on outcomes, ignoring the Behaviors that have caused them, and as a result fail to get results, because they've skipped over the source of the problem.

This is one of the most common, and most commonly missed, of all managerial errors. It happens because, as I said earlier, many managers are wary of addressing personal Behaviors—they're embarrassed or think it's none of their business—and prefer to focus on "results." "I don't give a damn how they do it," an executive told me once. "I want a 30 percent share of that market." But he wasn't willing to investigate, and "manipulate," the various activities (Behaviors) of his people that might get him the 30 percent. Predictably, he didn't get it.

I've run across a lot of corporate honchos in positions like this executive's. They're used to reading the quarterly P&L reports, but they take them in as if they were created in a vacuum—as if some magical machine spewed out a 14 percent increase in volume one month, and a 2 percent drop the next, without any *people* being involved. The truth is that every P&L statement is an outcome that is created by an accumulation of thousands of "insignificant" Behaviors, from the drafting of the report itself to the pushing of a little yellow button down on

Line B approximately fourteen times an hour. If the guy responsible for pushing the button doesn't perform that Behavior correctly, the P&L is going to be different. And the president can yell all he wants to about the need to "lift the profit picture." Unless he—and all his managers—understand that the yellow-button Behavior is part of that total picture, the P&L is going to stay where it is.

So the first lesson of Pinpointing is that, if you want to get anything done in business, you have to start at the beginning. You have to start by focusing on Behaviors.

In my company we do that in a very precise manner. When we teach managers in our client companies how to Pinpoint their people's Behaviors, we ask them to ask themselves the following questions:

1. Is the Behavior *observable*? That is, can it be seen and/or heard? If it can't be, it's not a Behavior. We've found this question to be a good check against the all too common tendency to confuse "attitudes" and "personalities" with real Behaviors. Say a production line has a high rate of breakdowns. We might ask the supervisor of the line to define the Behavior problem: to Pinpoint the activity that's causing the problem. A lot of managers will say, "Those guys are just screwing up; they're too lazy to work up to speed." Maybe that's true, but it's *not* a Pinpoint. In this case an example of a Pinpoint would be: "The foreman is calling for a slowdown three or four times every hour." To use Pinpointing properly, you start with that *observable* Behavior; later you can figure out why it's happening.

2. Is it *specific* enough that two independent observers could agree the Behavior is happening? Again, this is a check against subjectivity. A manager plagued by breakdowns or a sales director hampered by unfilled quotas might have a "general" idea that the problem is faulty maintenance or seasonal industry slowdown. Maybe he'll Pinpoint the problem by saying "Alex doesn't do the daily PM checks he's supposed to" or "Janet isn't making enough sales calls." That's possible, but if another observer swears that the checks or the calls *are* being made, you'd better check for subjective bias on the part of the first observer.

If two *independent* observers can say, "Alex does checks on Monday, Wednesday, and Friday," then—and only then—do you have a Pinpointed Behavior.

3. Can the Behavior be *quantified*? That is, can it be measured accurately in times performed and/or rate of frequency of performance? We ask our clients to describe each "Behavior" they witness in terms of *numbers per unit of time,* rather than in vague and subjective terms like "a lot," "pretty regularly," or "not enough." If the units you're supposed to be shipping out are piling up on the loading dock, it's reasonable to assume that they're not moving "fast enough." But in analyzing a problem like this in terms of the P.R.I.C.E. motivation system, you've got to start with specifics: To Pinpoint the Behaviors involved, you don't say, "They're loading the trucks too slow." Instead, you quantify: "Last week, the eight-to-four crew loaded an average of 1.3 trucks an hour."

The value of making sure that the Behaviors you're talking about are observable, specific, and quantifiable should be clear. It brings the whole business of analyzing problems down to the nuts-and-bolts level. It clears away the vague, accusatory garbage that often gets in the way of real problem solving, and it forces people to look at what is actually *happening.* If you start your motivational process with Pinpointing, you've gotten to a level of understanding that is already light years ahead of the level attained by the guy who only wants to know "Why the hell aren't we doing better?" By focusing on specifics, you know what's going on, step by step, in your plant or department's operation. You know exactly where you *are,* right now.

The next thing you need to know is how to get from *here* to *there.* You do that by using Pinpointing in the setting of your *objectives.*

PINPOINTING AND OBJECTIVES

Setting precise and quantifiable objectives can be just as much of a hassle as identifying Pinpointed Behaviors, and a lot of the time this has as much to do with organizational structures as it does with personal idiosyncracies. Every large business operates on a series of organizational levels, and the objectives relevant to each of those levels—although they're supposed to reinforce each other—sometimes don't. Divisional objectives may seem unrealistic to an individual plant manager, his objectives may seem poorly defined to one of his line supervisors, and so on. It's easy to state in an annual report, "Our overall corporate objective for the coming fiscal year is to increase penetration in our core market," but what does that mean to the accounting department, or the two new sales representatives you just hired, or the guy who pushes the yellow button? They all have their objectives, too, and if their objectives aren't met, your increased penetration goal isn't going anywhere. But how do you get all their objectives together? How do you get everybody geared up so that the fulfillment of their individual objectives contributes to overall success?

There are two main approaches to this problem. One is the "top down" approach, where the guys in the blue suits on the twelfth floor define the "Big Picture" that the company is supposed to paint, and then pass orders down the line that everybody has to "pull his weight" so it gets done. Managers who use this "top down" approach tend to think of the "real" work of management as long-range planning ("shaping the corporate vision," or some such malarkey) rather than actually running the business. The idea is that, as long as you state the mission with enough energy and conviction and pizazz, all the things that need to get done to bring it into being *will* get done. Somehow. By somebody. The vision is so exciting; who's *not* going to want to pull his weight?

You know what happens with that approach to corporate objectives? Top management starts to forget that it's *people* who actually make a business work. The blue suits start to spend all their time in the air-conditioned offices, and flying around to conferences, and sitting on the boards of other businesses, and they hire cadres of smart young kids from Stanford and Harvard to show them how to rearrange paper assets, and pretty soon they're making so much money in stock options and enjoying the company plane so much that they can't quite remember what the business *does*, which is to make windshield wipers or door frames or stuffed dolls. And when they forget that—when they start to believe that the business of management is to manage figures rather than Behaviors—they're done for, and so is the business.

I've seen this again and again in modern corporations. We're so damn paper-oriented and number-hungry and "visionary" about long-range goals that we don't know what's going on day to day. The average "chief executive" today knows the annual figures all right, but he doesn't have a clue as to what *put* them there. And that distant, heady view of management filters down through the ranks of junior management, because of course everybody wants to be like Mr. Big. Eventually nobody in management wants to get his hands dirty, and when that happens, you're sunk.

The other way of setting objectives in a large organization is the "bottom up" method, that "radical," dangerously democratic approach to goal-setting where the people who actually do the work get to decide what they can do, and how, and by when. The overall company "vision" might still be set at the top, but the ways of implementing that vision are established, and constantly revised, by people who understand that getting your hands dirty is the only way *anything* gets done. I'll tell you from my experience on the football field and in dozens of American companies—in everything from heavy manufacturing to banking—that this second method, the "participatory management" method of setting objectives, is the only one that works, long term. I can explain why with two examples, the first one from my Viking days.

Example One: Getting to the Super Bowl

In 1975 the owners of the Vikings wanted to send us to the Super Bowl more than Dumbo wanted to fly. They were obsessed with the idea, and we didn't have anything against it either. We knew, and they knew, that wanting to get there was essential, but it wasn't exactly a game plan. The question was this: How could we transform that Super Bowl objective into a reality? What specific, individual steps did we have to take to get from where we were to New Orleans?

We had a solid defensive team, but had been coming up short on offense. So before we could achieve the Super Bowl objective, we'd have to secure a preliminary objective, that of making our offense the best in the business. We did it by using Pinpointing. We didn't call it Pinpointing; we called it something like "offensive game plan." But it amounted to the same thing.

It worked like this. At the opening of the 1975 season, I sat down with the Viking offensive coordinator Jerry Burns and our offensive line coach John Michaels and made a list of the critical variables to success that would have to occur if we were going to carry our load. For example, we knew from the record books that playoff teams, over the previous years, had averaged four yards per rush during the regular season. So we made one of our preliminary objectives "an average gain of four yards per rush." We found out what the previous playoff teams had done in terms of numbers of first downs, percentage of time scored once they were inside the ten, and so on. And we made each one of those items an objective on our offensive strategy list. These were the Pinpointed objectives that we were going to have to attain if we wanted to get to the larger objective of playing in the Super Bowl.

Then we took the analysis one step further. In order to attain these preliminary objectives, we knew the team members would have to perform certain designated activities—certain Behaviors—that would lead to the required outcomes. So we Pinpointed those Behaviors too.

For example: one of the most common mistakes made on any football team is a lineman's blocking the wrong person. This isn't surprising, considering that a pro football playbook might contain two hundred running plays against eight or ten different defenses, and considering that on any given play the linemen have to decide which way to turn in about two or three seconds. It's not an easy thing to remember, and yet forgetting it can be disastrous. A guy could have steam coming out of his ears and hit the left defensive tackle like a freight engine, but it wouldn't do us any good if his target was supposed to have been the middle linebacker. So the Pinpointed objective in this case would be simply to block the right person, not necessarily to block with the right "attitude." Like good behaviorists, we focused not on attitude alone, but on the *specific activities that* would give the attitude *direction.*

We made it to the Super Bowl that year, and I give a lot of the credit not just to the drive and motivation of my teammates (that was *always* there), but to the Pinpointing technique that enabled us to *focus* that motivation where it would do the most good.

What we'd done, in effect, was to *isolate the ingredients of winning,* and then concentrate on making them second nature. There's an awful lot of data in a football game, and it can get lost in the shuffle unless you break it down into its components, and then work on each one individually. Putting that strategy together was a little like putting an airplane model together. We didn't throw one hundred and fifty pieces in a box together, shake it, and say, "Let's go get 'em." We sorted everything out, labeled the pieces, put it together step by step—and came up with a championship offense.

Pinpointing your problem areas and areas where performance has to change can be just as critical in business, since you have just as much free-floating data there as anybody does in football. It's fine to say "Let's win one for the Gipper," but your team is still going to have to know *how.* Remember old "Wrong Way Corrigan"? He was the young pilot who, in 1938, started a night flight from New York to California, and ended up in Ireland. That boy was motivated as hell. Which would have been enough if wishes were horses. Because they're not, you need the Pinpointing technique: it points you in the right direction from the start.

Example Two: Inverting the Pyramid

My company was called on once to solve a productivity problem that illustrates perfectly the limits of "top down" objective setting. The firm with the problem had just hired a new CEO, and the guy was fanatically gung-ho about boosting profits in his first year. Nothing wrong with that, of course. But, like a lot of "distant" top managers, he thought he could bring that about by exhorting his people to "work harder." One of his favorite expressions was the "up from your bootstraps" slogan "When the going gets tough, the tough get going."

Great expression. But it wasn't going to get the job done. One of the first things we told the fired-up CEO was that if he wanted his people to "get going" he first had to tell them *where*. And the way to do that was by Pinpointing.

The company in question owned one large manufacturing plant out on the West Coast. It contained six different assembly lines, each one employing about ninety workers, divided into three shifts, or "teams," of thirty. Top management wanted "the plant" to produce faster and better, so that profit would rise. What they seemed to be forgetting is that "the plant" didn't run by itself. It was productive or nonproductive as a direct result of the many individual Behaviors on those six lines. "If you want more profit," we told the CEO, "and if your profit is linked to more production, then you start by looking at the factors that control production. Those are human factors. And you've got five hundred and forty of them in that plant."

If you want to achieve your overall, general corporate goal of "higher profits" this year, we told him, you have to translate that goal into a meaningful objective at *every level* of the organization. And the farther "down" you go in the organization, the more *specific* the objectives have got to become. For example, at the level of plant-wide operation, the general goal of higher profits might be linked to two Pinpointed objectives:

1. to "increase productivity by 15 percent by June 30"
2. to "increase volume by 3 percent by March 31"

At the next "lower" level, that of the team operations of the various lines, the Pinpointed objectives would have to be more precise: they might include "increase hours of running time by 25 percent by June 30" and "increase units produced per day by 10 percent by September 30." For staff functions, they might include "deliver all monthly market reports by the 15th of each month" or "decrease R&D overhead 10 percent by April 10."

Finally, at the level of individual team members, Pinpointed objectives would include such "unimportant" activities as "feeding the line at seven units an hour," and "fixing jam-ups within five minutes" and "performing daily lubrication checks."

"That daily lubrication check," I remember telling the CEO, "is just as important to your profit picture as anything being done in finance or marketing. If you don't believe that—and if the managers down on the line don't believe it—it doesn't matter what else you do. You can forget about the profit advance."

In directing the CEO's attention to the "bottom" level of his operation, I was flying in the face of conventional wisdom, which says that the really important decisions in an organization are made at the top, and that if those decisions are sound, the day to day will take care of itself. It comes from the old picture of the "organization as a pyramid," where "orders" flow down from the apex, and are carried out dutifully at the bottom. It doesn't work that way. You should really think of large organizations not as traditional pyramids, but as "inverted pyramids," or as "funnels," where the necessary work gets done at the broad, multi-member "top" of the funnel, and the goodies (productivity, profit) flow *down* to "top" management.

The bottom line is this. You can't motivate the guy making $12.35 an hour to care about your billion-dollar profit with the same intensity that the CEO cares about it. You *can* motivate him to do the daily lubrication check and other Pinpointed Behaviors, if he sees that it makes a difference to him to perform them. When (and only when) he cares about making that check will the billion-dollar profits follow.

HOW TO PINPOINT AN OBJECTIVE: FIVE CRITERIA

Start at the "bottom," start small, and start specific. Those are the general guidelines you want to follow in using the Pinpointing technique. Let me expand a little bit on those guidelines, by outlining a few criteria that we use to make our clients' Pinpointing more reliable. If you're facing a problem that relates to motivation and are considering remedies to solve it, I suggest you look at each objective with the following questions in mind:

1. *Can it be measured accurately?* Objectives, no less than Behaviors, have got to be quantifiable in order to make any sense to the people who are supposed to be aiming for them. "Higher productivity" means nothing. If you set your objective as "higher productivity," an 0.01 percent increase in production can be interpreted as "objective attained." Unless you're turned on by flat growth curves, you don't want to settle for that. A good, Pinpointed objective always includes the following information: it says specifically (that is, numerically) *what* needs to be accomplished, by *whom*, and by what *date*. In our seminars we use the following model for writing objectives:

"To (action verb) (quantifiable improvement in designated area) by (date)."

And we add the name of the person or persons who are going to be responsible for the objective.

Some examples, following the model. "To reduce waste on Joe Gaffey's production line by 0.8 percent by July 1." "To deliver 75 percent of outstanding shipments by end of this month; shipping department foremen responsible." "To complete half of the ABC financial statements by April 10; supervisor Judith Carson."

The advantage of setting objectives in quantifiable terms like these is twofold. First, you know exactly what you're aiming for. Second, you know exactly when you've achieved it. If there are eight ABC financial statements in all and Carson completes three of them by April 10, you know the objective has not been attained. You can't know that if you originally set the objective as "getting some headway on the ABC statements."

There's a motivational benefit, too. It's a hell of a lot easier to psych people up for going somewhere if they know the destination in advance. Sure, some folks just like to drive, and I'm not saying there's anything wrong with that. But do it on your vacation time, not in the office or the factory floor. Because if you just "drive" in the general direction of "improvement," you're going to get nowhere. And you'll get there alone.

2. *Is it realistic?* In other words, can it be done? And—even more to the point—can it be done by improving the effectiveness of *human* (rather than mechanical) performance? Maybe you'd like that production line to churn out three times as many units as it's doing now, so you can fill a sudden, increased demand. Fine. But if the running capacity of the line is only twice its current speed, you can motivate the hell out of your people there and you're still going to fall short of your goal. Even if you can perform the dubious task of getting the human actors involved to double their speed of operation.

The first big client I had when I started my consulting business was a North Carolina-based Cannon Mills plant. They had a headache with turnover, and they didn't know why. At the time I had one employee: a sharp young behavioral specialist. After checking out the Cannon operation for several weeks, he told me that the line managers there were so gung-ho about meeting production quotas that they were creating their own "law of diminishing returns." You know how that works. You whip a horse a little bit and you might get him to run a little faster. Overdo it, though, and you're eventually going to *de-motivate* the poor nag: if the horse sees that *no* amount of super effort is going to satisfy you, he's going to buck you off, lie down, or both.

It was the same thing with the Cannon Mills workers, and we cut down on the turnover problem in what was really a very simple way. We explained the diminishing-return principle to the line managers, and got them to set more realistic production goals. Not only did turnover drop, but production actually went up!

Setting your objectives at a realistic level means making sure that they are *consistent with the resources you have.* That means human and nonhuman resources. The best-defined, most clearly quantified objective in the world is still going to fall flat if your physical resources can't handle the extra load—or if the people who will be involved in reaching the objective aren't convinced it can (or should) be done. If Carson doesn't think she has a sparrow's chance in a tornado of getting the ABC statements in when you want them, the date you're looking at is by definition unrealistic.

I don't mean you should set your goals so low that a well-trained baboon could attain them. Setting realistic goals is a matter of balancing the *attainable* with the *challenging*. That's a tricky balance to find sometimes, but it's an often overlooked fact that the people who have to perform the objective usually have a pretty fair sense of where that balance lies. So ask them.

3. *Is it meaningful?* Is it worth doing? Will the objective that you're considering really, visibly, improve a key performance area in your organization? And will that performance improvement feed in naturally to the larger, long-term goals that are going to keep your operation healthy?

In the great old movie *The Caine Mutiny*, Humphrey Bogart, playing the rattled Captain Queeg, gives a classic portrayal of a manager who doesn't know the difference between meaningful and meaningless performance. Queeg, a case study in how *not* to motivate a crew, uses the typical "four insults to one word of praise" of the bad manager, and at one point in the story turns his entire ship upside down to find a pint of strawberries that he believes has been stolen from the officers' mess. The Great Strawberry Hunt, which finally convinces the crew that he's bonkers, is a classic example of using a sledgehammer to kill a mosquito.

Granted, no manager wants stealing going on under his nose. Stealing is definitely the kind of Behavior that you want to demotivate whenever you can. But Queeg in this case was doing what many "rule-oriented" managers end up doing: confusing his own authority with his team's performance and effectiveness. He was able to convince himself that finding the strawberry thief was a worthwhile objective, but he was unable to convince the crew. As a result, the energy he put into the search—and forced the crew to put in—eventually *lowered* their performance rate rather than increasing it. The same thing happens every time a gung-ho administrator transforms one of his own pet projects—say maintaining a rigid agenda for management meetings—into a crusade against company "inefficiency."

To be effective as an incentive toward greater motivation, an objective has to be understood as *important* by everyone in a position to impact it. Everyone. If that doesn't happen, you're going to have every department head off on his own Great Strawberry Hunt, with no coordination—and no results.

4. *Is it easily understood?* Start small and keep it *simple.* It's the old story of "one step at a time." Leave it to the financial wizards upstairs to plot out your company's every move for the next five years. If you're trying to motivate behavior at less than the boardroom level, you always do better by focusing on immediate gains. And on those *single* Behaviors you need to make them a reality.

I once saw a sales manager give a year-end address to his reps that showed the relative value of simplicity and detail in Pinpointing objectives. His company was about to move into a potentially lucrative new territory, and he spent about forty-five minutes telling the salespeople why that was a good thing. He had charts and overheads and magic markers coming out of his ears. He traced the competition's experience in the territory over the past three years. He itemized the potential revenues available, explained the company's expansion plans, went into detailed demographic breakdowns of the area, practically street by street. He described everything but how to ring each individual doorbell, and then finished with this conclusion: "The upshot is that we should be able to capture 40 percent of this new market within the first eighteen months."

That was the objective, clearly stated. But he had taken so long to state it that half his audience got lost along the way. I'll never forget the comment I overheard from one young sales rep after the manager had tied up the talk. "If that's what he wants us to do," he whispered to his neighbor, "why didn't he just say so up front?"

A word to the wise is enough. If you can't state the objective you want in the "model" form I mentioned above, maybe you don't know what it is. Maybe you have two or three objectives.

If so, you should split them up, talk about them with the people to whom they apply, and attack them one by one. You want to row across the Atlantic Ocean, fine. But you start with one pull of the oars.

5. *Is it "owned"?* This is probably the most important criterion of all, and it's the one most managers forget. We're back to Square One in the analysis of motivation: people will only perform—will only change their Behaviors—if it makes a *difference* for them to do so. The way you show them that difference is by ensuring their *stake* in the objectives you want.

The general manager of my company, Hank Conn, has a favorite expression that illustrates what I'm saying. Hank says, "People don't resist their own ideas." So if you want them to contribute to your goal, make sure they see it as *their* goal, too. People will work for their own goals. And those are the *only* ones they'll work for.

Now, there's a straightforward and reliable method for getting people to "own" an objective, and it's *not* the common ruse of selling them a bill of goods. I've been talking in this chapter as if you, the individual manager, figure out what your objectives are and then transmit that favored information to your teams. Actually, that's not what happens. Not in any effective team setting. The way you achieve group ownership of goals is to involve every member of your team in the original *setting* of those goals.

There's a critical distinction to keep in mind here. It's the difference between simply *having* an objective and helping to *set* that objective yourself.

Say I'm supposed to push the yellow button six times an hour and you're my line foreman and you tell me, "Fran, I want you to increase it to eight." I can be said to *have* a new objective, but I sure as hell can't be said to *own* it. But say you take me aside on a break and say, "Listen, Fran, we have an inventory backlog that's driving the bookkeepers crazy. How much faster do you think you can move the size forty-two units through your section? What's a reasonable speed-up time until we get the backlog under control?" What's my reaction going to be then? I've tried this hundreds of times, and I can tell you what it will be. It'll be to set myself a *higher* objective than the one you had in mind. Because you've had me set it myself.

Traditional management doubts this. There's a strong suspicion of mere "workers" on the part of traditional managers, and many of them remain convinced that, if you let the guy on the line set his own objectives, he's going to set them too low. In a lot of cases this is true, but do you know why? It's because the workers involved have only learned to fear the consequences of failing to meet an objective, and have never been properly rewarded for success. Naturally if your primary focus is fear of failure, when you get a chance to set up your own target you're going to put it two feet in front of you, not twenty.

But if you're part of an organization where people are consistently encouraged to perform better, where they're reinforced according to the "4:1 Syndrome," and where performance really does make a difference to them, you're going to find them setting objectives that find that difficult balance between "attainable" and "challenging" every time. And you're going to find that, when they miss the balance, it's because they set their sights too high, not too low.

I'm not saying that the guy on the production line should necessarily have the last word in deciding how fast the line should run or how many quality checks should be performed or how often the lubrication can should be brought out. Any effective objective has got to be acceptable to *everybody* involved in its implementation—and that means supervisors and management, too. In fact, the establishing of "ownership" means that managers have to own the objective also.

The way you establish management ownership is a very simple one: you get the relevant supervisor to give *approval*.

Getting approval for the objectives that you've Pinpointed is the last step in the "P" stage of the P.R.I.C.E. motivation system, and it's critical. When I say everybody involved in achieving the objective has to *believe* it will work and *want* it to work, I don't mean that these people should make unilateral choices without consulting management. We're talking about cooperation, not revolution. You know damn well what will happen

41

to a game plan that only the line workers see: unless it's so brilliantly conceived that it outstrips management's wildest dreams, eventually it's going to run into trouble. Eventually a department head or division manager or financial whiz from corporate headquarters is going to get wind of the plan and say, "This thing's no good because I didn't sign off on it." And you're right back to Square One.

You can't avoid approval, and you shouldn't try. But approval from the top alone is just as useless in establishing ownership of objectives as unilateral consensus from the "bottom." That was true in every huddle I ever "managed," and it's true of every successful business group: the objectives that *work* are the ones that everybody agrees can and should work. The reason hooks right up to motivation. It's that when you feel an objective to be your *own*, you're going to want to make it a fact. So you're going to be motivated to perform those Pinpointed Behaviors that can bring it into being. And the reverse is equally true: no ownership, no motivation. No motivation, no Behavior change. No Behavior change, no results.

To summarize the Pinpointing process, then: you start with objectives that are easily identifiable and measurable, and you check to make sure that those Pinpointed objectives are also realistic, meaningful, simple to understand, and perceived as personally worthwhile by everyone involved in their implementation. That process comprises the first, essential step in motivating people toward their achievement.

The second step is to establish a scorekeeping system by which people can tell how fast and how far and in what direction their motivation is taking them. I call that step Recording.

TWO

RECORDING

> There's nothing wrong with putting all your eggs in one
> basket. Just *watch that basket.*
> —HENRY FORD

Everybody likes to know how he's doing.

In sports that's so obvious that it's barely worth mentioning. Whether you've just finished eighteen holes of golf, or three sets of tennis, or a two-mile run, one of the first things you're going to want to know about it is how you did: in other words, your *score.* This is true for spectators even more than for participants. You think the millions of people who watched the last Olympics on television understood all the intricacies of gymnastic floor routines or bobsled balancing? No—but all of them understood one thing. They understood who won and who didn't, because they saw the figures.

Sometimes I think that scorekeeping is what accounts for the popularity of sports: we all like to keep tabs on ourselves and our competitors, and in sports, at the end of every competition, you've got a straight-out presentation of the data that tells you how everybody did. That's got to be one reason that spectators get so revved up, and that amateur athletes push themselves so hard, from the local sandlot to the Olympics. Nobody pays an amateur to perform, so there's got to be another reason he plays. Part of that reason is scorekeeping.

This ties in directly to motivation. If you want to pick out the factors that contribute to good motivation, one way to go about it would be to look at activities that people choose to engage in on their *own* time, with no conventional, external incentive such as pay. Sports and other recreational activities come into this category. Ask yourself what activities like tennis and bowling and computer games have in common, and why they are able to motivate people so strongly to spend their *leisure* time in improving at them? One answer is that they all have a well-defined scorekeeping system, one that gives immediate feedback to the individual. That feedback on "how you're doing" is an essential aspect of motivation.

Think of what these activities—of what any leisure activity—would be like if you didn't keep score. Take golf, for example, which happens to be one of my favorite forms of culturally sanctioned insanity.

Golf has taken its raps over the years. It's been called "slow" and "boring" more times than Abraham Lincoln has been called honest—usually by characters whose idea of excitement is being able to hit thirty words a minute on a typewriter. The sportswriter Westbrook Pegler once referred to it as "the most useless outdoor game ever devised to waste the time and try the spirit of man." Mark Twain was more succinct: he called golf a "good walk spoiled." And when you look at the actual physical activity of the sport, it's hard to claim that it's taken *entirely* a bum rap. I mean, getting up with the roosters so you can walk three miles in the hot sun lugging a golf bag, and then lose your temper and your balls in the rough—is this a sane man's idea of fun?

It is for millions of people. Like me, and a number of American Presidents, and comedian Joe E. Louis, who once proclaimed, "I play in the low 80s; if it's any hotter than that, I won't play." Why? I think it's because of the scoring. Recording the score on each hole, you get instant feedback, and when you're done with those eighteen holes, you know exactly how you've performed. You might not always *like* your score. But even coming in at 30 over par is preferable to having no score at all. And the hope of being able to better your score the next time out is one of the chief motivating factors that keeps you going.

This is true in professional sports, too, of course. There's a direct, observable connection between good internal score-keeping and success in professional sports. By "internal score-keeping" I mean the data retrieval and analysis that constitute performance measurement on every professional sports team: all those play-by-play records that let the team members know, for any individual game, how the final score was arrived at. The most successful pro teams spend an enormous amount of time developing these internal records. Their scorekeeping systems are incredibly detailed and personalized. They don't just tell you how many yards were gained, how many penalties were incurred, and so on; they provide a score for each individual on the team, so each one knows how well he played the game. This establishes an incentive for each player to improve—regardless of the outcome of the game itself. Overall team improvement is the composite of all those individual performances, and they in turn can only be improved if they are constantly monitored and reviewed by means of individual "scores."

This is obvious to any professional sports manager. It used to be obvious to managers in business, too, but in the past couple of decades they've begun to forget it. The results have been disastrous.

WHY DON'T BUSINESSES KEEP SCORE?

There are a lot of things American businesses do extremely well, but scorekeeping is not one of them. In fact we do a terrible job in this area, and our failure to keep score more effectively is one of the principal reasons that the "human side of management" programs have not gotten any further than they have. We say over and over again that "People are our most important asset" (I wish I had a buck for every time I've heard that bromide in the last ten years), and we forget that *information* is a damn close second. Even worse, we forget that the two critical assets of people and information are linked so closely to each other that you can't manage either one well by itself. In all the flurry of interest about "humanistic management," we often forget their connection. We forget that, to be successful, you have to manage simultaneously and with equal effectiveness both your data *and* the people who make the data *work*. You can't have one without the other. Try to "treat people nice" without finding out how they're doing, and you're going to go bankrupt. Try to process all the reams of information that a modern business generates without relating it to your people and you're going to be crunched in your own number machine.

Now, when I say that people and information have to be related, I don't mean just that you have to "gather data" on "the workers," and then make managerial decisions designed to improve their score. I mean that everybody who affects, or is affected by, the information your company gathers has got to be made *aware* of that information, so he can use it to assess his *own* performance, and so his supervisors can work on his motivation in those areas where performance is lacking.

And I do mean everybody. In the last chapter I spoke about how the guy who pushes the yellow button on Line B ultimately affects not just his shift's performance, but the whole P&L picture of the company. Well, if that's so—if everybody's behavior contributes to the final result—doesn't it make sense to give everybody in your organization some regular feedback on how they're doing, on how they're contributing (or not contributing) to the overall final score?

Of course it does. But this is seldom done. You can be sure that when Mary Lou Retton and Tim Daggett finished their high-bar routines in the Olympic trials, their coaches told them exactly how they'd done: "That was an 8.6," or, "That wobble at the peak could have cost you a point." Business "coaches" don't do this nearly enough—or precisely enough. A line manager with a motivation and performance problem will complain that his people aren't working "well enough" or "efficiently enough," but won't give them specific, measurable data to track their progress. That's like saying to a gymnast, "Not too bad, Mary Lou," or, "Great performance, Tim." Without a specific score to hang your understanding on, that's a pretty useless piece of feedback.

Generally speaking, we do a much better job of record-keeping and performance measurement the higher up we go in an organization. The CEO and the highly paid bean counters that surround him get all the performance data they want— generally about the company's long-term prospects and quarter-to-quarter "scores." But even they are relatively ignorant about the day-to-day business on the line: about the millions of measurable tasks that *make up* the Big Score.

They don't know because they don't demand to know. Somehow the nitty-gritty work of production, and overhead, and quality control, is not as exciting to them as marketing and differential investment scenarios—and so these critical elements of the final score are left to chance.

That's bad enough. But the real bottleneck comes from the fact that the guys who are actually out there on the line don't have access to measurement of their own performance. Neither, in many cases, do middle managers; they don't know either how they affect the Big Picture. Nobody collects the data. Nobody shows them a scorecard. So they don't know how they're doing and, without knowing, how can they possibly be motivated to improve? So when the division head screams, "We've got to do better," they have every right to respond, "Better than *what?*"

The reasons that are usually given for failing to let people see their own scorecards would be amusing if they didn't have such terrible results. I can think of three that are particularly common:

1. *"It's not the workers' business."* You hear this piece of baloney all the time from managers who think of themselves as the "brains" of their outfits and who don't want to acknowledge that the "brawny" workers are critical to company success. This is division of labor with a vengeance. It's the attitude that everybody in an organization has a distinct and invariable sphere of operation, and that productivity is best achieved by everybody remaining in his sphere. In this addled scenario, of course, the "management sphere" involves access to financial, performance, and other data—it involves keeping The Big Score. The "labor sphere" doesn't involve any of that, because the "role" of the "worker" is to follow orders without wondering why. So there's no point in posting performance results, because (a) the worker is too stupid to understand them anyway, and/or (b) if we give him that data, he might use it *against* us.

Of the two versions I'm mentioning here of the "not their business" argument, the "stupid worker" argument is the more common one; it explains why the sales force in many companies has access to quarterly revenue charts and the bean counters have access to cash-flow diagrams (salesmen and accountants have been to college, see, so they know how to *read*), and why, in the same companies, the production line worker knows nothing from month to month about how many widgets come off his line or how much scrap is typically involved in his process. Don't burden the poor dope with statistics; he's just learned that two plus two is four.

The other version of the "not his business" argument is a little less common but more pernicious. Nobody seems to notice that it contradicts Argument A—that if the worker is smart enough to use your data against you, then he must be smart enough to understand it. In addition to being illogical, the idea is about as up-to-date in today's labor environment as a horse and buggy would be at Le Mans. It's the old idea that the worker isn't really part of the organization at all, but a mere necessary evil, who will turn on management at any moment, if you give him the least provocation or ammunition.

Maybe there is a risk (to "security" or "competitive integrity") in posting weekly waste-retrieval results. But I guarantee you that that risk is going to be more than offset by the added motivation supplied to the waste-retrieval department when they're able to track, from one week to another, exactly how well they've been doing.

Failing to give workers information about their own week-to-week scores is like refusing to give feedback to a football lineman on how well he scored on a given play. If he doesn't know how he did on that play, how is he going to improve? Why is he even going to *care* about improving? What's going to motivate him to move from Point A to Point B on any performance continuum if he doesn't even know where Point A is?

2. *"The workers won't stand for it."* The assumption that workers do not want—and in fact will actively resist—record-keeping on their performance ties right in with the "stupid worker" argument, but carries it one step closer to absurdity. This excuse for not telling people how they're doing rests on the theory that people are suspicious of having performance data posted. Sometimes, I admit, that's true. I've seen plenty of organizations where, when we first suggest the Recording element of the P.R.I.C.E. motivation system, it's the unions and not the management who balk. That's only natural. But do you know why? *Not* because workers are "inherently" resistant to higher productivity, but because historically attempts to quantify and measure their production have always been linked to *negative* Consequences.

Think of the time-and-motion man caricature. Is he an earnest researcher trying to make life—and livelihood—better for everybody by making the company more efficient? Not at all. In every portrait I've ever seen, he's a vicious company stooge whose only real interest in rooting out inefficiency is in firing as many people as possible. The image you get of the "efficiency expert" is that he's only secondarily interested in efficiency. He really gets rewarded by the number of people eliminated.

The stereotype wasn't born in a vacuum. Factory workers have good reason to be suspicious of a tightening-up of record-keeping. Since negative Consequences have so often followed the implementation of better record-keeping, you can hardly be surprised at labor's negative reaction.

But it's ridiculous to suppose that Recording can have only negative Consequences. That's certainly not the point of keeping score, and it's not why we use it. Truly efficient Recording, in fact, would lead to as many (or more) promotions as firings, as many bonuses as dockings of pay.

We recently did some of our own "time and motion" studies in a company where the labor-management history had been less than progressive, and in which the labor contract specifically *prohibited* the public display of individual performance measures. Talking to labor and management leaders, we discovered why this clause in the contract had been introduced:

the union thought it was a necessary safeguard against "intrusion" by management, and specifically against the peremptory firings that they expected would follow the posting of the performance data. The general idea among the workers was that, once such data was collected, it would be used as an excuse for getting rid of people that management just "didn't like."

It took us about two weeks of convincing, but we were finally able to persuade the shop foremen involved to accept performance posting on a trial basis. The result didn't surprise us, but it shocked the hell out of the labor leaders. Within two weeks after the Recording element had been introduced, workers had become so enthusiastic about finding out how they were doing that they would not let their supervisor leave in the evening before posting that day's results! The contract clause prohibiting such "intrusion" was promptly forgotten by labor and management alike.

Why this abrupt turnaround from suspicion to cooperation? Because the way we had introduced the Recording element stressed the importance of *positive*, not negative, Consequences. As part of the trial arrangement, we agreed that demotivated or poor performing workers would be privately counselled and aided by their supervisors to improve. The graphs indicating the daily "scores" would focus only on those workers—or teams of workers—whose performance had been *above* average. You should have seen the rush at the end of each day to see if a worker's name had appeared on the list. With that simple example of positive Consequences—the public acknowledgment of a job well done—we were able to transform an entire factory supposedly full of "lazy, irresponsible" people into people who were *driven* to excel.

There's a similar lesson to be learned, in a more humorous fashion, in the old Spencer Tracy/Katharine Hepburn movie *Desk Set*. She's the supervisor of a public information service employing several people in an antiquated library. He's an efficiency expert with a computer who wants to make their work easier by putting the library on disks. Only they don't know that. When he comes in with his charts and data banks, they assume (like the workers in the plant we upgraded) that he's out to eliminate their jobs. They begin to sabotage the computer until it goes haywire, and it's only after they understand that the machine is meant to assist them, not get rid of them, that the researchers begin to use it to advantage.

The moral goes back, as usual, to Consequences. Recording can be a critical element in the upgrading of motivation and performance—but only if the people being recorded understand that the scorekeeping will make a *positive difference* in their lives.

3. *"We're doing just fine without it."* Management often tends to track and monitor bad performance more closely than it does good work. It's strange, but true—and we saw it happen with dire results in the boom-and-bust economy of the 1970s. When things were sloping downward, everybody wanted to know "what's wrong," but when things were moving up, people were far less interested in knowing why things were going right. And because they didn't take the time to track upward motion—to find out why it was happening—they eventually found themselves going downhill again.

In a very perceptive article called "Made in America," business writer M. R. Montgomery, a few years ago, linked this dangerous penchant for forgetting about keeping score when you're winning to a physical manifestation of scorekeeping, the manufacturing gauges known as "process controls." His description in the *Boston Globe Magazine* shows how closely these controls are linked to what I'm calling Recording:

One of the ways to get the insensitive supervisor off the worker's back . . . is to give the worker instant and objective information on the quality of his work. Modern factories have machines that automatically gauge the dimensions of parts, confirm welding temperatures, and otherwise keep track of what's happening to a piece of metal as it goes down the line. These are "process controls," and when the worker has access to them, he has that instant and objective measure of how he's doing his job.

"Instant and objective information" about "how he's doing his job." You couldn't have a better thumbnail definition of a good

Recording system at work. The trouble, as Montgomery describes it, was that as the economy of the early 1970s began to expand, these critical performance gauges were dropped. "In the booming economy, our companies accepted high-scrap rates and passed on costs rather than instituting quality control."

You can get away with that kind of penny-wise/pound-foolish approach for only so long, and eventually the chickens will come home to roost. That's what's been happening more recently—and not surprisingly, as scrap overrun costs begin to eat into profits, top management begins to look again at the value of process controls.

They could have saved themselves a lot of grief if they had continued to "keep score" on scrap figures in the boom days as well as the bust ones. The fact is that you *always* have to know how you're doing—whether you've shot an 80 or a 65, whether you've got a 40 percent share of an ad market or 14. If you forget that in good times, sooner or later you'll get clobbered, because there is nothing more demotivating to good performance than the attitude that "We can't be hurt." In this economy, *nobody* is immune from downturns. Ask Braniff, or General Motors. One of the best ways I know of to guard against an "unforeseen" dip in your fortunes is to keep your eyes open while you're sailing high.

Alabama coach Bear Bryant said it well. "Most coaches study the films when they lose. I study them when we win—to see if I can figure out what I did right." He didn't get where he was by assuming winners don't need to know why they've won. He got there by studying the films—by tracking the scoring Records—after every game, win or lose. And I'll guarantee you he didn't keep the scorecards to himself. I'll guarantee that, in every one of those filming sessions, the entire 'Bama team was watching *with* him.

HOW IT'S DONE: GRAPHING

In my company we use the most common and most easily accessible method of displaying performance progress that social science affords: the simple line graph in which the performance

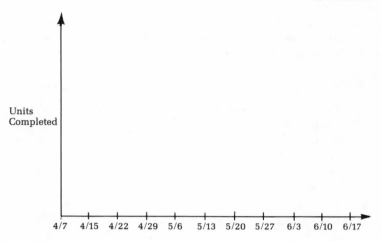

Figure 2

variable being measured is plotted on the vertical axis and units of time are plotted on the horizontal. For example, if you wanted to record the weekly change in output of a given assembly line, you would set up the graph like the one in Figure 2. This graph illustrates the charting of a line productivity variable, but of course you could just as easily plot a "management" variable like R&D expense, or sales calls, or reports delivered.

It's a simple enough concept, but it's important to call attention to a couple of often ignored features of this type of graphing.

First, notice that, on the vertical axis, we're measuring the performance variable—in this case, a line's output—in terms that are strictly *quantifiable*. We're not tracking "output" or "efficiency" or "productivity," but "units completed." Secondly, the same general observation goes for the horizontal axis: we're not tracking some vague "sense" of improvement "over time," but the units that come rolling off the line in question at the end of each week. Specificity is everything in keeping good records, and that's why the weeks are designated along the bottom border of the graph.

You've also got to keep specificity in mind when you're choosing the variables to measure. A major error made by managers in recording and tracking performance is that they choose the *wrong* variables to track—variables that, in terms of the P.R.I.C.E. terminology, are just not Pinpointed enough to make sense to the people who are tracking them. To help you avoid this problem, we suggest that, in deciding on which performance variable you want to measure, you ask yourself three questions:

1. Is the measurement going to be relatively *easy to get,* and not result in a lot of extra work for someone? There's no point in setting up a Recording system to improve the efficiency of your operation if the system itself cannot be efficiently run. Look for variables that are immediately accessible, easy to identify, and clearly quantifiable.

2. Will your people readily *understand* the measurement and the graph that pictures it? If not, they're not going to be responsive to the data, and the whole purpose of the score-keeping will be lost. Since you're aiming for changes in human behavior, look for small, discrete Behaviors that can directly and obviously affect your performance picture.

3. Can the variable be *controlled?* That is, can you improve it by human, rather than simply mechanical, modification? Again, since Behavior is the key, you don't want to post data on your machinery's compression ratios or on depreciation curves. Focus on those things that your *people* are saying and doing, and that can be changed for the better. There's nothing more frustrating than getting negative feedback on a condition over which you have no control.

Once you've chosen the performance variable—whether it's a "blue collar" variable like units completed or a "manager's" variable like sales calls—you should establish a *baseline.* You do this by collecting relevant data for a brief period of time, averaging that data, and then plotting this baseline average on the left end of your graph. This baseline then becomes the standard against which change in performance is measured: it's like par in golf, or what I referred to as that hypothetical "Point A" on the journey from poor to good performance.

Remember when I talked about my 1975 season with the Vikings, when Jerry Burns, John Michaels, and I established the objectives the team would need to accomplish if we were going

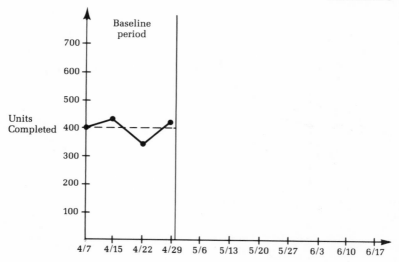

Figure 3

to win? We began that exercise in Pinpointing by determining in the record books what playoff teams had averaged over the years in terms of various variables; by doing that, we were establishing the baseline that we knew we needed in our own performance.

Or take the example I gave in Figure 2, where we were plotting the number of units completed per week. Let's take the first four weeks of the horizontal time line as the baseline period, and assign hypothetical numbers to the "units completed." Say four hundred units came off the line in the week ending April 7, then in the next three weeks four hundred and twenty units, three hundred and fifty units, and four hundred and ten units. Those four figures are identified by the four points plotted on the graph in Figure 3. The *baseline average* is the average of those four figures, and it's represented on the graph by the horizontal dotted line. What this graph now tells a worker or manager is that at the beginning of the scorekeeping period, "par" was established as three hundred and ninety-five.

From there it's easy. At the end of each week, you simply plot on the graph that point indicating units completed for that

55

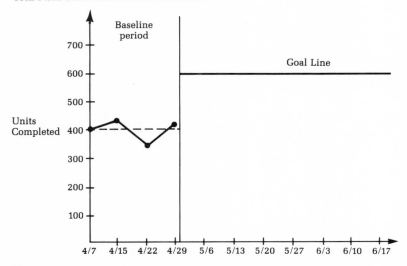

Figure 4

week, and connect them over time with a solid line, as I've done here for the first four (baseline) points. The resulting graph will give immediate, visible feedback to the people involved on how they're doing, week to week. Which is the point of the system.

But there's one other feature of graphing that is important to get in. I've said that the Recording element of the P.R.I.C.E. system is a way of showing people how they're progressing from Point A to Point B. Point A is the baseline we've just set up. Point B is the goal, or objective, you want to get to, which I talked about in the last chapter. In the companies we work with, after we've determined a realistic, Pinpointed objective with regard to a given variable, we draw that objective in on the relevant graph as the "goal line" that everybody should be working for. If it's been determined that six hundred units a week is a reasonable objective, for example, we would draw that in on our graph as shown in Figure 4.

Once you've drawn the goal line in, you have the required Point A–Point B "journey" pretty well mapped out. All you have to do is to fill in the intermediate points on that journey week by week, to keep yourself and your people aware of how you're all doing. In the chapter on Evaluation, I'm going to give some detail about how to "interpret" the developing map, so that it becomes not just a snapshot of where you are, but a real motivational tool. Here I just want to mention two fundamental points about using Recording and graphs:

First, in order to be effective, a graph like the one given as an example here has to be *publicly posted* so that the people whose performance is in effect creating the data know what that data is. Remember, the whole point of this element of our system is to give people scores on their work, so they can change and improve. If you're graphing a very specific performance variable of one person, of course it makes sense to give him or her the results privately. But in today's industrial and corporate environment, you're not going to be doing that very often, since everything is so interconnected. Most of the time you'll be tracking data that has been generated by an entire working team: every member of that team should have access to that data.

Secondly, they should have access to it as *soon* as possible after it is collected, and as *frequently* as possible over time. Ideally this means every week, and in some cases—where a performance variable is very critical to the overall operation and delay in improvement would cause major losses—it means every day. Scorekeeping is a useless exercise unless it follows immediately upon performance—which is why the quarterly report approach to industrial motivation is just not acceptable. If you want to hike the unit figure up to six hundred or cut down on the number of days lost to accidents, let your people know *now* what they're doing wrong and doing right. Waiting for the "Big Picture" in areas like these is like waiting until your boxer is on the canvas before telling him to keep his guard up.

THE BENEFITS OF SCOREKEEPING

What are you going to get out of all this? How will you know it's worth the trouble? After all, I'm asking you to spend a considerable amount of energy and attention in producing public records for folks who probably haven't asked for them, and probably aren't used to seeing them. Where's the payoff?

There's one very obvious payoff, and that's the simple fact that, with a clearly posted and properly maintained performance graph, you always have an objective, visible picture of where you are. If you're asked by front-office management how your department is doing, you don't have to resort to weasel phrases like "an acceptable rate of progress." You can just haul out your graphs. But there are other, less tangible benefits to using such a Recording system, and you're going to find in the long run that these intangible benefits are what make the system really work.

First, the mere *fact* of Recording lets people know that you are interested in what they are doing, and that nearly always provides a motivational incentive to do better. That's an incentive that no amount of "You're all part of my family" blarney can buy. The workers in the businesses I visit are—every one of them—from the great state of Missouri. You can yammer all you want about being interested in what they're doing, and they'll just stare at you. Which is what you deserve. But post a graph on the individual Behaviors that comprise their performance—that is, *show* them you're paying attention—and they'll start paying attention, too.

This is not exactly a new discovery, although today's number-crunchers frequently forget it. Back in 1927, in fact, a Harvard Business School professor named Elton Mayo proved the value of "paying attention" in a series of classic experiments at the Western Electric company's Hawthorne plant in Illinois. He and his colleagues went in to that plant to see if making changes in lighting conditions would improve the morale and the performance of the workers. What they found set the whole "science" of industrial hygiene on its ear.

If you improved the lighting in a certain department, the Hawthorne experimenters found, sure enough productivity went up. But it also went up in those departments where the lighting was actually made *worse*. The only departments where productivity didn't improve were those the experimenters ignored. Their conclusion, described as the "Hawthorne effect," was that improvement in motivation and performance resulted from the simple *fact*, and not just the content, of attention. I've seen that lesson borne out in every industrial operation where we institute a clearly posted, up-to-date Recording system.

A second benefit of using Recording is that it provides your people with an *objective* measure of their work that cannot be talked around or marked up to personal factors. Every manager knows somebody who seems insensitive to either positive or negative reinforcement, because he figures that praise comes only when the manager is "feeling good," and criticism comes when he's "feeling lousy." And the assessment isn't always off base. Some managers *do* mete out their rewards and punishments based not on actual performance but on how the marriage is going or on how much heartburn they're getting from last night's pepperoni pizza.

The combination of Pinpointing specific performance variables and Recording their change on a graph makes it impossible for either managers or workers to explain away a bad situation as a spinoff of marital strife or indigestion. The facts are staring you in the face. Since the figures are generated by performance factors, not personalities, you can't condemn them as subjectively judgmental. That means they're going to be seen as *fair*. I guarantee you that a fair, objective appraisal of my performance is going to get me motivated, every time, better than one that I see as unjust.

Third, a scorekeeping system like the one I'm describing here tends to make work *fun*: in other words, more like the games that we choose to play even though we don't really *have* to. I'm aware that, to some people in business life, the idea of work being fun will come as a startling, even dangerous, doctrine. Work is supposed to be hard, I can hear them saying. Tough, and necessary, and the sweat of your brow, and all that Protestant work ethic stuff: the last thing it's supposed to be is enjoyable.

This attitude toward work is essentially a puritanical one, and you know what H. L. Mencken said about puritanism: he called it "the haunting fear that someone, somewhere, may be happy." We've gotten a little more enlightened about work since the Puritans' day, and even since Mencken's day, but the attitude that work is a cousin to misery has not entirely died out. There are still plenty of Theory X managers around who subscribe to it, and who use it to justify the notion that the average worker needs to be coerced or threatened into performing. But the idea is simply baloney, and one of the quickest ways to prove that is to inject into the workplace some of the elements of play. Elements like striving for a goal, and putting out 100 percent effort, and enjoying the sheer activity of what you're doing, and the sports addict's system of scorekeeping that ties the whole business together.

In whatever we do, we all like to win. Winning may not be everything, but it sure as hell is difficult to get fired up for an activity if you lose at it all the time—or, even worse, if you never know whether you're winning or losing. A Recording system like the one I've described in this chapter lets you know, week by week or day by day, how you're doing. It allows you to keep dreaming, and aiming, and reaching. It lets you keep trying to improve because, however you're doing today, someday you're going to be a winner. If that ain't fun, I don't know what is. And it's because it's fun that it *works*.

Finally, a scorekeeping system allows an individual to see how his personal performance ties in with the larger, overall performance of the organization. The guy who pushes the yellow button or does the payroll can read the quarterly report and discover that the company increased its profits by 7 percent. But so what? Why should he care about that unless, as I said at the outset of the book, it makes a *difference* to him? And how is it going to make a difference to him? There are only two ways I know of. Either the difference can be external and tangible, like an increase in pay or a bonus or a cut of a profit-sharing plan. Or it can be internal: it can be the satisfaction of knowing that he has contributed to a winning team.

There's nothing wrong with pay incentives and bonuses, but in my experience they always play second fiddle to the intangible, internal motivating factors like feeling good as part of a good team. Knowing that you've done your part to bring about that 7 percent increase is what really turns most workers on:

it's what gets them motivated in the first place, and keeps them coming. Establishing that connection between individual effort and overall improved performance is a critical element in any team motivation system. The Recording element of the P.R.I.C.E. system is one solid way of making that connection.

A broader, and equally important way of making the connection is to involve the worker, at all levels, in the setting of objectives and establishing of baselines and making of decisions that affect him. Once you've set up a reliable scorekeeping system, you next need to make each team player a part of keeping those scores as high as possible. You do that by developing the "I" element of the P.R.I.C.E. system, the element we call Involvement.

THREE

INVOLVEMENT

> The outstanding mistake of the employer is his failure to
> realize he is dealing with human material.
> —ROGER WARD BABSON

Remember the good old days when the only thing you had to do to get a nonmotivated worker to push harder was to yell at him, "Shape up, Riley, or ship out"? Remember when the Boss was a kind of fourth person of the Trinity in pinstripes, and managers were lords in their own domain, and the guys in blue collars were happy slaves? Remember when the word "authority" meant something, and you could get a lazy employee to be more productive just by kicking his ass, and you never had to worry about lip because as long as you gave them their paychecks, they'd shut up and do what you told them?

You don't remember those days? Me either. In fact *nobody* remembers them, because they didn't exist. Back in the nineteenth century maybe, when workers were treated like children because half of them *were* children; but not in your lifetime or mine. As far back as any of us can remember, the image of the manager as an omnipotent galley master whose job was to find out where the lashes ought to fall—that image has been nothing but a myth. And the dream that some managers still have of the docile, dim-bulb employee who just wants to be told what to do—forget it, that bears about as much relation to reality as Broadway does to a farm.

But there's a funny thing about myths. Sometimes they last a lot longer than "realistic observers" give them credit for. That's certainly the case with this one. In a lot of companies I see, there's always a small group of managers who seem to think that, even if this is 1986, they ought to be able to behave as if Grover Cleveland was still in the White House. Even in "enlightened" businesses, you see the attitude hanging on: that the "good old days" had it right, and that the best way of getting people to put out more is to act tough and boss them around.

In some places I've visited, the management even goes so far as to say that this is the way workers *want* to be treated. "They want to be told what to do," a first-line supervisor told me once. "They're being paid to turn that damned screw, not to think."

Since I've been talking a lot about involving your people in decision-making, you can guess what I think about this attitude. In deference to the memory of my preacher daddy, I'll refrain from calling the spade a spade here, and just say that, as a way of motivating people to better performance, the galley-master mentality is completely useless.

A few years ago a private research firm called the Work in America Institute studied the conditions in society that were changing the way people thought about work. In a report that every manager in America ought to read, the institute's president, Jerome Rosow, listed a number of conclusions that bear directly on the problem of motivation. Some of his findings:

1. *Attitudes toward authority are changing.* As the polls are always telling us, there's been a steady decline over the past couple of decades in public confidence in institutions—whether you're talking about government or educational institutions or business, people just don't have the same knee-jerk respect for institutional power and authority that they used to have. In addition, the growth of permissiveness in society—starting with the so-called sexual revolution of the 1960s and proceeding into the current grab-bag of alternate "life styles"—has tied in with a general suspicion of all authority, all received ideas, all traditional ways of doing things. Therefore, the roles of authority figures, as well as of the people who are supposed to be "under" them, aren't nearly as well-defined as they were in Grandma and Grandpa's day.

2. *"Work" is no longer at the center of people's lives.* People still have to work, that's true, but today more than ever before they feel they "have" to do a lot of other things as well. A hundred years ago, a young worker was satisfied with a steady paycheck and a roof for himself and his family. Today the average worker also wants a car, a color television, two-weeks' paid vacation, weekends on the beach, and so on. The old Protestant work ethic is gradually dying, and being replaced by an attraction for the "good life," with all the emphasis on pleasure and leisure that that implies.

This attitude has even entered the workplace itself. "Quality of Work Life" is now an agenda item in scores of companies around the country; a hundred years ago, "quality" of work life meant that you got to work by the light of a 40-watt bulb rather than a 20-watt one. Workers have discovered the revolutionary idea that it's all right for them to *enjoy* their lives. Even from nine to five.

3. *Workers expect to participate in decision-making.* That doesn't mean necessarily that they want to take over the factory and put the boss's head on a pike; it does mean that, where they are performing tasks about which they know as much or more than their supervisors, they expect to be consulted about those tasks—to have their input sought, and listened to, and taken seriously.

Taken together, these three developments—a change in attitudes toward authority, a change in the relative importance of work, and a heightened expectation for participation in decisions—have dramatically altered the texture of the workplace, and have given today's business managers an unprecedented challenge. That challenge is to see if we can incorporate into our working lives the same elements of cooperation and joint decision-making and democracy that we keep bragging about in our political lives.

I can tell you from working with businesses as diverse as finance, and textiles, and steel, that the solution to that challenge is found in Involvement.

You've heard about Involvement before, under other names. One of them is "participatory management," and I like that term a lot because it links the two essential features of a viable (not just visionary) workplace democracy: full involvement, and a continued emphasis on management direction which is the only thing that can make the involvement pay off.

A lot of our business leaders already understand that Involvement, or participatory management, has got to be the wave of the future. Take William Hewlett, whose company Hewlett-Packard was practicing participatory management about twenty years before the term was invented. In a speech entitled "The Human Side of Management," Hewlett noted the following:

> Productivity is the name of the game, and gains in productivity will only come when better understanding and better relationships exist between management and the work force.
>
> We must find better solutions to the adversary relationships that have so long dominated the American labor scene. Management is in a position to take the lead in such a new relationship. Managers have traditionally developed the skills in finance, planning, marketing and production techniques. Too often the relations with their people have been assigned a secondary role. *This is too important a subject not to receive first-line attention.*

That tells it like it is. Productivity *is* the name of the game, and as Hewlett rightly points out, the only way you're going to get it is to get beyond the old garbage of bossman versus workers, them versus us. If you want to win ball games, this is *no longer optional.* Adopting a more participatory form of management has become a matter of business survival. It's what's going to make the difference, in the rest of this century, between industries that act like yoked oxen that hate each other's guts and industries where management and labor pull together like a team. Only teamwork is going to get results.

INVOLVEMENT: WHY PEOPLE RESIST IT

Of course, you've got to fight to get this message across. There are plenty of obstacles to getting workers at all levels more deeply involved in the running of businesses. And there are plenty of great sounding justifications for setting up and maintaining these obstacles. They break down, I've found, into three basic attitudinal blocks: ignorance, inertia, and fear.

The three are obviously related, since ignorance of something novel is often joined to a fear of what would happen if that something were adopted—and the result, in many cases, is the personal and institutional inertia that makes it impossible for any change at all to take place. Anybody who has spent any time in an organization that has been run along traditional lines since Methuselah was in knee pants has come across the kind of resistance I'm talking about. "It just won't work," you hear a manager say, and you know that what he means is "I don't want to find out if it will work because if it does I'll have to scrap 80 percent of what I know and that scares the crap out of me."

It's easy for managers to get away with this know-nothing approach because, let's face it, in most companies "participatory management" is still just an abstraction. It's by definition "untried," and when something is untried there's always the chance it won't work. So why try? In addition, in places where this revolutionary approach to management *has* been tried and hasn't resulted in instant productivity bonanzas, it's easy for people who were suspicious of it in the first place to say "I told you so" and revert to traditional structures. One of the built-in limitations of participative management is that it takes a while to get off the ground. You don't get quick fixes or immediate, visible bottom-line gains, so managers who are looking for those things are naturally wary of the new style.

But asking for instant results from something as innovative and far-reaching as participative management is like asking a quarterback to learn how to block in one weekend. For a quarterback, blocking is just not in the job description. Sure, a quarterback can learn to block, but you can't expect him to be good at it right off because there's about as much call for blocking quarterbacks as there is for Wimbledon finalists to juggle their tennis balls between sets. So you can't expect him to make it all come together right away. The same for participative management. This is unmapped terrain for most firms. Nobody should be incredibly surprised when, after a month or two of the new style, profits aren't up by 12 percent. Managers who expect that to happen have been grossly oversold on the technique.

But resistance to the Involvement style of management rests only tangentially on the suspicion that "it won't work." The real reason that it's such rough going when a company starts up with participative management is that a lot of the vested interests in the company are deathly afraid it *will* work. I mean, you start letting one guy on the line tell you what he thinks about his job, and pretty soon everybody is going to want to do the same thing, and you're going to end up with management by committee, or no management at all.

By "vested interests" I don't mean just the stereotypical hard-nosed supervisor who can't stand the idea of sharing power. A lot of the resistance you get to participative management comes, ironically, from the workers themselves—or, to be more precise, from shop foremen and other union leaders who see in such a "reformist" system the erosion of their own power bases. One of the weirdest aspects of the current American business system is that the "adversary relationships" William Hewlett spoke about are actually *satisfying* to a lot of folks who ought to be pissed off about them.

The collective bargaining apparatus that has been set up to provide "exchange" between workers and management, after all, is basically a way to *maintain* the adversary relationship that made unions necessary in the first place. So, whether you're talking about the boardroom or the union hall, Involvement can be viewed as a threat: it threatens the conventional hierarchies on both sides of the worker-management "fence," because its ultimate purpose is to tear that fence down. If your job function is intimately tied in to keeping a watch on that fence, naturally you're going to be suspicious of the misty-eyed "revolutionary" who says the fence needs scrapping, not repair. Naturally you're going to say "this new-fangled junk just won't work."

BENEFITS OF PARTICIPATIVE MANAGEMENT

It does work, though. I found this out in my Viking days when—against the conventional wisdom that said the quarterback was supposed to be a combination of a mainframe computer and The Flash—I practiced what came to be known as the "participative huddle" approach to play-calling.

In the mythology of professional football, the quarterback is supposed to be only one step down from the almighty Coach in terms of field generalship and overall savvy. Everybody else on the team is supposed to be inanimate matter. The only reason you need linemen at all, so the theory goes, is to protect genius scramblers like yours truly.

Now, I've never been real upset at being called a genius, so in my Viking days I didn't take out any ads announcing that the theory was a crock. Take this as a belated confession. All those sportswriters who said I was a fair to middling runner and passer but a topnotch caller of plays, take note: I called about 25 percent of our plays myself. The rest were called by "lunks" like guard Ed White and end Ahmad Rashad, and my good buddy and roommate, center Mick Tinglehoff.

When you stop to think about it, this is just common sense. Nobody can solve every problem, every time, on his own, so if you're already working with a group, doesn't it sound pretty reasonable to find out what that group thinks?

I always figured that if you didn't need the team's input, then you ought to be able to make it to the Super Bowl on your own. I needed the team, and I knew it. After any number of plays, when I was trying to get an offensive drive going and getting nowhere, I would go back to the huddle and say, "What do you have out there, Ahmad?" And Ahmad would let us know what he saw, and because I knew he was *out there*, we would often go with Ahmad's suggestions, and we would get the drive moving. And we would keep it moving with the added input of Ed and Mick and everybody else in the huddle.

At the Vikings, we developed that "participative huddle" approach to play-calling gradually over the years, and I'll be the first to tell you that the play sequences we developed together were an awful lot more effective than any I could have come up with on my own.

That's why I kept using the participative approach. Like most competitors, I'm results-oriented. I don't care how brilliant your idea sounds. If it doesn't get me yardage, I'm not interested. On the Vikings, the linemen's input got us yardage.

Our unusual style of play-calling worked for the same two reasons that all participative management programs work, when they're actively encouraged and endorsed by managers at every level. One, it's a simple fact that two heads are better than one—a cliché with a lot of truth to it. Other things being equal, you're going to get more creative solutions to your problems by involving as many different viewpoints as you can—especially when those viewpoints come from directions you don't have access to.

Second, when you involve somebody in a participative management decision, you reinforce everything about him that makes him a smarter, more willing team member. You draw on the resources of his mind, not just his body. And everybody wants to feel that his mind—his unique understanding of a situation—is valuable, and valued. When somebody feels that, you can bank on his self-esteem improving. You can bank on his motivation going up. You can bank on the fact that he's going to be quicker to draw the connection between the overall objectives of the team and whatever his personal objectives may be.

But you have to do it, not just talk about it. Speeches about how "people are our most important asset" won't cut it, unless you act on that belief. To do that, you've got to get beyond the old "brawn versus brain" hangup and start to manage on the conviction that everybody in your organization—whatever his position and no matter how much money he makes—has got something to give to the team effort.

At participative management companies, the top people have been practicing that belief for years. Ask Fred Allen, chairman of the Connecticut-based company Pitney Bowes. In an article in *Leaders* magazine a few years ago, Allen talked about the connection between his own company's productivity and its commitment to Involvement of all its employees, and he made it very clear that the basic reason you want to reach toward Involvement is not because it's "nicer" to do that, but because it gets you results:

It is probably not love that makes the world go around, but rather those mutually supportive alliances through which partners recognize their dependence on each other for the achievement of shared and private goals. . . . Treat employees like partners, and they act like partners.

At Pitney Bowes the "partnership" aspect of employee Involvement has a very pragmatic, institutionalized side, because the company has a well-publicized Suggestion Plan that gives workers financial rewards for contributing in ways that save the company money: in other words, the company links Involvement with positive Consequences on a "We'll pay you for your ideas" basis, so the commitment to shared goals and mutual support can't possibly be seen as a gimmick: you get involved at Pitney Bowes, and you can take the results to the bank.

But, to stress one of the most important points about the entire P.R.I.C.E. system of motivation, you don't *have* to link Involvement to *financial* rewards in order to make the principle work. When I asked for Ahmad Rashad's and Ed White's input in my "participative huddle" days, I wasn't holding out the hope of an after-game bonus if their play suggestions got us yardage. I was just saying, "Look, your ideas are valuable to this team; I *need* your contributions; let's get your brains as well as your brawn involved here." That plea was, on one level, its *own* reward. It let every member of the Vikings team know that we were a "mutually supportive alliance" working toward the same shared goals.

A *Business Week* article from a couple of years ago demonstrates perfectly what I'm saying. The article profiles a Ford Motor Company foreman named Donald R. Hennion who, before the introduction of "participative management" techniques at his Edison, New Jersey, plant, was a typical "hard-nosed, loudmouthed disciplinarian." (Those are his own words.) You could hardly think of a less likely candidate for learning Involvement principles than an auto company foreman, but listen to what happened to Hennion.

He started to change his management style, the article points out, when he was assigned to a supervisory position where he didn't really understand the line operation, and so, for the first time in his career "had to rely on the workers' knowledge." That's a critical first step in any motion toward an Involvement style—the recognition that the people doing the work know *more* about that work than you do. That's the step I took as the Vikings quarterback when I asked Ahmad what was going on "out there." When Hennion took that step, he was amazed. "It's surprising," he told *Business Week*, "how much an employee can see that's wrong with a job."

A second step was for Hennion to redefine the nature of his own job, away from the idea that he had to crack the whip to get results and toward the notion that he was really not so much a taskmaster as a "facilitator." The implications for what a manager or supervisor actually *does* are startling. If you see yourself as a "facilitator," it means that when something breaks down, your job is not to find the bozo who caused the breakdown and kick his butt into next Sunday. It's to do something much easier than that. Something that, when you think about it, ought to be every manager's obvious first choice: it's to find out *what went wrong*, and then to get it fixed.

This focus on "what went wrong" rather than on "who screwed up" is not a semantic distinction. And it's definitely not a trivial one. Because when you focus on getting better results rather than kicking more butt, a remarkable thing happens to your team members. Instead of covering up defects and shifting blame—which are the usual responses in a "galley" style production team—they actually start to *look for* defects before they happen, and to call them to the foreman's attention. So, instead of one supervisor, you really end up with a whole team of supervisors, all motivated to pull together to create a better product, better quality control, and so on.

They put this "multiple supervisor" feature into place at Hennion's plant by allowing assembly line workers to do something that a lot of traditional "top down" managers would consider akin to Bolshevism: they let them *stop the line.* "The thought of an hourly worker stopping the line," the *Business Week* article says wryly, "would have made old Henry Ford apoplectic"; but the "stop concept" is one aspect of a worker participation program that invariably improves quality, reduces absenteeism, and lessens hostility between bosses and workers. We have found this to be true consistently in the plants where we introduce our Self-Managed Work Teams—teams of workers at every level who themselves are responsible for work schedules, quality, and general performance. It turns out the robber barons were wrong: you give the worker an inch, and he gives you *back* a mile.

It isn't really surprising. When you let the guy on the line have this kind of basic control over his own pace of work, you're demonstrating that you trust not only his judgment but his *loyalty.* You're saying, "I know you care about what we're doing here, and I know that if you push that button, you'll have a good reason for doing so." It's letting the lineman call the play again—because he's the one on the line, and he knows better than you do exactly what's going on "out there."

The same principles apply when you're trying to motivate white-collar people. Take sales, for example. Traditionally, control over how much work, and what kind of work, a sales representative does is established at the top—by a branch or division sales manager, and not by the "field troops" themselves. Sales management sets the quota and then tells the people who have to meet it what it's going to be. Sales directors may seek the input of marketing managers, and production managers, and the overall company brass, but they will not ask the opinion of the field representatives themselves—even though they are in the best position possible to say whether a quota is reasonable or not.

It's a pretty ridiculous system, and it survives only because managers are afraid that, if they are left to their own devices, sales representatives will never come in anywhere near quota. In every company I've seen where field people have a say in setting sales quotas, exactly the opposite takes place. If, instead of *telling* a salesman what he has to sell, you ask him what he thinks he *can* sell, a remarkable thing happens: he sets a figure for himself that is *higher* than the one you had in mind. Every time. Because people like to stretch. They just don't like to *be* stretched.

This means that, if you're a division sales manager or a factory line manager and, following tradition, you refuse to solicit your people's input into their own jobs, eventually you're going to be cutting your own throat, not just theirs. That's one of the ironies of ignoring Involvement. Refusing to practice Involvement in today's increasingly democratized environment can be just as fatal to the *manager* who likes to think he's on top of things as it can be to the "underlings" who make him feel superior. If you've got the whip and you're barking out orders in a galley, it means you never find out about the leak near the bow, and you drown right along with your slaves. If you're a quarterback and you don't find out what the linemen know, it means you have Astroturf for lunch. There's an old expression about the slaveholder being just as much in chains as the slaves he thinks he's controlling, and that's true when you're talking about workers and "controllers" as well.

And the opposite is also true. Free a slave, get freed yourself. Another irony of participative management is that—contrary to what its critics fear—it actually gives managers *more* scope than they have under traditional methods of control. Under a real workplace democracy, the guys "in charge" gain just as much freedom as the people they used to boss around.

Donald Hennion calls attention to this curious phenomenon in talking about his changing job at the Edison Ford plant. He points out that, once line workers began to take responsibility for spotting defects and for stopping the line when it was necessary, he was freed of a whole level of managerial responsibility that wasn't really getting anybody anywhere anyway: for the first time in his management career, he didn't have to spend half his day looking over people's shoulders—and looking over his *own* shoulder as well. Because he now trusts people to do their jobs without being constantly monitored like mischievous children, he "has considerably more time to work with maintenance people, draw up better plans for the flow of material, and make minor engineering changes without calling the plant engineers." In other words, he can become a real *manager*, because he no longer has to be a guard.

What's the bottom line? Hennion has no doubt that Involvement has boosted the overall profits of the plant as well as the morale and motivation of his people. "You're more productive in the long run," he says. "People on the line seem happier. You still have . . . boredom, but the attitude is changing. We're working as a team."

THE SYNERGY EFFECT

Happier workers, more responsible workers, higher productivity—those are the principal effects I've seen in the companies I visit from adopting a more involved style of motivation. But there's one other effect I want to mention, because it really explains why you get all the others. I call it the "Synergy Effect."

I believe that people want to be contented with their work, they want to be responsible for what they're doing, they want to pull their weight to achieve lower waste and higher productivity. And I believe that, in today's increasingly interconnected work environment, they can best accomplish those personal goals by being part of winning teams. In fact, being a member of a winning team becomes in itself a high priority achievement, because it makes the attainment of all those other goals so much easier.

The Synergy Effect explains why this happens. It explains why good teamwork and an institutionalized system of Involvement lead to better motivation and performance: it explains why groups achieve things that individuals alone cannot achieve.

Every team athlete has experienced synergy at one time or another. It's that strange and almost indefinable phenomenon that happens when you get three or four reasonably good players together and find out that, when they function together, they perform on a much higher level than even the best of them could do by himself. You know the old expression that the whole can be more than the sum of its parts—that sometimes one plus one plus one can equal four? That's the Synergy Effect. And it works even more obviously in business than on the playing field.

In our seminars on productivity, we do a "group survival" exercise that illustrates the Synergy Effect extremely well. First, we separate the seminar into groups of six or seven people each. Then, we ask them to imagine that they have just crash-landed above the Arctic Circle, and that there is no way of repairing their plane. They are uninjured and reasonably warmly dressed, but at least thirty miles from the nearest town and in totally unfamiliar territory. In addition to a barely decipherable map, they were able to salvage from the plane only fifteen items. These include several wooden matches, a compass, an axe, a flashlight, some rope, three pairs of snowshoes, and a fifth of Bacardi rum. The exercise is to rank these items in order of importance to the group's survival, with the most important item being ranked 1, the next most important 2, and so on down to 15.

We ask the seminar participants to perform this ranking exercise in two stages: first, individually, and then working in their groups, in a consensus fashion: that is, the group has to agree not by voting but by "talking it out" and compromise, what each item's ranking will be. We also tell them at the outset that, for the theoretical purposes of the exercise, there is a "best possible" ranking: it's a ranking that was provided to us by a Canadian wilderness rescue team, experts in Arctic survival techniques. This expert evaluation is the standard against which we measure the accuracy of both the individual and group rankings. We perform the measurement by taking the expert's ranking as a "zero base," finding the difference between this base and the other rankings for each of the fifteen items, and finally adding up the differences to reach a composite score.

For example, if Joe Barnes feels that the flashlight ought to be ranked at 3, we compare that figure with the expert's ranking—in this case, 10—and give Joe a score of 7 for that item. Likewise, if Roberta Malley ranks the flashlight at 12, she would get a score of 2 for that item. Once we've done that for each of the fifteen items, we add up the differences, and the person (or group) with the lowest total "wins."

Since our clients vary widely in their backgrounds and interests, we find a broad range of accuracy in their rankings. Some individuals and some groups get quite close to the expert's ranking, and some are light years away. That's not surprising. What is surprising is that, no matter how good an individual may be in ranking the importance of the items, I have never yet come across a case where an individual's score was better than that of his group.

I remember one guy from a banking firm who was an avid weekend backpacker, and whose individual score was incredibly low (that is, good). The average individual score in this exercise is something like 55, and his was 31 or 32. Nobody else in his group knew anything at all about the outdoors, so you might have expected that, when they came up with a consensus ranking, it would have been much worse than the wilderness wizard's own ranking.

Exactly the opposite happened. Somehow the interaction of the backpacking "genius" with the ignoramuses on his team made them come out with a game plan that was better than his alone. And this happens every time one of our client groups does the exercise.

We talked about the outcome later, and the backpacker showed some insight into why people who knew "less" than he did were able to give him lessons. "I was thinking about the problem," he said, "in the ways I had been trained to think. On most of the items that was OK. But on a few it was taking me in exactly the wrong direction. On some of those items the best ideas came from people who just didn't know what they were talking about."

In other words, they came from group members who were not burdened with "experience" or "tradition" or with the self-defeating knowledge that "you just can't do it this way." They came from people who were willing to throw in their two cents because they were too stupid to know that two cents won't buy anything. The result was the Synergy Effect—proof, once again, that even geniuses can be made smarter by an infusion of fresh ideas. That's a revelation that every manager troubled by low motivation would be wise to take to heart.

I'm going to talk about this survival exercise again in the last section of the book, on building and managing teamwork. Here I'll just make the basic point: not only are two (or ten) heads usually *better* than one, but they are also dramatically *different* in "partnership" than they could possibly be alone. Since the best solutions to business problems are seldom just accretions of former solutions, that differentness is an essential ingredient of really getting things done.

The way you get at that differentness is to make teamwork not just a word but an everyday, working reality. And the ultimate reason you want (or should want) to do that is very bottom-line and pragmatic: it gets better results than relying on the geniuses to show the way. Because sometimes the only way they can show you doesn't lead anywhere you want to go.

FOUR

CONSEQUENCES

In nature there are neither rewards nor punishments—
there are consequences.
—R. G. INGERSOLL

If you've ever tried to train a dog to do something he's not used to doing—whether it's rolling over, or hopping on his back legs, or refraining from biting the mailman—you know that you never get anywhere until you link up the desired new Behavior to clearly defined rewards and punishments. No dog in his right mind is going to get up on his back legs unless he knows there's a bone or a pat on the head waiting for him at the end of the trick. The only time your snapping Doberman is going to stop looking at the mailman as if he were a T-bone steak is when he gets a snootful of Mace. The lesson is the oldest one in behaviorist psychology, and it's the one I stressed at the opening of the book: to change a given Behavior, you've got to start with its Consequences. In talking about Consequences before, I said that there were basically three ways that you as a manager could impact the performance of the people with whom you work. You could give them *positive* reinforcement by making the Consequences of their Behavior attractive. You could give them *negative* reinforcement by making the Consequences unattractive. Or you could give them *neutral* reinforcement—that is, no reinforcement—by simply asking for a new Behavior without tying it in to Consequences. In this chapter I'm going to be talking a little more about these three choices, and I'm going to start with the last one—the virtual ignoring of Consequences that leads to what my company calls the Extinction Effect.

THE EXTINCTION EFFECT

Because most managers are not familiar or comfortable with the idea of "giving Consequences" for Behavior, it's very common in industry for a worker to be asked to do something, to do it, and then to get *no* reinforcement for having done it. I know you've seen this pattern in your place of business. A plant supervisor, for example, will ask a line manager who has been absent from work a good deal to increase his attendance rate. Asking him that is what I've been calling an "Antecedent": it precedes the desired Behavior of higher attendance. For the next three or four weeks the manager never misses a day of work: he performs exactly the Behavior that the supervisor has asked for. But instead of complimenting him on his newly learned diligence, the supervisor says nothing because coming to work every day is something the manager ought to want to do, something he shouldn't have to be told about. So there is no reinforcement—no Consequences either positive or negative—for the operator's obvious improvement. And he quickly regresses: five or six weeks after the initial reprimand, he's back to his old pattern of skipping work—and the supervisor can't figure out what happened. "He was doing so good for a while there," he says to himself. "I wonder why he's backsliding?"

The reason is simple. Unless you reinforce good Behavior, that Behavior will inevitably *decrease*. By failing to supply desirable Consequences for the manager's efforts, the supervisor *extinguishes* those efforts. He sets up the Extinction Effect.

And it's no good for a supervisor in this kind of situation to say, "Look, all I asked for was a return to normal. Why should I give him strokes for that?" Because in this kind of situation 100 percent attendance is obviously not "normal." "Normal" for this particular person was skipping work three or four times a month, and so when the supervisor asked him to come in every day he was requiring a Behavior that, for him, was much *better* than normal. Naturally, when he performed it and nobody said boo about his effort, he thought to himself, "What am I knocking myself out for? He doesn't care if I come in or not." And so he reverted to *his* "normal."

You know the expression "The squeaky wheel gets the grease." That expression is demonstrated all the time in business, with predictably lousy results. Managers are plenty willing to give out negative Consequences when somebody is screwing up his job, but they're not interested in applying the grease unless and until the wheel is really making a racket. That's like waiting until the bicycle just won't pump any more before you reach for the oil can. Intelligent management today has to do not only with "fixing" the bad spots when they show up, but also with "preventive maintenance" on the *good* spots, so they never turn into problems. If you don't apply the grease to the bike parts that evidently don't "need" it yet, eventually you'll be pedalling a pile of scrap.

Another transportation analogy. In our productivity seminars we sometimes talk about the "the 55 mile-per-hour ratchet." It illustrates very well what I'm saying about Behavior reverting to "subnormal" if it isn't constantly reinforced.

You know that in most of the United States there's a 55 mile-per-hour speed limit. To the people who "manage" our highways—police officers, legislators, other public officials—the link between Consequences and Behavior here is very clear. But it's not always clearly enforced—or consistently enforced—and that can lead to problems. The "ideal" Behavior would be for every motorist to drive at no faster than the legal 55 mph limit. But every motorist knows that, unless he drives *significantly* higher than 55, he is probably not going to be ticketed. The average rate of speed on our highways is not 55 or 57 or 58, but something like 62 or 63. Why? Because people know from experience that, when they drive at 65, they are going to be stopped. But they can drive at 63 or 64 without incurring any negative Consequences—and, therefore, that's where they drive. They perform at exactly that subnormal level that will keep them from getting pulled over.

It's different on big holiday weekends, when motorists understand that the cops are out in force, and that they are taking the 55 mph limit more seriously than at other times. In other words, on holiday weekends, the Consequences for driving at 62 are probably going to be more severe than they would be at other times. As a result, people drive slower. They change their driving Behaviors to more closely approximate the ideal, because the boys in blue have made it clear that it will make a *difference* to them to do so. Once the weekend is over, though, most drivers revert to type: their good Behavior gets extinguished because it's no longer linked to real Consequences.

This doesn't mean that everybody starts driving at 125. Just that performance drops to a level *just better* than the level that will earn negative Consequences. That's a basic rule of the Extinction Effect in business, too: In the absence of positive reinforcement, performance will stay *just above the level where punishment occurs*. Anything better than that will be extinguished. This means that, unless you bring out the grease gun frequently—and even when it's not needed—the best you can possibly hope for is a universal "Muddle in the Middle," where every one of your people is motivated just to *get by*, because there's nothing in it for him to do better.

Because of this universal human tendency to backslide, to do just what you can get away with and no more, managers eager to motivate their people have got to pay stricter attention to *reinforcement of the middle*—not just throwing flowers at the performance superstars and rotten apples at the fumblers.

John D. Rockefeller put it well. "Good management," he said, "consists in showing average people how to do the work of superior people." This means learning to balance negative and positive so that the general level of achievement in the middle is raised. Let's start with the down side of that balancing act: the problems and potential advantages of using constructive criticism.

PUNISHMENT AND CONSTRUCTIVE CRITICISM

I guess there aren't too many people in the world who actually like to get negative criticism, but I am one of those weird souls. I've got a good reason for it, too. As I used to tell one of my coaches—a smart man who was just a little too gentle for the team's own good—"If you don't give me negative feedback, if you don't give me good, hard constructive criticism of my performance, you *rob me of the chance to improve.*" And improvement is what it's all about. As a manager, if you really want your people to improve, if you want to motivate them toward the most productive Behaviors that they're capable of, you've got to use the stick as well as the carrot. Without it, everybody on your team is going to be driving at 125 miles an hour, and getting nowhere fast.

I'll be the first to admit that this is easier said than done. Even though more managers are used to giving out criticism than praise, very few of them know how to do it well, and that's not because they're mean or insensitive people. The fact is that it's *hard* to knock somebody's performance—at least if you're a reasonably decent person yourself and care about your people as people and not just cogs in the machine. It would be a lot simpler to hand out negative Consequences if we all had the sensitivity of Atilla the Hun.

For one thing, people who are hearing negative things about themselves tend not to be the most accommodating or cooperative individuals themselves. The operator that you tell to improve in terms of his attendance may make an effort to do that, but he's not likely to say, "Thanks a lot for pointing out that defect; I appreciate your giving me a chance to do better." Maybe that's what he *ought* to say. But realistically speaking, he's likely to be not rational but defensive. Whenever you give negative Consequences, you run the risk of setting up what we call the Punishment Effect: a reaction to criticism that includes evasiveness, excuses, refusal of responsibility, and in some cases outright aggression. All of which, of course, tends to decrease, not increase, the level of performance you want.

Unfortunately, the Punishment Effect often comes with the territory, which is why managers have to use caution and more than a little sensitivity when delivering negative Consequences. That's not easy, but I can give you one piece of advice that might lighten this particular load: you always make punishment more acceptable when it's not seen as the only game in town. When it's used not as an end in itself but as part of a total "performance improvement package"—that is, if your people understand that you're not out to get them but to make everybody's life smoother—they're less likely to resist or deny your negative Consequences. I'll go into this a little more in a moment.

A second reason that punishment is difficult to deliver is that, to be effective as a motivator to better performance, it has to be severe enough to hurt. You don't get the Doberman away from your throat by tapping him lightly on the muzzle, and you don't get the absence-prone manager back on track by frowning at him and saying, "You're not pulling your weight." The kinds of negative Consequences that are likely to be effective in the workplace—docking of pay, removal of worksite privileges—are also precisely the kind of Consequences that can lead your union people to call their shop steward and middle managers to have their resumes retyped. Again, that's a built-in hazard that only a "broader scope" approach to motivation can address.

Finally, the use of punishment as a corrective technique can set up a company atmosphere where this most severe kind of negative Consequence is seen as the appropriate one in all situations—and where, as a result, people tend to perform at that minimum level which will ensure that the whip does not fall on their backs. You see this dangerous effect occurring all the time in military organizations, and while it may have a provisional value in such situations, it has almost no value at all in the modern, increasingly democratized workplace. I go back to what I said above about the Extinction Effect. In the absence of positive reinforcement, people who are under the gun from supervisors will tend to revert to the *lowest acceptable* level of performance—that is, to a level just barely above what the organization needs to get by. So you get the manager who realizes that skipping one day every two weeks will not get him docked any pay. Or the soldier who does exactly the minimum number of pushups that can earn him an overnight pass.

In order to guard against the negative results of using punishing Consequences, consultants from the Tarkenton Productivity Group give our clients a number of general guidelines to apply in selecting punishments. Here are the most important of these guidelines:

1. Give a *warning* before applying punishment. This is another way of saying that, before you give Consequences for an action, you should already have given an Antecedent that let the individual know exactly what Behavior you wanted. I remember a situation in a small Midwest factory where spoilage on one shift was very high because line operators' hairs were falling into a lubrication system that was extremely sensitive to foreign matter. Before our consultants got there, the shift supervisor typically blew a gasket every time hairs were found in the oil—but made no suggestion to the operators about what they could do about it in the future. We advised him to give them hair nets, and to tell them, "If you don't wear these nets on this line, we're going to have to stop the line to retrieve hairs, and you'll be docked for the lost time." That was a combination of Pinpointing a Behavior and of giving an exact Antecedent (a precise warning) to ensure that the Behavior changed. It did change, too. And it wasn't just because of the nets. It was because every person on that line understood that, unless they adopted a new Behavior, they would suffer a punishing Consequence (the loss of time-down pay).

2. Make the punishment *timely*. This is just common sense. If you want the dog off your throat, you don't threaten to Mace him for twenty minutes while he's working his way toward your jugular vein. You Mace him *now*. It's the same in industry. If you have Pinpointed an ineffective Behavior, and everyone understands that it has to change, then the first time it occurs again, you've *got* to deliver the bad Consequences. Otherwise you're a paper tiger. And the hairs are going to stay in the oil.

I don't mean that you can't give "preliminary warnings" or give somebody who's really trying to improve another chance. But carry that on too long, and your entire team is going to suffer. Which is unfair to everybody—including the person who's falling behind.

The head coach of the Vikings, Bud Grant, was very exact and exacting about this. He knew he was in business as well as in sports, and he wasn't about to waste everybody's time and money giving people who just couldn't (or wouldn't) perform a hundred chances. A rookie came on to Bud's team and he was told *precisely* what he was expected to do (that was Pinpointing). If he didn't manage to do it the first time, Bud would take him aside and explain—again, precisely—what it was he was doing wrong. Maybe Bud or his coaches would do that three times, if the rookie was really busting his gut, but that was it. After repeated failures, you were out. And I truly believe that was *kinder* than allowing the kid to hang on, dropping hairs in everybody's oil, until he brought everybody's chances of success down along with his own. I have no doubt at all that it was a more efficient style of management. If somebody needs a kick in the ass, do it *now*.

3. Make it *appropriate*. The more intense the punishment, the more effect it has in cutting down unwanted Behaviors. I've already noted that, in today's workplace, you can't use really punishing Consequences (peremptory firings, for example) for structural and legal reasons—and it's a good thing you can't. But wishy-washy punishments are often worse than no punishments at all, because they give people the idea that your threats are empty. It's not a giant step from that realization to the suspicion that your promises of *good* Consequences are probably empty, too. And once your people believe that there is no solid connection between what they do and what happens to them as a result, you're sunk.

I can't tell you what would be appropriate negative Consequences for your industry or your particular site of operation. I guess that a ground rule would be the simple one of justice (which is not really all that simple). I mean that you look at the "crime"—whether it's absenteeism or falling asleep on the job or letting hairs drop in the oil—and you try to devise negative Consequences that "suit the crime," and that are neither too soft nor too hard. You don't fire somebody for being five minutes late a few times a month, and if your secretary takes two weeks to hand you a letter marked "Urgent," you don't let her off with a "Gee, be more careful, OK?" Since punishment is so hard to deliver—for both the person delivering it and the person taking it—I advise our clients to concentrate on devising "punishment schedules" that will accomplish the desired Behavior change with the *least* hurt possible that will still do the job. And I remind them to think of Dodger manager Tommy Lasorda's sage comment. In aiming for a balance between the "hard" and "soft" schools of control, he said you should remember that managing is "like holding a dove in your hand. Squeeze too hard and you kill it; not hard enough and it flies away."

4. Be *consistent.* The only way that you can, in the long run, reduce ineffective Behaviors in a team is to apply your punishment schedules consistently, whatever the overall work picture and whoever is involved. This means that you've got to be very suspicious of what somebody caught in the act is liable to call "mitigating circumstances." I don't mean you should always consider them irrelevant. Only that, if you're being asked to suspend the rules in an individual circumstance, you'd better make damn sure that the circumstances are more *important* than the rules. Not just for the guy who left the wrench in the engine, but for your entire organization.

Peter Drucker has a great definition of the purpose of an executive. He says it's "to make sensible exceptions to general rules." Very true, but there's a world of questions left open in that little word "sensible." If you want to find out whether or not an exception is sensible, ask yourself this question: "What's going to be the long-term effect on the motivation of my people if *everybody finds out* I've made this exception?" If the long-term effect is to generate a sense of innovation and openness and possibility, fine: it makes sense to bend the punishment schedule. But if the long-term effect is to let everybody know that you can be bought (or wheedled into submission), you won't need a Doberman to tear you apart. You'll be doing it to yourself.

5. *Correct the Behavior, not the person.* Getting anything done in a large organization involves the intelligent management of various Pinpointed activities just as much as it does the management of the people doing those activities. And it's a lot easier to focus on the activities—the Behaviors—being performed than to correct the "deviant" or "defiant" personalities of the actors. It's not only more humane to concentrate on the specific unwanted Behaviors; it also gets better results.

One example: the worst single case of coaching I ever saw in my eighteen-year NFL career. It happened after we had lost a close game two minutes from the final buzzer because the blocking had been a little fuzzy, causing me to eat the old Astroturf before getting the pass off. Back in the film room the following day, a veteran line coach was going over why we had blown it. When he came to the critical play where I had been sacked, he turned to a young teammate of mine—an all-Pro lineman who had been playing well for us all season—and said, "You see that, where you missed that block? *You cost us the football game.* And you know why? You didn't want to block him enough. He wanted to get to the quarterback more than you wanted to stop him. I guess he just had more character than you, that's all."

More character! This was the 1970s, in the Big Time, with a room full of adult professionals! Hearing that was one of the most embarrassing moments I ever experienced in my career, and I wasn't the one being chewed out. And you know what great results came out of that sensitive application of negative Consequences? The Punishment Effect in spades: that young lineman never played another good game for us all season, and at the end of the season we had to trade him. He went to a team where the handbook on coaching apparently didn't talk about "character," and he played just *great* for them.

What our line coach should have done was to focus on the Behavior, not the person. He should have said, "Look, you see where you missed that block? The guy got you turned around. You didn't have your feet planted square enough; and you were off balance. That's why he got by you. Let's work on that this week." That would have been sound coaching. It would have

Pinpointed specific Behaviors that needed work, and focused on correcting those Behaviors. I guess that's the approach that the young lineman's new coaching staff must have taken, because he sure tore up the track with them. And it was our loss.

The bottom line? You want to change a person's Behavior, focus on that Behavior. You don't know squat about his character anyway, so forget about the armchair psychoanalysis. Just *work on what you can control.*

6. *Reinforce the change.* Finally, a lesson that the supervisor I spoke about before failed to remember, and that is essential to the long-term use of negative Consequences. Whatever you consider "normal" and whatever your employee considers "normal," be sure to *follow up* on the criticism by identifying any improvement, and by giving *positive* reinforcement for that. Remember that when negative reinforcement is the *only* type of Consequences you hear, you're going to fall prey to the old "Muddle in the Middle," and perform "just above" the punishment level. If you want to motivate *peak* performance, not just adequate performance, you've got to link your negative Consequences with positive ones. If somebody on your team is handing in reports four days late, and you express your disapproval, he might start handing them in three days late. If you want to get them in on time, you have to say at that point, "Jeff, thanks for trying to cut down on the lag time on these reports; I really appreciate your effort. But I've still got a problem here, so I'd like you to get them in on time." If all you say is "Thanks," or (worse yet) if you say nothing, the report-delivery is going to stay at three days late—and eventually drift back to four.

In fact, when you're devising your punishment schedules, it's always a good idea to keep the old 4:1 Syndrome in mind. Remember that most people behave "at least adequately" about 80 percent of the time (four times to one). But most managers— whether they're on a football staff or in a manufacturing concern—tend to reinforce Behavior in exactly the *opposite* proportion: they give four strokes for every slap, even when their folks are doing fine. Effective management of motivation reverses that tendency. The best managers understand that, as the old bird hunter might have observed, you need both honey *and* salt to get the birds to come to your hand. But while a diet of constant honey might not be your idea of nutrition, it's much more important for the motivator to remember that *nobody*—bird, Doberman, or human—will live on salt alone.

FIGHTING THE EXTINCTION EFFECT: POSITIVE REINFORCEMENT

Many of the guidelines I've just given with regard to negative reinforcement apply equally well to positive reinforcement. Good positive Consequences should be delivered in a *timely* manner, they should be *appropriate*, and they should be given *consistently* to anybody who performs the Behavior. Beyond that, though, there are some guidelines that apply particularly to positive reinforcement that I want to go into now.

In my company we make a distinction between *extrinsic* positive reinforcers and *intrinsic*, or "naturally occurring" reinforcers, and we tell our clients the Consequences that grow naturally out of the work environment are almost always more effective than the extrinsic variety. In a lot of places we work, this sets the conventional wisdom on its head, so it's important to emphasize it here.

An extrinsic reinforcer would be something like an annual Christmas dinner for employees, a team picnic, or tickets to a play or other entertainment offered as a reward for good performance. The expectation of these kinds of rewards can be motivating, sure, but there are some problems involved with using them exclusively, because they tend to get institutionalized and expected, and so they come to be seen not as Consequences but as mere perquisites of the job. The first time you invite your department to a holiday bash as a reward for services rendered, they may see it as real reinforcement. But the second and third time you do it, the event is going to start seeming like the norm, and the motivating benefits will go down, because people will begin to get the idea that they've got the annual party "coming"—whatever their performance has been.

Not that traditions like Christmas parties and team picnics can't serve a useful function in the workplace. They can. They can help to create that atmosphere of community that generally helps Involvement, and helps to make people identify their personal satisfactions with those of the team at large. Such traditions are just not especially useful as *reinforcement*, that's all.

For example, I know of a small New England computer company where the management-initiated practice of Bonus Day has been in place for about ten years. "The first couple of years," a production supervisor told me once, "Bonus Day was a blast. It meant not only that you got your year-end bonus, but also that you drank a lot of beer and had a great time celebrating a productive twelve months. By the third or fourth year, though, people started to expect it. They knew that, whatever the year's productivity had been, the beer would still be flowing. So they started taking it as a given, and they didn't push themselves to make it happen. Pretty soon the beer blast was happening even in lousy years, and by that time it was just a hollow gesture. We're thinking about doing away with the tradition."

Why was Bonus Day in this company becoming a hollow gesture? Because it was no longer tied to real performance improvement. In addition, it violated a principle called *differential reinforcement* (which I'll talk about in Chapter 8) because it gave everybody in the company the *same* reward, regardless of his or her personal contribution to the team. In other words, it was a "noncontingent" or "unnatural" perk of employment—it happened every year, no matter what else had gone before it.

To motivate people to peak performance, you have to concentrate on what we call "naturally occurring" or *contingent* rewards—that is, rewards that are dependent upon specific Behaviors, and don't "just happen" in a vacuum. A contingent reward, when you think about it, is the only kind of a reward that can really be called a Consequence. It's also the only kind of reward with true motivating power.

There are as many examples of contingent or naturally occurring reinforcers as there are people and situations in your work environment. Just one example. Think of the "hairs in the oil" problem that I was talking about earlier. Say you are supervising the line where that problem occurs, and you tell the foreman that he's got to be more attentive, right now, to the lubrication purity of his line: that's the Antecedent that you give him to modify his Behavior. And say that he does modify his Behavior. Say that, at the end of the following week, when you check your Recording graph to see how the problem is going, you find that "hairs in the oil" is down by 40 percent. It's time to give the foreman positive reinforcement for his good Behavior. How are you going to do that? What naturally occurring reinforcers do you have available that are going to motivate him (and his team) to continue to improve their work?

Actually, I get asked this question all the time. Managers who are just not used to giving good Consequences are constantly shrugging their shoulders at me and saying, "I just don't know what to do so he'll continue to perform well." I tell them they've got an unlimited number of things they could say or do. They could:

1. Verbally praise the person
2. Write a note of commendation to the plant or department manager
3. Post the person's name and/or picture on a bulletin board or in a company newsletter
4. Give him an opportunity to address a meeting
5. Ask him to join you for lunch
6. Give him time off
7. Offer him a choice of a new work assignment
8. Treat his team to coffee and donuts

I could go on and on, but you get the idea. The point is that, if you want a newly learned good Behavior to keep coming, you've got to let the person who's done it know that you've seen it, and that you appreciate his work.

Now, all the examples I've given here, you'll notice, relate directly to the work environment. We call such Consequences "naturally occurring" reinforcers, in fact, because they develop naturally out of the job itself. That's why they're so effective. Employees like such intrinsic rewards because they allow them to make the connection between better work and more satisfying work. I've already said that people *want* to do a good job when given the chance; if you give them immediate, contingent strokes for doing that, they're going to be all the more eager to continue.

But there's another, more mercenary reason that naturally occurring reinforcers like these are (or should be) attractive to managers interested in motivation. It's that they are nearly always *free*. Look at the list I've given here. The only items on it that are likely to cost a manager any money are lunch and the coffee and donuts—and even those are a hell of a lot cheaper than a year-end beer bash for all employees. One of the most gratifying ironies of using positive reinforcement in business is that the Consequences that seem to matter the *most* to employees are not the giant bonuses and tickets to the World Series, but the small, intangible evidences of gratitude that any manager can deliver with minimum expense. If you've got the least interest in making your motivation system cost-effective, positive reinforcement like this is a Godsend. There's no other way to increase a team's motivation that gets you so much return for so little time and energy invested.

Amazingly, you still hear resistance to this idea. You hear managers refusing to give out positive reinforcement because "You shouldn't praise somebody for just doing his job." You hear people saying that the only reinforcement that really matters is the kind you can stuff in your wallet. And you hear people claim that the employee who is already performing well doesn't *need* reinforcement.

All of these fallacies are related, and I can demonstrate why they're inaccurate by relating a couple of brief football stories.

The first concerns the only time in my eighteen-year football career when I called a play that required the quarterback to block. I've already pointed out that the blocking quarterback is about as rare a creature these days as a dope-smoking TV evangelist, and with good reason: we just don't *learn* that Behavior. Back in 1974, when I had just returned to the Vikings from my stint with the Giants, I had to learn it, and learn it fast. With an 0–3 record behind us, we were facing the St. Louis Cardinals out in Bloomington, and getting nowhere. I knew we had to pull out a surprise play to save the game, and there is nothing more likely to surprise a defense than a play where the quarterback blocks.

The play in question was a reverse where I handed off to Ed Marinaro (now on TV's "Hill Street Blues"), Ed handed off to John Gilliam, and I took out a tackler who was trying to get to John. The way I took him out was a little unconventional: I fell down on the ground in front of him, and he tumbled over me. But what the hell, it worked. John went in for the touchdown, and we won the game.

The next day, watching the films, I was all hyped up for Coach Bud Grant's readout. When it came around to "my" play—the one where I had sacrificed my body for the team—I was all ready to sit back and bask in the glory. It never came. Bud praised everybody involved in the play: Marinaro, Gilliam, the entire line, but not me. After the filming, I asked him why. "You saw my block, didn't you, coach? How come you didn't say anything about it?"

Now, some folks would have said, "Look, Tarkenton, you're the highest-paid guy on this team, and that ought to be enough for you, so can it." Bud wasn't that stupid, but what he said betrayed another kind of "You don't need it" fallacy. "Yeah, I saw the block," he told me. "It was great. But you're always working hard out there, Francis, you're always giving 100 percent. I figured I didn't have to tell you."

"Well," I told him, "if you want me to block again you do."

The lesson is clear. It goes against what a lot of managers seem to believe about the "good" performers on a team: that they'll continue to be good if you just leave them alone. That's bull. If you want somebody who's performing well to keep performing well, tell him so—or extinguish the good Behavior.

The second story involves Max Winter, the president and founder of the Minnesota Vikings, who was one of the most understanding and decent men I've ever worked with. When I retired from the field in 1978, I wrote him a brief letter saying how much I appreciated the guidance and support he had given me during our long association. This was a man who was a millionaire many times over, and who had access to every luxury money could buy. You wouldn't think a letter from a former quarterback would have meant very much to him. But you know what he did with it? I later found out that he had it framed and hung it on the wall of his office. For all his money and success, Max wanted what everybody else wants: recognition for a job well done. That was something nobody's money could buy. And it hadn't cost me a cent.

One last piece of evidence, if there's any doubt left in your mind that you can motivate better with intrinsic rewards than you ever can with hard cash. A number of years ago, Psychological Services of Pittsburgh, a social-science research group, surveyed the attitudes of two hundred and twenty-eight people who had one thing in common: they clearly liked their work. They chose workers at all levels in a number of different occupations—from steelworkers, to shipbuilding engineers, to managers in light industry—and they asked them in interviews to identify what it was that made their jobs particularly enjoyable to them. Remember that these were people who, whatever their status, had very *positive attitudes* and very *high motivation* regarding their work.

The results? Of the variety of people who responded, very small percentages mentioned such factors as working conditions, status, and interpersonal relations as reasons for their positive attitudes. A fairly significant percentage (between 20 and 26 percent) mentioned the factors "the work itself," "responsibility," or "advancement." Now here's the kicker. "Recognition" got voted for by 33 percent of the workers, "achievement" was identified as critical by 41 percent—and only 15 percent thought they were happy in their jobs because of "salary." That is a very poor argument for giving your people a paycheck and saying that you've motivated them enough. And it's an excellent argument for using the "naturally occurring reinforcers" that I've been talking about in this chapter.

THE REINFORCING MEMO: A CHECKLIST

One of the easiest—and cheapest—of these reinforcers is the simple Reinforcing Memo. Because you get so much back in motivation from this simple device, it's worthwhile tying up the chapter by explaining briefly how to write one. As my story about my note to Max Winter illustrates, everybody (no matter what his position) likes to see in print that he or she is appreciated, and the Reinforcing Memo is one of the best ways I know of getting that critical motivational task done.

A memo designed to reinforce a good Behavior is a somewhat more formal way of saying "Thanks, keep up the good work" than a personal, face-to-face comment would be. For that reason the Reinforcement Memo is a good tool to use when you have relatively little contact with the person whose Behavior you're reinforcing. It's also valuable when you're trying to reinforce *exceptional* or *continuously high* Behavior; when you want a *record* of the Behavior for publicity or performance appraisal use; when you want to include *graph-based* Recording data to indicate specifically why you value the person's contribution; when you're reinforcing a series of *complex, interrelated* Behaviors; and when you just want to *vary* your verbal reinforcements, and let your people know that this is not just another simple "Thank you."

The actual content and style of a Reinforcing Memo, of course, will depend on the situation and people involved. As an example, here's a sample memo that might be written from a production manager to a line worker who had contributed exceptional performance in an emergency situation:

From: Art Davis, Production Manager
To: Jim Ryan

Jim, on Friday, March 30, when the #3 presser broke down and we asked shop people for assistance, you responded by working through the night and into Saturday when the problem was fixed.

I wanted to write this memo to express my sincere appreciation for a job well done. Your energetic response to the plant emergency made everybody's job (especially mine) a lot easier last week. As you've shown many times in the past, your dedication and dependability have made an outstanding contribution to the high performance standards of our plant.

My thanks for a super job.

cc: *Personnel file*
Florence Moore, assistant plant supervisor

You can vary the presentation suggested here depending on your particular situations, but I'd keep a number of guidelines in mind. In our productivity seminars we suggest the following guidelines:

1. Keep it *short.* The three paragraphs indicated in the sample are probably optimum. A good Reinforcing Memo should never run on effusively, but should come on as a *slightly* expanded "Thanks." The longer the memo, we've found, the lower the degree of credibility.

2. Be *precise.* In other words, Pinpoint the Behavior that you're praising. It's never sufficient to call a person "cooperative" or "dependable." Make it clear why those adjectives apply in the specific instance you're referring to: "Thanks for your cooperation in agreeing to work overtime last Friday." The more Pinpointed the memo, the less chance the person will see it as insincere—and the greater chance that you will effectively reinforce the specific Behavior you found desirable.

3. Say *why* you're writing the memo. Explain specifically why it's important—both to the company and to you personally—that Behaviors like his be repeated. In the sample above, the production manager highlighted Jim's contribution to "high production." "Thanks a lot for coming in" means nothing. A memo that effectively reinforces Jim's coming in will identify his value to the plant ("high production") *and* to the writer of the memo ("You made my job a lot easier last week"). The point is that people want to know not only *that* they are helping the team, but also *how.*

4. *Quantify* it wherever possible. If Jim's overtime work on Friday saved the Production Department six hours of down time, say so. Refer to your Recording graphs if they are relevant to the problem at hand. People want to know as specifically as possible how they have contributed to team success. Figures won't always be relevant in a Reinforcement Memo, but where they are relevant, use them.

5. Keep it *personal.* Not mushy, just personal. You don't need to send Jim roses, but you do have to let him know that you're talking to *him*, person to person. Excessive formality ("Management appreciates the diligence with which you continue to perform your job functions") is always going to be less effective as a motivating style than the use of "I" and "we" and of such conversational kudos as "great work" and "super job."

6. Make it *timely.* To reiterate what I said earlier about the need for immediate Consequences: make sure a Reinforcing Memo follows by no more than a couple of days the Behavior you're trying to reinforce. The farther away from the event, the less power it's going to have to motivate. You wait two weeks to tell somebody you appreciate his exceptional performance, and you're just setting yourself up for the Extinction Effect.

7. Make and/or post *copies.* Notice that in the sample given here, the manager sends a copy of the Reinforcement Memo to the personnel department and to the assistant plant manager. It's always useful to let the highly motivated worker's superiors know that he's performing well—and to *let him know that you've done so.* If those people can be encouraged to write brief comments on their copies (or simply to initial them) and return them to the person being praised, so much the better: using this technique of "synergistic reinforcement," you can get triple or quadruple the recognition benefit with the same amount of initial work. And you can't tell me that a person who receives three or four positive comments for doing one good Behavior is not going to perform that Behavior again.

Those are the positive guidelines that we use to strengthen the impact of Reinforcement Memos. One negative guideline also should be mentioned. One of the common errors in using positive reinforcement is that managers will confuse their *own* rewards with the ones that they're giving their employees, and offer as a reward something that the employee really sees as a punishment. In a typical Reinforcement Memo scenario, this means that the bottom line of the memo will read, "You wrote that report so well that you can do them all from now on." Fine if the writer of the report really wants to keep writing them. Not so good if he sees report-writing as a burden he will take on to help out, but one that he actually despises.

There was a great *Business Week* cartoon a couple of years ago that illustrates what I mean. An executive is "praising" a subordinate who seems less than pleased with the situation. Why isn't he pleased? Because his boss is saying, "I'm so happy with the way you handled that lousy, thankless job I gave you that I'm going to give you another one."

Hence the negative guideline: In writing a Reinforcement Memo—and indeed in delivering any kind of positive reinforcement—*do not ask for additional Behavior* unless you are absolutely certain that the Behavior is something that the person eagerly wants to take on. In "rewarding" a motivated employee by giving him more work to perform, you're playing the part of the Indian giver—and demotivating him in the long run.

One final word on reinforcement. Although both negative and positive reinforcement are valuable in motivating teamwork, you should always keep sight of the fact that honey *does* work better than salt. And it's generally more appropriate, too. If you're in business for the long run, you've got to keep the 4:1 Syndrome constantly in mind. You've got to give people positive encouragement even when they're doing "average" work. Because that is the only way to avoid extinction.

It's a lesson that's long in the learning, but one that even the hardest of managerial taskmasters can learn, if they put their minds to it. I saw that down in South Carolina recently, when I was sitting in the office of a textile plant manager where the 4:1 Syndrome was just being introduced as part of our overall performance-improvement package. This was one of Roger Millikan's plants, and because Roger is fully committed to our P.R.I.C.E. motivation system—and has the P&L figures to prove it—I knew we'd get the management here on board eventually. It was slow going with this particular manager, though. He had been a galley master style of manager for so long he thought that "ability to yell" was part of a plant manager's job description.

But he was learning, and as I sat there I saw that even a galley master can be taught to change his ways, if he knows his people will row faster for it. The manager was on the phone for about three minutes, yelling at a foreman for some production slow-down, and he was making Vince Lombardi look like a lamb. After a couple of minutes he slammed the phone down, took a deep breath, and turned to me. "Well, I guess I owe him four," he said.

That's a lesson we all could learn. I've never said a good manager shouldn't correct people when they deserve it. But just remember, every time you throw somebody down the stairs, you owe him four trips back up.

FIVE

EVALUATION

> The minute you think you've got it made,
> disaster is just around the corner.
> —JOE PATERNO

As the philosopher Yogi Berra once remarked, "It ain't over til it's over." He was talking about baseball, but the message is equally applicable to business. One of the only fatal diseases I know of in the business world is to think that you have all the answers, and to assume that the game is won because you happen to be on top of things at the end of the fifth, or seventh, or eighth, inning. The hard fact is that, as long as the game is still being played, you can win it or lose it; relax your guard, and you can bank on one thing: after it's over, you're going to have less on the board than the competition.

I'll go one step farther. Since business—like baseball, or football, or any competitive endeavor—doesn't end after one game or one season, "it's" not really over even *after* it's over. There's always next season, the next accounting period, the next fiscal year. You may be twenty market share points ahead of your competitors in July. But if you think that's enough, if you think you can forget about motivating your people to greater effort because your current system is perfect, don't bet on having that market spread in December. I've always liked Bert Lance's comment about leaving well enough alone: "If it ain't broke, don't fix it." But as Lance found out—and as unwary managers find out every day—everything is always a *little* broke; every operation in which people are involved is by definition running at less than 100 percent efficiency, and can be made to run better by the continual application of better motivational energies.

Earlier in this book I mentioned the importance of doing regular preventive maintenance. Anybody who works with machinery knows you've got to do that to protect your "capital base." Number Six engine might be purring like a kitten today, but kittens grow into crotchedy cats, and that's why you've got to keep an eye on them all the time. The same thing goes for people—those human "machines" which are, after all, your most valuable and delicate asset. People need preventive maintenance, too. The manager who forgets that is setting himself up for "Muddle in the Middle."

In my company's seminars we address the problem I'm raising here by insisting that our manager clients frequently, and consistently, *evaluate* the results of the motivational system we teach them. And we provide them with on-site help to let them do that better. We've found over and over that relying on training alone is a losing game, because the minute you leave the factory, all those well-trained people are going to be reverting to their old Behaviors, and your work will have all been for nothing—*unless* you keep tabs on what's happening by an ongoing Evaluation system.

Evaluation is the fifth element of our P.R.I.C.E. motivational system. I'm going to talk about this element in this chapter, and show how using it can help you consolidate the drive of your teams, and ensure that they're going to be just as up for peak performance six months down the line as they are when you first start to deliver Consequences.

THE ABC MODEL REVISITED

In discussing the ABC Model of behavior back in the Introduction, I said that an Antecedent is anything that you say, or do, to *initiate* a Behavior, and that a Consequence is anything that happens as a *result* of that Behavior being performed. I also said, parenthetically, that many Consequences can *become* Antecedents in their own right—and thus create new Behaviors. This circular aspect of behavioral response is particularly important to managers. It's what lets them keep feeding data in to the human "capital base," and getting it "fed back."

Take an example I used in the last chapter: the case of the chronically absent line manager. Say you're that manager's supervisor, and you've just found it necessary to deliver the negative Consequences that you warned him you would have to deliver if he continued to take days off from work: you've written up an official discipline report and put a copy of it in his personnel file. For him, that report is a Consequence. But it's also an Antecedent, because you have designed it to initiate a change in his Behavior. Obviously, what you want to know now is whether or not it's done what it was designed to do. Has it motivated him to straighten out his act?

In other words, you want *feedback*. In the last chapter I spoke about the feedback that the employee you're trying to motivate needs if he's to understand where he's supposed to be going. The positive and negative Consequences you provide—from the docking of pay to the writing of a Reinforcement Memo— are examples of that necessary feedback. But you need feedback, too. You need to be able to read the "consequences of your Consequences," to see if they need adjustment. You do that by Evaluating.

It makes sense that, when you go back to assess the effectiveness of an operating system, you start at where you were *before* you put in the system. In our system that means, to measure your current rate of success or failure with regard to motivation improvement, you check out your data-based Recording, and go back to your initial baseline.

This doesn't necessarily mean that you're going to be reading line graphs. Maybe you don't even have a posted, week-by-week track of your absentee manager's attendance. But you'd better have some numerical idea of when he's been in and when he's been out—or your entire project of getting him to keep better hours is going to founder on the shoals of subjectivity.

The point is that, with or without an actual graph, you need

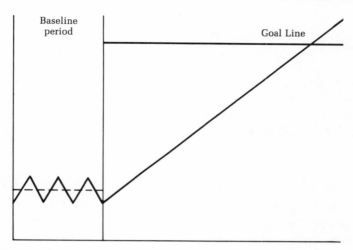

Figure 5

to begin your Evaluation by knowing exactly where you started. Since it's easier to demonstrate this by using figures than by using "impressions," let's go back to the example that we developed in the chapter on Recording. There we were setting out to measure the improvement, over time, in the number of units produced on a designated assembly line. We started there with a baseline—that is, an average per-week number of units produced—of three hundred and ninety-five. Let's say that we've Pinpointed certain Behaviors that can increase the efficiency of the line, that we've Involved all workers in the setting of realistic goals, and that we've been implementing reinforcing Consequences for the past several weeks, as the units produced have gradually gone up. We look at our chart now to Evaluate our progress, and this is what we find (Figure 5).

Fat chance, right? The chart I've given here would be ideal, of course—steady, solid growth brought about as a result of the P.R.I.C.E. system—but you know and I know that this kind of a chart exists only in mathematics textbooks. When we go back several weeks after the implementation of a P.R.I.C.E. system to see how it's been working, what we're likely to find will be something a little more erratic, a little less unidirectional, than

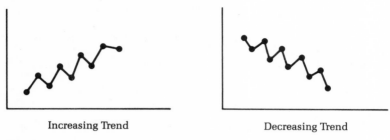

Increasing Trend   Decreasing Trend

Figure 6

this ideal diagram. What we're going to find, probably, will be a pattern that illustrates one or more of three basic designs: trends, range, and cycles.

TRENDS, RANGE, AND CYCLES

At the Tarkenton Productivity Group, when we use the word *trend*, we mean simply the *direction of change*. This direction can be either increasing or decreasing. An increasing trend would look like the figure on the left in Figure 6; a decreasing trend would look like the one to the right. You could also find the virtual absence of a trend, as when there is some fluctuation in the direction of change from week to week, but no long-term upward or downward motion. In cases like these, we would have to focus on those small, week-to-week changes to get an indication of how we were doing. We call the distance between the weekly points on a week-by-week graph the *range* of variability, and we identify this second variable of graphing as either "narrow" or "wide." The greater the fluctuation between points from week to week, the wider the performance range.

You can find Recording measures that show a combination of trend and range in any of six patterns. The six patterns look like those illustrated in Figure 7.

In addition to trend and range, there is one other pattern of variability that you have to be on the watch for when you are

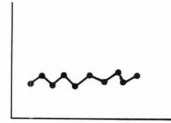

Narrow Range; No Trend
(i.e., No Increase or Decrease)

Wide Range; No Trend

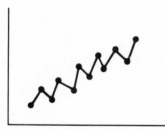

Narrow Range; Increasing Trend

Wide Range; Increasing Trend

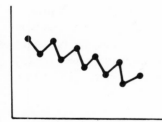

Narrow Range; Decreasing Trend

Figure 7

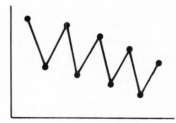

Wide Range; Decreasing Trend

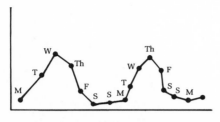

Example: Performance patterns
related to the 5-day work week

Example: Performance patterns
following periodic training
(without follow-up)

Figure 8

Evaluating the rate of your progress. That is the *cycle* pattern, where the points indicating advance or retardation repeat themselves over a given period. Two common cyclical patterns are indicated in Figure 8. In the chart on the left, a performance variable rises and falls in approximate synchronization with the work week itself, with peak performance coming in the middle of the week and poor performance tracking the weekends. In the chart on the right we see a typical pattern observed in companies where "training alone" is thought to be enough to raise motivation: you see a spurt of improvement, and then a dip in performance as the training is forgotten and things get back to normal (that is, the Extinction Effect).

The value of these kinds of graph patterns should be obvious. In a perfect world, where the first application of a P.R.I.C.E. system brings bonanza results, you wouldn't need to know in what direction you were moving, or whether you were getting there smoothly or in zigs and zags. In the world every manager inhabits, you do need this kind of assessment to be able to sort out what's working and what's not. Evaluation of the Recording system at regular intervals gives you the essential feedback you need to be able to fine-tune the system.

But how do you do that fine-tuning? What do you look for in Evaluating performance, and how do you use what you find to continue to motivate your teams? Especially if you find that the goal line you set for yourself is not within reach, how do you know what's going wrong?

FINE-TUNING THE SYSTEM

The answer is to review all the elements of the P.R.I.C.E. motivational system in turn, checking for weak spots, areas of strain, and places where the principles of motivation are not sufficiently understood, or inappropriately applied, or both. Even cars that have just rumbled off the assembly line break down sometime, and that's not necessarily because their design or basic structure is faulty. Sometimes it's just because somebody has forgotten to tighten a screw somewhere. So you go back and check all the screws.

You start with Pinpointing. You started to apply our motivational model by Pinpointing specific Behaviors that you determine to be holding your coworkers or teammates back. If you're not to the Super Bowl yet, maybe you picked the wrong Behaviors. Maybe they weren't the source of your problems. Maybe Alex, the guy you suspected of not doing daily preventive maintenance checks, actually was doing the checks, and the real problem was that his machines had an internal malfunction that couldn't be picked up by a routine PM check. Maybe the slowdown in sales didn't have anything to do with seasonal variations in market demand; maybe it was the result of a new competitor that your marketing department had overlooked. So the problem to be Pinpointed was in marketing, not in the sales department. If you find out information like this on a second investigation of the problem, it's time to Pinpoint again.

The same thing may go for your objectives. Remember that they have to be Pinpointed, too, and that they have to zero in on *quantity* to be changed (increased, decreased) in a given *location* (the market research department, for example) by a specified *date*. If you haven't made your objectives specific and quantifiable in this way, the problem might very well be that your people, who *want* to work harder, just don't know what they're aiming for.

Finally, is the Pinpointing being used in a way that will effectively highlight Behaviors *and* objectives that can realistically be "owned" by the people who are supposed to be affecting them? Do they all see your goal line as realistic? Have they been involved in setting the mid-term goals themselves? Do they believe that it's important and meaningful for them to be working toward the specified goals? If not, your goals can be as high (or as low) as you desire, but they're just not going to get accomplished.

What I'm saying here relates not just to Pinpointing, but to the Recording and Involvement elements of the P.R.I.C.E. system as well. The goal is (or ought to be) to set team and individual goals that everybody has contributed to, that are clearly understood by everybody who needs to work toward them, and that are frequently assessed and posted so that the folks who need to pull harder know what it means to them when they do. When you've got those kind of goals set from the outset, your fine-tuning is going to be a snap. When you don't have those goals, you're going to have to work that much harder to instill confidence and energy and commitment in your people— no matter how smart or skilled they are.

Part of this comes from your personal commitment as a manager, and your ability to make that commitment contagious. If *you* don't believe the new system (whether it's a P.R.I.C.E. system or a new cost-accounting method) will work, you've tied your people's hands behind them before they've even begun. I've found this out a hundred times on the ball field. Going in to any game without believing you're going to come out on top is a flat-out waste of time. The best quarterbacks, and coaches, and managers can get that message across to their teams. All of them. Because if they don't buy it, it ain't sold. Total Involvement isn't something a good business organization can take or leave today; it's one of the few things keeping you from being plowed under by the competition.

In the next chapter I'm going to come back to this, and talk about ways I know of to convince your folks that they can win—

that you all can win together, and only together. But here's the basic point. In Evaluating your progress from Point A to wherever you are on the graph right now, keep in mind that, in business and in sports, superstars don't make it, and genius generals don't make it, and people who see workers just as "human capital" don't make it. The only thing that makes it today is teamwork. That means Involvement. So if you haven't yet reached that first goal line, find out if everybody's pulling. Find out if everybody has a *reason* to.

After you've reviewed the Pinpointing, Recording, and Involvement elements of the P.R.I.C.E. system, you only have one element left. That's Consequences, and it's what makes everything else rise or fall.

In the last chapter I explained how to give positive and negative Consequences, and I don't want to repeat all that here. Let me just focus on the three points that I think are most critical to this kind of performance-improving feedback.

First, I said you should keep your Reinforcements of good and bad Behaviors *timely*. Are you sure that you are giving the relevant Consequences *soon* enough after the performance of the desired new Behavior? In the management of people's motivation, "better late than never" just doesn't hack it. If it doesn't come soon, it might just as well not come at all. I knew a financial manager once who was doing handstands at lunch because his team of accountants had saved their company six figures in taxes one year by close attention to the tax laws. "They really outdid themselves," he told me shortly after the April 15 filing deadline. "Why don't you tell them that?" I asked him. "I'm waiting until Christmas," he confided. "Their year-end bonuses are going to be a big surprise." The only problem was that, by the time Christmas rolled around, two of his seven accountants had departed for new jobs. *They* knew they had performed well, and wanted to be told so, right away.

You can overdo the timeliness, of course. I found this out in the winter of 1975, when the Vikings and I had just fought our way to a Super Bowl slot. I was so high on my offensive linemen that, the Wednesday before Super Bowl Sunday, I took them all out to dinner at New Orleans's most famous restaurant, the elegant antebellum watering spot Antoine's. We ate like royalty, and I think it's fair to say that every member of the line was pleased at the positive reinforcement. On Super Bowl Sunday, however, we gained a smashing total of seventeen yards rushing against the Steelers. From which I learned an important lesson: sometimes you can reinforce *too early*. What I was trying to do (unconsciously, of course) was to ensure a Super Bowl victory by giving positive Consequences in *advance*. It didn't work. It never does. If you want continued improvement, continued high motivation on the part of your working team, you've got to reinforce them immediately after they've done the good work. No later. And no earlier, either.

Second point. Keep it *appropriate*. Are you sure that the Consequences you've been meting out suit the virtue being rewarded or the vice being punished? I don't mean asking simply, "Did I kick his ass hard enough for screwing up?" and "Was that letter of thanks enthusiastic enough?" Those are important questions, sure, but they're not enough. In giving out Consequences you've got to be attuned not only to the "objective" facts of individual cases, but also to the people involved. Different people need different reinforcement. The rewards or punishments you give out have got to fit the people, or they'll be meaningless.

Or worse than meaningless. The distribution of inappropriate Consequences can backfire badly on you. Most of the time this happens because a manager gives out a punishment which *he* thinks is a reward—or vice versa. All of us in business could learn a lesson from old Tom Sawyer. Remember when he has to whitewash the fence—a punishment from his Aunt Polly—and he convinces his friends that it's actually a reward? Everybody in the neighborhood comes flocking, because Tom has managed to convince them that they ought to enjoy what he's doing. If we were all that cagy, motivation would be a snap. But we're not. So we have to investigate—to track the "consequences of the Consequences"—in each individual case and for each individual person, to determine whether a given Consequence is a plus or a minus. Otherwise we fall into the position of the manager who gives out "extra responsibility" to his best workers—and wonders why the others don't improve.

A final point about Consequences: they must be *consistent.* That is, they must follow the hallmark of justice, which is to treat like things alike, or to reward (or punish) according to the quality of the performance, not because you like or dislike the person involved. If the reward-and-punishment system you're working with is not giving you the results you expected, this might be a problem area. There's nothing as hostile to performance, nothing as ultimately demotivating to a team member, as realizing (or just suspecting) that the coach or manager is playing favorites—and that he's not one of them. The one way I know of to avoid this type of demotivation is to observe the behaviorist's basic ground rule: reward (or punish) the *Behavior,* not the *person.*

This doesn't mean you have to be cold-hearted about giving Consequences, or adhere to some rigid schedule, like a scientist would do in programming rats. Sure, there are opportunities for individual, differential reinforcement that don't do harm to the morale of the team, and a wise manager takes advantage of them. But he does it with one eye open for trouble, because he knows envy and resentment are very strong human emotions, and that the "at least adequate" performer can easily be demotivated toward poor performance if he feels he's being given the shaft.

In the Gospels there's a tantalizing story about a vineyard owner who hires a group of workers early in the morning, another group at midday, and a third group late in the afternoon. At the end of the day's work he pays them all the same and, not surprisingly, the second and third group take exception. "We busted our butts all day long," they say in effect, "and these guys only worked a couple of hours, and you're paying us all the same. What gives?" The vineyard owner explains that they have no cause to complain, because they agreed to work a given period of time for a given rate, and he hasn't cheated them. If he chooses to pay the others the same money, it takes nothing away from them.

The parable is meant to illustrate the fact that, in the "competitive race" for God's kingdom, we are all equally sinners and all equally indebted to the grace of the Lord. Charity and common sense both dictate that, if a greater sinner than I is admitted to Paradise, I should be grateful that I got in at all, and not complain because God is all-merciful. Theologically, this is watertight. But don't apply it to motivating others. As a manager of human beings, you've got to pay your workers *differentially,* based on their *works,* not grace. God can get away with being generous to everybody alike. You can't. If one of your junior marketing managers delivers twice as much good work as the others, you can't send him the same kind of "Thank you" message as the rest, or he's going to ask (quite reasonably), "What gives?" You've got to be consistent.

One caveat, though. I mean consistent, not rigid. In Evaluating your progress as a motivator, you have to ask not only, "Am I giving everybody the same message for the same Behaviors?" but also, "Are my same messages getting boring?"

In our productivity seminars, we talk about a Satiation Principle as the key to maintaining an effective, not a rigid, consistency. Something as simple as asking an earnest worker to have coffee with you can be an effective motivator if it's used consistently for every earnest worker. But if coffee is the *only* reward you give out, people are going to get tired of it very quickly. The Satiation Principle is going to set in, and the motivating value of the reward is going to be lost. At that point—and ideally, well before that point—it's time to change the reinforcement schedule. Consistency tempered by variety is the key.

EVALUATION AND EVOLUTION

We use technological metaphors a lot these days, because they've become part of the common coin of business parlance, and because they provide a nice scientific aura for concepts that are, after all, only related to those mundane creatures, human beings. So I've been talking about feedback and tracking mechanisms, and earlier I mentioned the post-game films that we used to watch in the National Football League to track our individual and team performance—another high-tech metaphor that illustrates the need for constant reassessment. For a change, consider a biological metaphor.

Scientists disagree as to why the dinosaurs—those hugely successful beasts that ruled this planet for 100 million years— suddenly vanished from sight. But whether it was a diminishing food supply, climate change, or some unknown catastrophe, one thing seems clear: the giant lizards went out of the picture because as a species they were *unable to adapt* to some critical new variable in their environment.

Many species are like that. There are probably as many species that now exist only in fossil form as there are species that are now thriving, and the reason for their extinction—the particulars aside—is always at root the same. They can't adapt. They're constructed a certain way, and that way fits in with the geography at a certain place and in a certain time, and when things change, the animal (or plant) that has been suited so well for its ecological niche suddenly doesn't fit any more, and disappears.

Businesses, sports teams, and other organizations that are composed of human beings are like living organisms in this sense. They come together at a particular time and in a particular place to perform certain functions, and they thrive as long as they can adjust to dramatic changes, internal or external. In the business world we're constantly threatened by changes in foreign competition, a shifting market base, worker expectations, the tax laws, and so on. We either learn to Evaluate and react to these changes, or we go under.

At least we have the choice. We're one up on the dinosaurs in this regard. Since the organizations we manage are composed of relatively intelligent creatures, and since we have access to enormously sophisticated and very rapid feedback about environmental changes, we have the opportunity to adapt—to change the way we live our organizational lives—before we are done in by the threats. Unlike the dinosaurs, we can *use* the feedback we're getting. We can Evaluate. And we can modify the systems we're using so we can become more competitive, more productive, better performers.

In other words, not only can we evolve, but we can *direct the course* of our evolution. Like an NFL team looks at the films of last Sunday's performance to do better next Sunday, we can use the feedback we have available to us to increase the motivation of our people, jockey into better position against the competition, and continue to evolve.

It's a sad, but unavoidable, fact of modern business history that the only time most businesses do that is when it's nearly too late. It's the old story of the roof that only "needs" fixing when it's raining. In fact it needs fixing even when the weather reminds you of Death Valley, but most of us still prefer to wait until there are Niagaras in the living room, and then to cry, "Where the hell did *that* come from?"

We could all use a little more trouble. It gets us off our duffs. It gets us sitting up straight, sniffing the wind, saying, "Where's that storm coming from?" That's why I think that the best thing that's happened to the American automobile industry in the past fifty years is the so-called Japanese invasion. For the first four or five decades of this century, the fatcats out in Detroit were getting pretty cocky. They had gradually lost that entrepreneurial spirit, that willingness to take risks, and trust people, and trust your instincts, that made this country great in the first place. And they were getting that fatal disease: Know-it-all-itis. Once you get that disease, you think like a brontosaurus. You start to imagine that nothing can hurt you. And pretty soon you're in a museum.

The Japanese changed all that. They made the fatcats wake up. You know what General Motors—the fattest of all the fatcats—did last year? They acquired a computer-research company, Ross Perot's famous EDS, so they could track the market better. So they could keep abreast of the changing environmental conditions in manufacture and data-processing and accounting and marketing and supplies. In short, so they could Evaluate what they had been doing wrong, and take steps to fine-tune the system.

It remains to be seen, of course, whether they, or any of the other industrial giants, will use that same sophisticated approach to "how the systems work" to the single most important feature of modern business life: how the people who work for you *feel.* If GM puts its new EDS database to work on getting its own people to perform—if it uses its enormous Evaluating skills to generate Involvement and plot Consequences and develop teamwork—the trade deficit might start to plummet overnight. If not—if they demonstrate that machinery is more important to them than the folks who run the machinery—then it doesn't matter how much they learn about compression ratios and robotics. They're still going to be thinking like old Bronto.

No matter how expert you are at what you do, you still need Evaluation. The best managers and the best players already know this. Back in 1965, when Jack Nicklaus won his first Masters tournament, golf legend Bobby Jones remarked, "Palmer and Player played superbly, but Nicklaus played a game with which I'm not familiar." Part of that unfamiliarity, I think, is Nicklaus's incredible precision, the way he seems to leave nothing to chance. And that doesn't happen by itself. Jack is known in golfing circles as a man who won't take the basics for granted. One of his staff members is a spotter whose job is to constantly review his boss's *basic* moves, and Pinpoint where they can be improved. That's an intelligent use of Evaluation—and you can see where it's gotten Nicklaus.

The leaders are constantly checking, constantly reevaluating their performance, and the performance of their team members, to see how they can do it better. That's what makes them leaders. I hope that the principles in the past five chapters have shown you how that can be done in the context of real people management. I hope it reminds you of Bear Bryant's great comment: "I watch the films when we've won. To see what I've done right."

PART II
TWO ESSENTIAL MOTIVATING SKILLS

SIX

REFLECTIVE LISTENING

He who has ears to hear, let him hear.
—MARK 4:9

In the wake of the corporate bribery scandals of the 1970s, a University of Georgia business professor named Archie Carroll interviewed hundreds of corporate managers to find out whether or not they felt they were being pressured to bend their principles in order to beef up the bottom line. One of his findings was especially disturbing. It was that there seemed to be a severe "breakdown of understanding" between various levels of the business hierarchy over issues like book-cooking, and bribery, and quality control. Apparently a lot of middle managers were hearing mixed or confusing messages, and as a result were "behaving unethically out of a fear of reprisal, misguided sense of loyalty, or distorted concept of the job."

You come across this problem a lot in big organizations, and not just with regard to ethical problems. The "mixed message" or "missed message" syndrome surfaces constantly where managers hint, or suggest, or imply that such-and-such an operation be carried out without actually spelling out what they mean. Their subordinates take a noble stab at what they think is being asked of them, and a lot of the times they guess wrong. So you get a quality control officer, for example, fudging an inspection report because his boss has said, "We're running way behind" and he interprets that to mean, "It doesn't have to be good, it has to be Tuesday."

The situation isn't only unfortunate, it's a little ridiculous, too, because there's really a fairly simple way out of the problem. It's for the confused subordinate—or the confused manager at any level—to come out and *ask* what is meant. It's for everybody involved in a mutual enterprise to *talk* to each other regularly, so that everybody knows what the rules are, and how the game is supposed to be played. In other words, the solution is *communication*.

This has a direct relevance to motivation. If you as a manager want to get anybody to do what you want, the one type of skill you *must* become good at is the skill of communicating with others. You can set up the most beautifully Pinpointed set of objectives in the world, and the most rigorous Recording system, and you can deliver those positive Consequences in exactly the right 4:1 ratio, but if you can't communicate with your people, it will all be wasted effort.

In this chapter, and the following chapter, I'm going to be talking about communication, laying out the specific interactional skills and techniques that my company has found effective in making the P.R.I.C.E. motivation system not just a well-designed blueprint, but a working reality.

There are two aspects to communication: listening to what others are saying, and telling them what you want. The first aspect, listening, is extremely important to anybody who wants to turn anybody on, for the simple reason that if you can't hear what is being said to you, you will have no idea who you're dealing with: you'll be in the ridiculous situation of the manager who *assumes* his people understand him—and ends up with a record run of defective merchandise because that's what they "knew" he wanted.

The good Lord gave us all two ears and only one mouth. Yet most of us, in and out of business, behave as if the allotment were exactly the reverse. In this chapter I'm going to be emphasizing the importance of those two essential organs, the ears, because they're so often neglected.

In my experience both on the playing field and in our company's business motivation workshops, I've found that there is a specific set of listening skills that most quickly and effectively serves to clarify who it is you're dealing with, and what he or she understands about what you want to get done. We call them Reflective Listening skills. This chapter will show you how to use these skills to improve the communication process in all your personal interactions, so that you can avoid the "missed" or "mixed" message syndrome.

REFLECTIVE LISTENING: HOW IT WORKS

Various psychological studies have indicated that the average human listener actually hears and understands only about 25 percent of what is being said to him. Obviously that leaves a huge area open to misinterpretation.

If you're an "average" listener in a family, therefore, you're going to be missing out on *most* of what your parents, siblings, or children are trying to get across to you. If you're an "average" listener in a business setting, you could pay the price for that 25 percent retention rate in lost sales, poor employee relations, and incalculable losses in performance.

Reflective Listening is the way out of this bind. It's the primary skill you need to perform way *above* average in communication, whoever you're trying to talk to or listen to.

The reason that most people are "average" listeners is that they buy in to the conventional view of "listening." In this view, listening is indistinct from "hearing." It is a quiet, *passive* process which requires only that you do not interrupt the speaker, do not walk away while he is speaking to you, and do not cover your ears with your hands while he is in the middle of a sentence. In the conventional view of "listening," the listener does not have to *do* anything, because he or she is simply a mute *receptor* of an active party's transmission of information.

If that were all there was to effective listening, the auto industry and the UAW would have resolved their difficulties long ago, and no line manager who was told to "meet this contract any way you can" would ever turn out a string of seconds because he heard the message "Quality doesn't count." But it's not that simple. To understand why, look at the diagram in

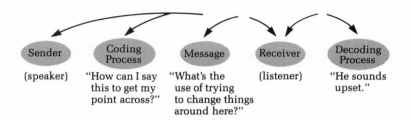

Sender	Coding Process	Message	Receiver	Decoding Process
(speaker)	"How can I say this to get my point across?"	"What's the use of trying to change things around here?"	(listener)	"He sounds upset."

Figure 9

Figure 9, illustrating in a schematic format the process that goes on every time one human being talks to another.

As the diagram indicates, every time one person speaks to another, you're dealing not just with the two people themselves (Sender and Receiver), but also with a Message being transmitted: that is, the actual words being "sent" by the Sender to the Receiver. And this Message is very often lost or distorted during transmission. The reason why this happens is suggested by the other two elements in Figure 9: the Coding Process and the Decoding Process.

The Coding Process is the Sender's internal mental process that determines *how* a given piece of information—an opinion, a feeling, an idea—is to be translated verbally, into the spoken Message. It's the Sender's private, unspoken "conversation with himself" by which he tries to put the information he wants to express into the most effective public form.

Imagine that you have been unwittingly insulted by a co-worker or a friend, and you want to let him know that you are offended by his unintentional slight. There are various ways you could get the idea of "I am offended" across, and unless you are one of those rare and invariably ineffective people who simply blurts out everything that enters his head, you will probably go through a brief internal dialogue with yourself be-

122

fore you comment. In that dialogue you will consider whether the appropriate response is "Jim, I think you were a little thoughtless in that comment" or "You no good S.O.B., I never want to talk to you again" or something in between. The Coding Process is the name we give to this silent (and usually unconscious) internal dialogue.

The Decoding Process, on the other hand, is the *Receiver's* internal process that determines how he or she *interprets* the Sender's spoken message. The interpretation, it's important to remember, always involves the Receiver's reaction to *more than the words alone.* To "decode" what the Sender has expressed, the Receiver—even if he's not conscious of doing so—always attends to intonation and expression, to gesture and body language, as well. And these nonverbal cues to what the Sender means to convey are often just as important as the basic verbal Message. If that weren't the case, Messages could simply be passed from person to person on slips of paper, with nothing being lost in the transcription.

Because we don't use slips of paper but rather a huge armory of verbal and nonverbal transmitters, it's easy for both the Coding Process and the Decoding Process to go awry. This happens for several reasons.

First there's the fact that language itself is ambiguous. Consider the simple word "plan." Even a child's dictionary gives half a dozen meanings for that word. If you as a Sender tell someone more "planning" is in order, you may mean, "You need to think about this some more before you make the final decision" or, "You've got to buy that forecasting software package immediately"—or any number of things in between. By giving someone whose Behavior you want to influence a Message that hinges on the interpretable word "planning," you are setting him up to hear information that you may not intend him to hear. For not only do words themselves have several shades of meaning, but each individual *uses* those words in slightly idiosyncratic ways, based on his or her background, education, personal experience with idiom, and so on. Since human beings are not computers, you always have to allow for individual creativity in conversation—and not all that creativity

123

is going to enhance understanding. When it doesn't, not only can you not motivate people to do what you want; often you can end up getting them to do exactly the opposite.

Second, the verbal and the nonverbal messages you give out can conflict, and even if you know exactly what you're trying to get across, your listener may get a different message because she's concentrating on the tone of your voice or your body language rather than the "official," verbal Message. We've all been so badly conditioned by sales people trying to stick us with garbage that we tend to be suspicious and defensive of a lot of nonselling Messages as well. A manager can say outright, "I want those reports in by Monday," but if his voice is weak and his eyes are wandering when he says it, the message may not get through.

Finally, the single most important reason that the Coding-Decoding process gets fouled up: simple inattention on the part of the Receiver. Later I'll be talking in some detail about inattention, and about how, in various pernicious guises, it can impede motivation and communication. Here I'll just point out that most communication breaks down because the Receiver has misinterpreted the Sender's message—and that in nine cases out of ten, this happens because he has not been paying attention. The motivational outcome is always bad: when you don't attend to what the other guy is saying, you can't hear; when you don't hear, you can't respond; and when you can't respond, getting him to do what you want is like getting him to read your mind. Unless he's Houdini, that won't work.

The phrase "paying attention" suggests *activity* on the Receiver's part. That is no accident. In contrast to the conventional passive listening style that most people fall into most of the time, the effective manager has a listening style in which the Receiver becomes actively—or to put it more precisely, "reflectively"—involved.

I use the term "reflective" for two reasons. First, it suggests that a good listener, a good Receiver, *thinks about* what the Sender is sending, rather than simply opening his ears and letting the sounds form background music; that is the first way in which he actively "reflects" on the Message.

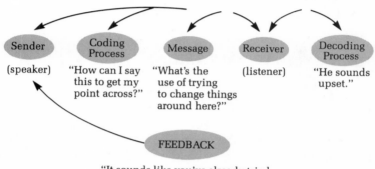

Figure 10

The second way is more important. In Reflective Listening, the Receiver is not content to just "think about" what the Sender is saying. He carries the active process one step further, and *reflects back* to the Sender what it is he thinks has been meant. In other words, he adds another component to the ongoing exchange of information—a component that, in the world of computers, would be called "feedback." Using the same diagram as I used in Figure 9, I'll add this "reflecting back" or "feedback" component (Figure 10).

Notice what the introduction of this feedback component does to the communication process. It provides an immediate check on the listener's Decoding of the message, by "playing back" to the speaker what the listener thinks has been said. The feedback serves as a sensing device to ensure that the message has not been garbled in transmission—or, if it has been garbled, to alert the listener to that fact so he can seek clarification.

The "playing back" technique is a major feature of the communication exercises my company uses in our productivity workshops. In those workshops we call the technique "Rephrasing." It's one of four critical listening skills that we have

125

found to be effective in improving motivation and performance for our clients. They comprise a package of "reflective motivational strategies."

REFLECTIVE MOTIVATIONAL STRATEGIES

First of all, it's necessary to remember that the four skills I'm going to describe are *learned* skills, not innate human capabilities, and that *anybody* can learn them. We often hear two objections when we describe these skills to our clients. One is that Reflective Listening may be all right for some people, but, "I'm just not a good natural listener" (or, "I'm too shy," "I'm not much of a conversationalist"). In other words, I'm not capable of learning how to listen any differently than I do now.

Not true. Nobody was born knowing how to talk; everybody learned that critical communicational skill, slowly, bit by bit, until it was mastered. It's the same thing with Listening. With practice, anybody can learn Reflective Listening. And it takes a lot less time to learn than it took any of us to learn to talk.

The second objection we hear is that these listening skills are "unnatural." Some clients say that they feel forced and uncomfortable when they first start practicing Reflective Listening—and that they are wary of the new skills because they don't want to appear insincere or phony.

This is not an unreasonable fear, but I can assure you that, as with any other newly acquired skills, the Reflective Listening skills become far less "unnatural" with practice, and at the same time more effective. In our experience, it takes very little time, especially in team workshop settings, for participants to become comfortable with the four skills I'm about to describe. And ultimately the proof is in the pudding: In the words of an East Coast plant manager who expressed misgivings when we first taught him Reflective Listening, "I've been using this stuff for two months now, and it's getting easier all the time. Considering how our performance has gone up as a result, I don't see how I ever got along without it."

That is a comment, we've found, that is frequently echoed

by our client managers. The reason is that Reflective Listening provides two enormous benefits to anybody whose job involves getting other people turned on to their jobs.

First, it helps to *clarify* the situation by enhancing the flow of information that anybody needs to get his job done in the first place. Reflective Listening techniques supplement the Pinpointing and Recording and Evaluation elements of our system by ensuring that both people involved in a communication process are starting with the same basic data.

Second, Reflective Listening helps to *validate*—and therefore *reinforce*—the person to whom you're speaking. It ties in with the Involvement and Consequences elements of the P.R.I.C.E. system, by letting the other person know that you have been attending to what he's been saying, and that you want to hear more. Whatever the specific content of your Reflective Listening response, the very *fact* that you give feedback to the other person about his or her comments becomes in itself a motivating factor.

The first of the four Reflective Listening skills is also the easiest to learn, and in fact many people who have never heard of Reflective Listening use it in their daily interactions all the time. We call it Prompting.

1. *Prompting.* Prompting consists of telling the speaker, with a minimum of verbiage, that you want him to continue speaking, to give you more information. We identify two types of "prompts": verbal and nonverbal.

Verbal prompts include such phrases as "Really," "No kidding," "That's interesting," "You mean? . . .", "Like what?", and "Tell me more about that." They function to keep the speaker talking, and therefore by definition Involved. Generally speaking, the actual words used in a verbal prompt are less important than the intonation used in expressing them. Probably the most frequently used of all verbal prompts is the nonword "Hmmm . . ."—an expression that is really little more than a grunt, and that certainly conveys no hard data to the speaker. Yet in spite of its lack of "information," the expression can be invaluable in drawing a hesitant speaker out, provided it is "stated" in a sympathetic voice, and with the appropriate facial expression and gestures of attention. That is, with the right "nonverbal prompts."

Nonverbal prompts include the whole "cues and prods" repertoire of the classic "good" listener. Think of a situation in which you have bent somebody's ear for an hour or two, unburdening your soul or seeking sympathy for problems. What "support" did that person give you as you rattled on about yourself? Most people who have been in this situation (which includes pretty much all of us) say that the truly good listener is admired not so much for the advice or information she or he conveys, but for the unspoken *support* that is evident in expression and gesture. The good listener's repertoire includes, therefore, the sympathetic smile, the raised eyebrow, the nod, the hand holding the chin, the body tilted forward toward the speaker, the laugh, the wince, and the knitted brow. All of these gestures signal the speaker that you are on his side, and want to hear more.

Nonverbal prompts can be tremendously motivating, and especially useful to a manager who is not by nature voluble or passionately "engaged." In my Viking days, I learned that lesson time and again from the way our head coach, Bud Grant, "prompted" me to better efforts on the field. Bud is a quiet, stoical man—the kind of guy you'd almost have to pay to laugh at a Marx Brothers movie. But he is one of the best motivators I've ever met, because he uses nonverbal prompts so well. I'd come off the field after a good pass, and Bud would stand there with his arms folded, not moving a muscle, and just nod at me as I came in. That was all—just catch my eye quickly and nod. And yet it was one of the best and most cherished reinforcements I had in all my years of pro ball. That nod meant more to me than carloads full of champagne. And you'd better believe I was out there strong the next series of downs, looking to get reinforced like that again.

2. *Open-Ended Questions.* The second Reflective Listening skill is a little more complicated than Prompting, and it focuses more precisely on missing information that the listener wants to get. It's called Open-Ended Questioning.

The difference between Open-Ended and Close-Ended questions can be stated very simply: the Open-Ended Question cannot be answered with a simple yes or no, and the Close-Ended Question can. For anyone who is interested in eliciting as much information as possible from a speaker, it's obvious which kind of question is going to be more effective: the Open-Ended Question, like the Prompt, encourages the speaker to keep talking, and thus reinforces and Involves him. The Close-Ended Question is designed to elicit only a specific piece of information—which may or may not be the information that you need.

Sometimes it doesn't even elicit that, because it's phrased in a purely rhetorical manner. The rhetorical question—where you don't really want a response—is the worst type of Close-Ended Question, and it's one that demotivating managers use all the time. You know the kind of person I mean. The division sales manager who storms into a meeting of branch managers and announces, "We're going to hit quota this month or all you guys will be getting your resumes retyped. Any questions?" Rhetoric. Intimidation. And no Involvement.

I used to have constant run-ins with an NFL coach who used this Close-Ended tactic before games. "I want you guys to enjoy yourselves out there," he'd say. "But I don't want any mistakes. If you drop that damn ball one time, and if you don't beat these turkeys' asses, I'm going to sack every last one of you. Do you understand that?" Sure, we understood it. And we understood, too, that he wasn't interested in hearing a response. That's no way to get the best from your people.

Open-Ended Questions never start in this limiting and intimidating way, but with those words that newspaper people appropriately call "openers": who, what, when, where, why, and how. "What are your questions about the new quota we're setting up here?" "When do you think we should put this new DP program on line?" Close-Ended Questions imply that you'd better not have any question. Open-Ended Questions imply that you do have questions and concerns, that they are worth talking about, and that the questioner is sincerely interested in finding out more about your confusion. Because the grammar of the question does not allow a monosyllabic answer, you allow the person to expand on his or her opinions, to express difficulties and confusions, to provide information rather than a grunted yes or no.

A couple of examples, the first from a factory floor situation. Say you're confronted by a "slow" worker who just doesn't seem to understand what he needs to be doing to make a new machine operate properly. To get that person's Behavior to change, you could ask either a Closed or an Open-Ended question. Here are the possible choices:

A. Do you understand what this machine does?
B. What's your understanding of this machine?

Notice that the A (Closed) version, aside from inviting even a totally ignorant machine operator to say "Sure," also unnecessarily challenges the listener to "prove" his expertise by giving himself an A+ rating on a device he may, or may not, understand. The B (Open) version allows for more hesitancy and humility: it allows the operator who is not absolutely certain of the workings of the machine to admit it, and ask for an explanation.

One caveat, though. Obviously, you could, if you were a particularly vindictive plant manager, make the B version sound pretty nasty, and you could also, if you were particularly attentive to people's reactions, make the A version sound like a real plea for information. To go back to the point I made in the section about nonverbal cues: The appropriate use of Reflective Listening requires an attention not only to grammar, but to nuance and "body grammar" as well.

A second example, from a situation that might confront you as the manager of a computerized marketing department. You've just signed a trial contract with a software supplier that includes a given amount of on-site training for your people each month. You're excited about the system, but your assistant marketing manager seems hesitant. You might ask her:

A. Don't you think this software training is exactly what we've needed?
B. What do your people think about the new software training?

In this example, the A (Closed) version of the question not only demands a one-word response, it even specifies what that response should be. This is an example of what is often called a "leading question" or a "pre-emptive query," because it pre-empts the listener's own response by subtly, but very strongly, indicating the "right" answer. This kind of question is the most extreme example of the limited Close-Ended question. It gets very close to being a mere rhetorical question, where the questioner really doesn't want an answer at all, but only silent approbation for his own already-formed opinions. In terms of conversational effectiveness, it has the same negative effect as politically barbed "inquiries" that assume the listener is in accord with the questioner: "You just can't trust the Russians, can you?" or "Don't you hate Reagan's new budget?"

By contrast, version B (Open) of this question allows a variety of responses. It's a realistic probe for information rather than a request for rubber-stamping. The political equivalents might include "How do you feel about the new Russian presence in Angola?" or "What's your opinion of the president's budget cuts?"

Some people, of course, are resistant to providing information, even about their own deep concerns, and I don't deny that there are communicational risks involved in working with Open-Ended Questions. The most obvious, and most prevalent, of these risks is that the person you're asking for "clarification" will say—or indicate to you without actually saying it—that what you're asking is simply none of your business. That can close you off from him, and make it extremely difficult for you to turn him on to whatever needs to get done.

When you run into this kind of problem—and you will—you might want to resort to a pair of Open-Ended Questions that we have often found to be useful in drawing out the more closed individuals. If Jim is reluctant to tell you "how he feels" about a given issue, we suggest asking him one positive, and one negative, question:

- The positive question: What do you *like* about this?
- The negative question: What are your *concerns* about this?

These questions, of course, will not guarantee that Jim will suddenly be transformed into a garrulous, enthusiastic fellow ready to talk with you for days. But they do tend to focus the need here for more feedback and more Involvement. Usually this will turn Jim around. If it doesn't, I suggest backing off and trying another Reflective Listening technique to get him Involved. Let's face it. There *are* people who see direct, personal questions of *any* kind as a threat, and there is no point in antagonizing those people just because the Open-Ended Question in general is an effective listening technique.

3. *Rephrasing.* I mentioned Rephrasing in passing when I introduced the Coding-Decoding diagram earlier in the chapter. In Rephrasing, you put into your own words what you believe the speaker to be saying, and then reflect that back to him or her—that is, give him or her feedback—to check the accuracy of your understanding.

A couple of examples. An assembly-line worker might complain to his supervisor about maintenance problems on a piece of machinery. His identification of the trouble is vague: "Things are really going to hell around here." The supervisor could *assume* he's talking about maintenance, and maybe he'd be right and maybe he'd be wrong. A surer way of identifying the problem would be to ask the worker, "You mean that machines are breaking down?"

Or a purchasing officer might tell a member of his department, "We're getting screwed on these overruns." The department member could, without asking, take that to mean that a supplier is overcharging—or he could ask: "So you think that ABC Industries is padding its invoices?"

In each case the Rephrased question accomplishes the dual purpose of Reflective Listening in general: It *clarifies* what the first speaker has expressed imprecisely, and it *reinforces* him or her to give you more information.

A couple of technical observations. Notice first that each Rephrasing statement in the examples begins with a kind of introductory "keyword" that identifies what is to follow as an attempt at clarification. In the first example it's "You mean? . . ." In the second it's the small word "So." Other examples of introductory words or phrases for Rephrased statements would be "It seems to me you feel . . .", "You seem to . . .", and the old reliable "In other words . . .".

Second, notice that the Rephrased statement in each case is *not* simply an echo of the speaker's own statement. In Rephrasing, always beware of the "parrot trap," and exercise your imagination to come up with a version of the speaker's comment that is more than a simple carbon copy. Remember that the double purpose of Rephrasing—as of Reflective Listening in general—is to clarify and reinforce. Neither of these benefits is achieved by a verbatim reproduction of a comment. In fact, if your response to "Things are going to hell around here" is "You think things are going to hell," it's likely to have a counterproductive effect because verbatim transcriptions can easily be read as mimicry, mockery, or both.

The most useful kinds of Rephrased statements are those which seek clarification by attempting to *specify* (Pinpoint) what the speaker is getting at. You'll notice that this is the case in each of the examples above. The assembly line worker expresses a general sense of dissatisfaction, and the supervisor then attempts to verify that it's the broken machines that are on his mind. The purchasing officer mentions "overruns," and his colleague tries to pin that down: is it overcharging she means, or something else?

Asking a Rephrased question in this kind of Pinpointed manner serves the purpose of clarification even when your idea about the other person's feelings are off base. Take the first example above. It's possible in this case that the worker would come back to the supervisor with, "Yes, it's the damn machines." It's also possible that he would say, "I'm not talking about the machines. That's just a temporary problem. I mean that management just doesn't seem to care. They have no contact with us anymore." But in either case—whether he was right or wrong about the machines—the supervisor would still have clarified the specific reasons behind his employee's frustration and enhanced his own ability to resolve them.

Ironically, there is a problem associated with many Rephrased statements that grows directly out of the fact that they are used to Pinpoint the issues. Rephrased statements are really a kind of Close-Ended question: in each of the examples given here, it would be possible for the initial speaker to answer the Rephrased question with a simple, and nonproductive, yes or no. Because this is so—because there's a danger that Rephrasing can close off rather than open out the conversation—we always advise the people to whom we teach Reflective Listening to use Rephrasing with caution, *and* to use this technique in conjunction with the Open-Ended questioning technique.

In the first example, for instance, suppose the worker responded to the supervisor's query about the machines with a simple, "No, that's not the problem." The supervisor could then resort to the Open-Ended questioning technique to further clarify the worker's concerns. "I don't quite understand what you're getting at, Roger," he might say. "Could you tell me more about why you think things are going to hell?" The bottom line here is a logical enough lesson: it's only when *all* the Reflective Listening skills are used interactively that you create the most fluid and productive communication.

One last point about Rephrasing. It is not appropriate for *every* communicational situation, but only for those where someone says something that is important, complicated, and/or confusing. Situations, in other words, where clarification is needed. I can give you a simple guideline for knowing whether or not it's time to Rephrase something you've just heard. Just ask yourself, "Do I understand what this person means? Do I know exactly (in a Pinpointed way) what he's talking about?" If you do, you don't have to ask. If you don't know for sure, go to Rephrasing.

Some people resist the idea of Rephrasing—of throwing a person's comment back at him—because they have the notion that it's insulting or rude to do so. That's nonsense, and to a manager who needs information so he can get his people moving, it's dangerous nonsense. In today's extremely compartmentalized and specialized business environment, it can be a fatal error. I've seen chief executives of major companies talking to their own financial officers or engineers, and obviously not knowing what's going on, and yet not being willing to say, "Stop and explain that again," because they don't want to be shown up as ignorant. Big mistake. Finance officers and engineers can lose *anybody* these days, and if you make a decision based on what you *think* one of them has said to you, you're stacking the deck against yourself.

The same principle applies no matter who you're talking to, or at whatever level. My partner of twenty years, Tom Joiner, is one of the most brilliant people I know, and for that very reason getting him to explain something to you *simply* can be like asking a physicist to explain relativity in twenty-five words or less. Tom has lost me a hundred times. But I learned a long time ago that if I stop him in mid-sentence, say, "Do you mean . . .", and ask for clarification, things eventually get simpler. And we stay partners.

It's *never* rude to ask somebody for clarification. What's rude is nodding when you *don't* understand. When you do that, it always comes back to haunt you later. The way out of that tangle is Rephrasing.

4. *Empathy Statements.* The fourth Reflective Listening skill is a sophisticated special case of Rephrasing. I've pointed out that the two major goals of Reflective Listening skills are to clarify and to reinforce. Rephrasing generally focuses on the first of these two goals. Empathy Statements are designed to satisfy both goals, but with a greater emphasis on any motivating system's linchpin, reinforcement.

Like Rephrasing statements in general, Empathy Statements encourage the speaker to talk, to elaborate on his or her comments, so that you can get further information. They also indicate to the other person that you have been listening to what he is saying. But in focusing primarily on how the speaker is *feeling*, rather than simply on the *information* he is expressing, they do one thing that other Rephrasing statements do not: they serve to defuse feelings of anger and resentment, and thus to calm an agitated speaker down. Obviously, someone who is calm and attentive is going to be far easier to motivate than someone who is preoccupied and distracted by his anger.

Consider again the first example from the section on Rephrasing. Let's assume that in response to his initial Rephrased statement, the supervisor learns from the worker that it is indeed the breaking machines that have him going up the wall. He might carry the conversation forward with the following Empathy Statement: "I can see how you must be feeling frustrated, Roger, with the machines going off all the time." Such a statement has the advantage not only of focusing on the real cause for Roger's frustration, but also of letting him know that the supervisor *understands* and *accepts* his emotion.

That is what every good Empathy Statement does. It lets an angry, or nervous, or otherwise upset speaker know that, as far as his feelings go, he is not alone: somebody else understands. This has the immediate effect, in the vast majority of cases I have witnessed, of defusing the negative feelings—even where the situation that has created them has not changed.

Given the centrality of emotion in every person's general psychology, this is not really too surprising. R. D. Laing and other students of schizophrenia have pointed out that the one sure way to isolate an individual from human interaction, the one way to ensure that he or she will be unable to communicate effectively with others, is to label his or her feelings as either "mad" or "bad." Empathy Statements do exactly the opposite thing: they label the speaker's feelings as acceptable, understandable, in short as *valid*. Someone who knows that you consider his or her feelings valid is going to be a lot easier to get Involved than someone who suspects that you don't.

There are good ways and bad ways to express Empathy Statements, however, and to ensure that the people we teach learn the proper use of the Empathy technique, we suggest in our workshops that they practice these statements at first by fitting them into a standard model. The "standard" Empathy Statement that we suggest has two parts: one part that *labels* the feeling, and a second part that lets the person know that you *understand* why he's feeling that way. Here's the form:

I can understand (or I realize, I guess, I see) that you feel ———— because ————.

In the first blank, managers write the specific (Pinpointed) emotion that they feel the person they're dealing with is having: upset, annoyed, confused, sad, and so on. Generally, we have found that this blank can always be filled in with some variation of the four "basic" emotions: anger, fear, sorrow, and joy.

In the second blank we ask managers to think of the specific, Pinpointed reason—a situational reason—why it would be all right for the person to have that emotion. Just as the specified emotion lets the speaker know that the listener is not merely nodding without understanding, the specified situational reason lets him know that the listener is making an attempt to relate the speaker's feelings to the circumstances that caused them. The following example will illustrate.

Ray, a line supervisor in a factory that has been experiencing a rapid increase in work load, learns at a management meeting that his people have just been "awarded" yet another time-consuming order. He looks bewildered: "This is nuts," he says. "We can't even get our current orders out on time, and now you want us to take on another major project!" A fellow supervisor replies: "You must be feeling pretty frustrated, Ray, because we always seem two weeks behind."

Notice the adherence to our "formula" Empathy Statement: a first part identifying the person's feeling, and a second part linking it to the situation. Naturally, as you use Empathy Statements more and more, you can vary this formula—as long as in phrasing it you make it clear to the dissatisfied speaker that you understand both his feelings and the situation. If he sees that, he's going to see you as being on his side—and be more willing to consider himself part of your side. You'll have created an instantly more Involved worker, eager to adopt and "own" your solutions.

But there's a subtle distinction to be observed between the situation and the feelings, and it's one that is often forgotten by people who use Empathy Statements incorrectly. Many people, when you advise them to use "empathy," will object to the technique on the grounds that it's "inappropriate" to the person or situation at hand. "What about when the guy's just plain wrong?" they'll say. "Why should I validate an opinion that's based on an inaccurate reading of the situation?"

To people who make this objection—and there are plenty of them around—we always say, "You're not validating the person's opinion, or his assessment of the situation. You're only saying that, given his feelings about what's going on, you can empathize with him, for the simple reason that *you have felt the same way yourself.*"

That's really the crux of the matter. Empathy Statements are actually the easiest kind of validation to use, and they only get fouled up when, in attempting to be "empathetic," you assume that you have to *agree* with the speaker as well—that is, that you have to recognize this reaction not only as valid, but as *appropriate* as well. You can avoid this misuse of Empathy Statements if you remember that their focus is feelings. You have to understand enough about the person's situation to be able to link it to his feelings, but you do *not* have to agree with his analysis of the situation, and you do *not* have to acknowledge that his feelings are justified by the situation.

SEVEN DON'TS OF REFLECTIVE LISTENING

I've said that the single most important problem encountered in human communication is the lack of a Receiver's attention to what a Sender is saying. To a great degree all other problems of communication derive from this basic problem of inattention. The most damaging of these subsidiary problems can be listed as a series of "Don'ts."

1. *Don't rehearse.* If you want to get 100 percent of what a speaker is saying to you, you can't give him or her 25 or 50 percent of your attention. That means more than simply not letting your mind "wander" on to irrelevant topics. It also means not letting your attention wander to your *own* (relevant) thoughts while the speaker is talking. We all have a tendency to do this—to prepare and rehearse our countering statement while the speaker is talking—and the habit can be fatal to understanding. Rehearsing what you're going to say when he shuts up may be an appropriate tool for a debater, but good managerial motivation has very little to do with debate. You simply cannot turn somebody on if you're turned off to him from Square One.

2. *Don't defend.* A related problem is allowing yourself to become defensive in the face of comments that can be interpreted as antagonistic. Defensiveness, even when it's justified by a speaker's attack, is a major barrier to understanding. It's a natural reaction, I know, and I'm not suggesting that you shouldn't *feel* defensive. But as a manager you've got to look to the long term. You've got to keep your public reactions to antagonism on hold, or turn a potentially motivating exchange into the worst kind of demotivating experience—a shouting match between opponents. Find out *first* what the person is saying and feeling; you can counter later on.

3. *Don't interrupt.* Unless the guy is rambling on like he's possessed, and you can't make anything out of the diatribe, interruption is always contraindicated. It is physiologically impossible to listen and talk at the same time, so the best you can hope for when you interrupt is the standard 25 percent retention rate that, as I've said, is a hallmark of poor communication. Again the lesson is to listen up first, then respond.

4. *Don't change the focus to yourself.* A common misuse of Reflective Listening, especially of Empathy Statements, is to try to "top" the speaker's story by relating it to one of your own. An effective Empathy Statement validates the speaker's feelings first. An ineffective one often reads something like this: "I know just how you feel. I had the same thing happen to me. Let me tell you about it." And the "listener" goes off on a tangent, talking about himself while the speaker (who is the one with the immediate problem) is left feeling half-understood. (If you have a story that *does* relate to the speaker's, there's nothing wrong with mentioning it briefly, of course; but if you want the clarification of information that Reflective Listening is supposed to bring you, you must keep the initial focus on the speaker.)

5. *Don't discount.* When Laing and other psychologists caution against identifying a person's feelings as "mad" or "bad," they refer to such a procedure as "negating" or "discounting." Discounting a speaker's reactions as irrelevant, or inappropriate, or misguided nearly always guarantees that the communication process has broken down. As I mentioned in the section on Empathy Statements, you don't have to *agree* with each speaker's analysis of a situation. But you always have to acknowledge that the *feelings* he has about it are valid. Your goal as a Reflective Listener is to clarify and improve the situation; if you have a minor in clinical psychology and you just *know* that the speaker is reacting inappropriately, keep your pearls of wisdom to yourself—at least until after you have clarified *why* he is reacting the way he is.

6. *Don't judge.* Similarly, if you have assessed a situation in dramatically different terms from those of your speaker, slow down until you get *all* the facts before making a judgment on his or her view. I mean positive as well as negative judgment. It can be just as damaging to the ultimate solution of a dilemma to agree with a person's analysis prematurely as it can be to denounce it prematurely. The goal of Reflective Listening is "*clarify* (information) and *reinforce* (the speaker)." Judging the rightness or wrongness of either feelings or information generally tends to cut the conversation short—the last thing you want to do when the problem you are facing is still unresolved. So you should be just as wary of reacting with an enthusiastic "Yes, and . . ." as you are of reacting with a less enthusiastic "Yes, but . . ."

7. *Don't solve the problem—yet.* Finally, the Reflective Listener must always understand that the skills I have outlined here are ways of accumulating data—*not* shortcuts to pushing the button that will explain how all that data fits together. In the chapter on Creative Problem Solving, I'll show you how to work with your various speakers and listeners to generate effective team solutions. As you practice Reflective Listening, don't jump the gun. One of the quickest ways to turn off a speaker with a problem is to respond to his initial complaints with a ribboned-and-bowed solution. In team problem solving, the guy with the problem has got to be part of the solution. You serve no useful purpose by saying, "I know just how you feel, Ms. McVie. And here's how to set things straight."

The final lesson here is very simple. A fundamental reason

that human communication goes sour is that people who are supposed to be listening are doing any number of other things instead. This is because listening does not come naturally, but is a learned skill that improves with practice; obviously, only those who *do* practice it are going to get good at doing it. In this chapter I've outlined a few of the most effective techniques that I know of to increase your Reflective Listening potential. By practicing these techniques in your own job, family, or other social situations, you will gradually rise above that depressing 25 percent retention rate that most people think is "acceptable." Ultimately, hearing more and retaining more of what you hear is half the battle in human communication—and in the various performance and motivation problems that are governed by communication.

The other half of the battle is making sure that, once you've heard what the other fellow has to say, he will then hear *your* side. That's the subject of the following chapter.

SEVEN

MOTIVATIONAL ASSERTIVENESS

> Be sure you're right, then go ahead.
> —DAVY CROCKETT

Listening is essential to communicating well with anybody, and because listening is frequently slighted by would-be motivators, I've talked about it first. But listening is only the first half of the good motivator's communication skill set. The other half is, naturally enough, talking. It's speaking to the people you want to turn on in such a way that *they* will listen to *you*, and be willing to change their Behaviors in ways that you want them to change.

You might think that this would be the simpler half of the skill set to learn: since most of us get so much more practice in talking than in listening, it might seem that coming out and asking for what we want would be an awful lot simpler than hearing what other people want. But it doesn't work that way. Instead of asking, your average manager/motivator resorts to telling, or selling, or yelling—and as a result runs into stone walls.

The problem is basically one of tone. In order to get your people to really listen, and respond, to what you say, you have to be *assertive* but not *aggressive*, and few of us know how to draw that balance. Hence this chapter.

It is a strange irony that, in a country so enamored of "rugged individualism" and personal initiative, many of us have to be taught to ask for what we want. Yet it's a fact. We're pretty good at demanding, and we're not too bad at backing off if somebody responds to our demands in a louder, more threatening voice than our own. We're not so good at stating, simply and straight to the point, "This is what I expect you to do." Very few of us are as adept as my old coach Bud Grant was in Pinpointing what needs to be done, *asking* for it, and then promising, "And if you do that, we'll win the ball game."

About ten years ago, a whole cottage industry got built up teaching people how to ask for what they want. This industry was created by popular psychologists who were convinced that the inability to be direct about what you want was a symptom of "ego problems"—of insecurity about identity. In a book typical of much work in this field, Drs. Robert Alberti and Michael Emmons identify a sense of "personal powerlessness" as the root of nonassertive behavior. They encourage their readers to experience their "personhood" in a "positive way," to "radically change" their "self-concept" and their sense of "self-esteem." "Poor self-concept," say the authors of *Stand Up, Speak Out, Talk Back*, is nearly always the villain in the piece, and learning how to change that concept from the inside is the "key to self-assertive behavior."

There's nothing wrong with this psychological analysis of nonassertiveness, and it's certainly true that changing your self-concept can have a dramatic effect on your behavior. But you know by now that my bias is away from theory and toward results, away from metaphysical speculation on the "real" meaning of a given Behavior, and toward a system that uses the manipulation of Antecedents and Consequences as the proven way to *alter* Behaviors, that is, to motivate others.

In teaching people in our client companies to become more effectively self-assertive—in other words, to get what they want out of others by *asking* for it directly—we've always favored a straight-on and, I believe, an eminently practical approach. First, we get our clients to measure how assertive or nonassertive they already are; in this we are applying the Recording element of the P.R.I.C.E. motivation model. Then we teach a set of simple, learnable Assertion Skills with which anyone—whatever the extent of his "unresolved superego conflicts"—can behave in a more assertive manner. And we show our clients how to apply these skills in real-life situations where the goal is to influence and change others.

We're going to do the same thing in this chapter. By the end of the chapter you will have been introduced to the "other half" of the communication skill package that you need to motivate people effectively and generate good team solutions. First, however, a couple of definitions, presented up front so you will know exactly what I mean by "assertiveness" and why I feel it is just as important a component of sound communication as Reflective Listening.

BEYOND THE "FIGHT OR FLIGHT" RESPONSE

"Assertiveness" is a healthy and balanced response to a perceived external threat. In nature, an animal who feels threatened typically experiences a "fight or flight" response. In the fight or flight response, which consists physiologically of increased heart rate, dilated pupils, and generalized muscular tension, the animal is getting ready to defend itself against the threat, either by running away (flight) or by meeting aggression with aggression (fight). Running away would be a *passive* response, and standing to fight would be an *aggressive* one.

All of this makes perfect sense if you are a rabbit being chased by a fox, or a fox being cornered by hounds. But the "flight or fight" response is ultimately very limited; it allows the threatened animal only two clearcut choices of action, neither one entirely satisfactory—and neither one entirely appropriate to human situations, in which the perceived external threat is likely to be the more tenuous "attacks" of insult, oversight, or noncompliance with something that you, the motivating manager, want to get done.

If you're not able to express yourself assertively, you're going to be continually caught in the simplistic "natural" response pattern, torn between running away from disagreement and causing outright conflict. And you can't get people to see things your way when you're in that double bind. Nobody will listen to a manager who is bleating about "getting no respect." Or to one who threatens to burn down the house if he doesn't get his way right now. And yet that's the way a lot of managers typically react to confrontation.

To be an effective motivator, you often have to walk a thin line between firmness and abrasiveness, and a lot of managers never negotiate that line effectively because they fall prey to one of two opposite, and equally demotivating, behavior patterns. In trying to get their points across, they become either inveterate "wind-testers" or unyielding "standers of the ground."

- The *Wind-Tester* is someone who is afraid to come right out and say what he needs to have done, because he doubts his own rights in the situation. He doesn't want to appear "forward" or "bossy," and he doesn't want to be disliked by the people he has to work with every day. So he overcompensates by becoming so "likeable" that he can never get anything done. Every directive he gives is merely a straw in the wind; the only reason he expresses an opinion at all is because it's expected of him, and if you shoot that opinion down in a team meeting or a one-on-one confrontation, he'll be happy to back off. Naturally, the Wind-Tester is a lousy motivator: since he's unwilling to commit *himself* to a particular course of action, he's hopeless in getting *others* to commit to what he wants to do.

- The *Stander of the Ground* knows he's right—even when all the evidence is going against him—and he's going to stick to his guns even if it kills him. Which it often does. This kind of manager is constantly overstepping the boundary between firmness and pigheadedness, and cannot be made to acknowledge that, in certain cases, he may be wrong. His way of getting others to follow his lead is to announce in a loud voice what he expects to have happen, and then sit back and let them do it—or, even worse, to look over people's shoulders until they all fall into line.

Ironically, even though he's *completely* committed to his course of action, this guy is no more successful in creating motivated players than the guy who passively retreats. As I've said before, people will not commit to a decision unless they feel that it's *owned*—and the manager who stands his ground at all times doesn't allow that ownership to develop.

These are extreme portrayals, obviously, but I think you will recognize the types. They're all over today's business world, mucking things up for the rest of us by making it impossible to develop consensus, impossible to sort out real decisions from hasty or hesitant ones, impossible to generate real Involvement.

The happy medium is Assertiveness. To the assertive manager, everybody's rights are equally important, and everybody's opinion is valued. That doesn't mean everybody's ideas are seen as equally sensible, only that the *expression* of opinions, from motivators and motivated alike, is seen as a necessary element of humans *communicating* together. In true Assertiveness, because everyone is perceived as an equal, you can express yourself openly and directly, without either the fear of being "beaten" by another or the need to win at another's expense.

To most people in most situations, the middle way of open assertiveness remains little more than an ideal. Most of us are bogged down, in most conflict situations, into choosing between the equally nonproductive responses of timid retreat and hostility. A few examples:

Example 1: The Stolen Parking Space

You are about to back into a parking place when another driver, ignoring your signal, scoots into the space ahead of you. It's clear that you were there first, and that he has violated your rights. What do you do? How do you get him to *change his Behavior*?

The passive response would be to shrug the infraction off, saying to yourself that it's not worth a hassle, and to drive on, looking for another place. That would have two major drawbacks. It would probably make your resentful and "used" (as indeed you have been), and it would allow the other driver to remain immune to punishment, or correction, for what was obviously an act of gross discourtesy. No Behavior change. No results.

The aggressive response would be to climb angrily out of your car, calling the second driver choice names, and to try to "persuade" him by threats that he had better relinquish the spot. The likely outcome of that approach would be to make him all the more convinced that the spot was his for the taking, and that you are a fool for objecting. In other words, the Punishment Effect. And, again, no results.

The middle-way, assertive response would be to calmly point out to the other driver that you were waiting to enter the space, and would appreciate it if he would vacate it. It is difficult to say how effective such a response would be in this particular situation, because it is so seldom tried. But it certainly can't have *worse* effects than passiveness and aggression.

Example 2: The "Expert" Speaks

You are a member of your company's planning committee, and are attempting with the other committee members to draft a set of new directions and goals. Your comment about the need for "more product innovation" is met with stiff hostility by the committee's chairman. His assessment of your suggestion is entirely dismissive: "We know those damn blue-sky schemes always fail; let's talk about something that can succeed."

The passive response would be to hang your head, sheepishly acknowledging the superior wisdom of the chairman, and to butt out of the rest of the discussion. The aggressive response would be to tackle his resistance head on, adducing evidence of "conservative failures" to match his allegation of innovative flops. The middle-way, assertive response would be to point out that his characterization of your suggestion as a "blue-sky scheme" was an unfair generalization, and to ask him to consider your specific proposals before jumping down your throat. It would be, in other words, to aim for an open *exchange* rather than a "one up, one down" altercation. That's communication. Which leads to motivation and Involvement. Which in turn leads to results.

Why is true Assertiveness so rare? Why do we have so many Wind-Testers and Ground-Standers, and so few people who—like Davy Crockett's motto implies—are able to listen carefully first, to check out the situation and to give everyone's opinion a chance, and then come out directly with what they want?

One reason is simple inertia. Given a variety of responses to a ticklish situation, most people tend toward the response that will bring them the least negative Consequences in the *short* term. Failing that, they'll go for the response that will allow them to suffer the Consequences with which they're already familiar, rather than taking on new, unknown ones. A kid will eat spinach any day rather than tackle an oyster, because he knows what spinach tastes like.

But in the *long* term, a policy either of acquiescence to injustice against you or of intransigent disregard of others' rights, leads to precisely the same dead end. The only policy, the only set of behavior, that ultimately enhances all those things we want from our social interactions—better communication, better motivation, better performance—is the middle-ground policy of assertion. That is why, in spite of the awesome power of inertia and convention, it is essential for anyone in a position to influence the behavior of others to learn assertiveness skills.

We will move to those skills in a moment. First, though, let's go to what I called the first step in our program of learning to ask for what you want: the preliminary "Recording" or assessment of where you stand right now, in terms of the ideal middle ground.

THE ASSERTION SCALE

I want you to perform an exercise here that participants in my labor and management motivation programs perform. Remember that, in the P.R.I.C.E. motivation model, the second step—after you have Pinpointed a Behavior that needs changing—is to Record precisely where you are with regard to that Behavior, so that you will have a "baseline" for future measurement. We've just implicitly Pinpointed a Behavior that all of us, to some degree or another, need to work on: the tendency to be either passive or aggressive, and thus to avoid being assertive. Now we move to the Recording step, and ask you to measure your own assertiveness with reference to an Assertion Scale designed to show you how effective you are in asking for what you want.

Begin by looking at the list of situations in Figure 11, most of which you have probably already encountered at one time or another. Notice that, for each situation, you are to measure two things. In Column A, put down, on a scale of 1 to 5, the degree of discomfort you would feel in performing the individual situational behavior. In Column B, using the same 1 to 5 scale, say how frequently you would perform that behavior anyway, in spite of your discomfort level. When you're finished making those two sets of personal measurements, you'll have two columns of numbers. Total these two columns, so that you have two sums, one indicating your "discomfort degree" and the other indicating your "response probability."

Now, using these totals, plot your personal "assertiveness" position on the Assertion Scale in Figure 12. This scale, developed internally at the Tarkenton Productivity Group, is designed to show you not only how assertive you are in your day-to-day interactions with others, but also how *effective* your particular assertiveness level is, not just in terms of your motivational impact on others, but also in terms of your own internal sense of well-being.

To identify where you stand with respect to these two variables, first take the Degree of Discomfort total and identify that number on the horizontal axis of the chart. Draw a vertical straight line through that point.

Then take the Response Probability total and see where it falls on the vertical axis of the chart. Draw a horizontal line through that point.

The place where the two lines you have drawn intersect is your "position" on this Assertion Scale.

Situation	Degree of Discomfort in Behaving This Way	Response Probability
	1 = none 2 = a little 3 = a fair amount 4 = much 5 = very much	1 = always do it 2 = usually 3 = do it half the time 4 = rarely do it 5 = never do it
1. Turn down a request to borrow your car.		
2. Compliment a friend.		
3. Ask a favor of someone.		
4. Resist sales pressure.		
5. Apologize when you are at fault.		
6. Turn down a request for a meeting.		
7. Admit fear and request consideration.		
8. Tell a person you are intimately involved with when he/she says or does something that bothers you.		
9. Ask for a raise.		
10. Admit ignorance in some area.		
11. Turn down a request to borrow money.		
12. Ask personal questions.		
13. Turn off a talkative friend.		
14. Ask for constructive criticism.		
15. Initiate a conversation with a stranger.		
16. Compliment a person you are close to of the opposite sex.		
17. Request a meeting with a person.		
18. Your initial request for a meeting is turned down and you ask the person again at a later time.		
19. Admit confusion about a point under discussion and ask for clarification.		
20. Apply for a job.		
21. Ask whether you have offended someone.		
22. Tell someone that you like them.		
23. Request expected service when such is not forthcoming; e.g., in a restaurant.		
24. Discuss openly with the person his/her criticism of your behavior.		
25. Return defective items, e.g., store or restaurant.		
26. Express an opinion that differs from that of the person you are talking to.		
27. Resist sexual overtures when you are not interested.		
28. Tell the person when you feel he/she has done something that is unfair to you.		
29. Tell someone good news about yourself.		
30. Resist pressure to drink.		
31. Resist a significant person's unfair demand.		
32. Quit a job.		
33. Discuss openly with the person his/her criticism of your work.		
34. Request the return of borrowed items.		
35. Receive compliments.		
36. Continue to converse with someone who disagrees with you.		
37. Tell a friend or someone with whom you work when he/she says or does something that bothers you.		
38. Ask a person who is annoying you in a public situation to stop.		

Totals:

Figure 11

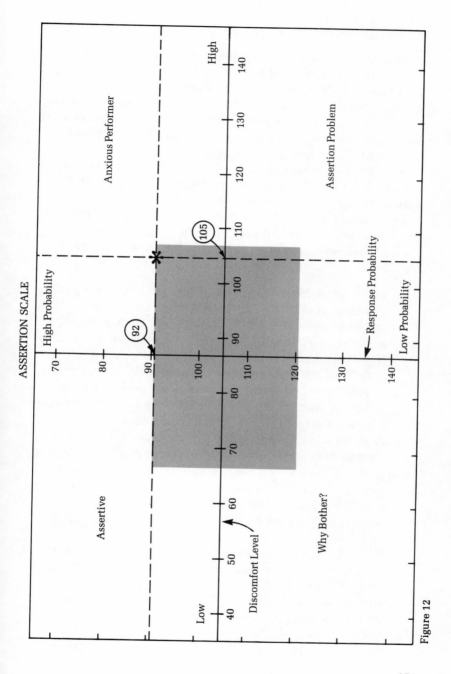

Figure 12

To illustrate the use of the Assertion Scale, I have plotted a hypothetical position on the chart as an example. In the example given here, the person's Discomfort level was 105, and the Response Probability total was 92. The place where these two values intersect is at the circled star, just "north" of the central box (we'll explain that in a moment) of the Assertion Scale, in the "Anxious Performer" quadrant.

You now have a preliminary "fix" on where you stand with regard to the two variables of Discomfort and Response Probability. How do you interpret this fix?

You'll notice that the Assertion Scale is divided into four equal segments, or quadrants. Here is how we interpret the general behavior patterns that fall into each of the four quadrants:

- *The Why Bother? Quadrant:* If you find yourself in this quadrant, it is likely that both your discomfort level with regard to threatening or disconcerting situations and your assertiveness in dealing with those situations are low. That is, you tend not to assert yourself in compromising social situations, but you experience little anxiety about denying yourself this option, because few of those situations seem to you to warrant a more assertive response. This could indicate that you're a very passive, retiring personality, or it could indicate that you have such a "philosophical" approach to social conflict that you're willing to take a back seat, even when the "actual" situation doesn't warrant it. Generally speaking, those who find themselves in the "Why Bother?" quadrant are ineffective at motivating others, and not especially interested in becoming more effective.

- *The "Assertion Problem" Quadrant.* If you are in this quadrant, you have, like the "Why Bother?" person, a low probability of reacting assertively to socially threatening situations. But unlike the "Why Bother?" person, this is likely to cause you some grief. Since there is a conflict between the high Discomfort level that you feel with regard to disturbing situations and the low Response level in those situations, you are likely to feel pressured and resentful in situations where the "Why Bother?" person would simply feel resigned to his fate. We say that a person in this quadrant may have an "Assertion Problem" not because he or she simply fails to respond, but because that failure to respond is causing internal anxiety for him—an anxiety that is bound to come out in the public arena as well, and to make him a less effective motivator or communicator than he otherwise might be.

- The "Anxious Performer" Quadrant. In the "Anxious Performer" quadrant, you show a high degree of Discomfort over difficult social interactions, and an equivalently high degree of probability that you will react in an assertive manner anyway. That is, you are perfectly willing to behave assertively, but you are not able to do so without incurring internal anxiety: you stand up for your rights at all times, yet this gives you little personal satisfaction, because you feel yourself continually on the defensive, and are not capable of drawing a healthy balance between speaking up and letting things slide. You find this syndrome of anxious performance a lot in highly motivated people who are never fully satisfied with their performance. They behave often in an energetic but self-destructive manner—like the newspaper writer whom Harry Truman once called "a four-ulcer man on a two-ulcer job."

- The "Assertive" Quadrant. In this quadrant, you achieve a reasonable balance between Discomfort about social pressures and assertive response to those pressures. Your anxiety level in the face of social threats is lower than that of the Anxious Performer, but the likelihood that you will stand up for your rights when threatened is higher than that of the person who says, "Why Bother?" Therefore, you draw the appropriate balance between the two equally unproductive extremes of fight and flight.

That's a general and very sketchy readout of where you stand in the Assertion Scale. Before you start going through the Yellow

Pages for the numbers of the nearest shrinks, however, let me make a couple of observations.

First, you should keep in mind that the "Recording" exercise you have just performed is subjective and highly personal: it is your *own* assessment of where you stand with regard to assertiveness. A professional "assertiveness trainer" might assess you differently, and I am not offering this chart as a surefire guide to anyone's personality. I do feel that a personal assessment is valuable, however, because it gives you a litmus test to work from. It is a window on how you *feel* about the way you interact with others in potentially problematic situations. The way you feel may not be the final word, but it's a pretty good initial guide to whether you're coming across as madly aggressive, wimpishly passive, or something in between.

Second, do not assume that the "Assertive" quadrant of this matrix is the only quadrant you "should" be in. All of us have different mixtures of assertiveness and compliance in our personalities, and it would be ludicrous to suggest that every officially designated "Assertive" individual was handling all his problems well—or that every Anxious Performer was doomed to be fretful and uptight. The box in the center of the four-quadrant matrix indicates *approximately* where "balanced" behavior might lie, whatever quadrant you might find yourself in. It's obvious, when you consider the need for this balance, that you could be way out in "left field" of the "Assertive" quadrant, and be managing your interactions very poorly. What a "low Discomfort, high Response" profile would indicate, in fact, is a person who always stood up for his own "rights," even when it was counterproductive to do so.

Finally, remember that the "fix" you have made on yourself here is just that: a fix, not a final position. When I talked about the need to establish a *baseline* of behavior and performance, I didn't suggest the baseline as the goal. The whole point of establishing a baseline is to understand where you're starting from, so you can measure your progress from that point. The same principle applies here. The Assertion Scale identifies a baseline so that, as you practice our repertoire of assertiveness skills, you can replot your position and move on.

It's time now to introduce those skills.

THE ASSERTIVE MOTIVATOR

In 1975, psychologist Manuel Smith published a popular book on assertiveness entitled *When I Say No, I Feel Guilty.* In that book he outlined several important skills for increasing assertiveness, and for increasing the effectiveness of your interaction with others. I've found four of Smith's skills of some value in the performance and motivation workshops we run. They have proved to be of equal value in nonbusiness situations as well; in fact, they have been demonstrated as effective in a huge variety of situations where you need to "ask for what you want"—that is, influence or motivate others—without trampling on their rights.

1. *Broken Record.* The lesson of the "Broken Record" technique is the lesson of the water that wears away rock: persistence pays. In using this technique, you state your side of the argument or discussion repeatedly, without either defensiveness or hostility, until the person to whom you're talking agrees to do things your way or, failing that, to what Smith calls a "workable compromise."

In *When I Say No, I Feel Guilty,* author Smith makes two good points about the Broken Record technique that I have found verified again and again in our performance-improvement workshops. First, for the technique to be effective, you have to repeat your assertion in a *calm and consistent* voice, refusing to be sidetracked by clever arguments against your side, and refusing too to become agitated at the refusal of the other person to concur with your conclusions. The magic of the Broken Record style is its infuriating uniformity—a uniformity that eventually convinces even the most intransigent opponent that the only way to turn off the record is to work *with* you rather than resist. A rising voice, increased volume, visible agitation on your part—all of these undercut that insistent uniformity, and undermine the effectiveness of Broken Record.

The second point that Smith makes explains why Broken Record is so effective in developing assertiveness over time: In sticking to your guns in a calm, unwavering manner, you are signaling to the other person—and, even more important, reminding yourself—that what you say and feel is not *dependent* on the opinion of other parties. This point reinforces the importance of using a calm tone. The manager who allows himself to get annoyed by a problematic subordinate is subtly locked in to the subordinate's own behavior pattern: he is controlled by the inappropriate behavior of another. Broken Record allows you to get beyond this common interactional bind by proclaiming your independence of others' behavior. With the Broken Record skill, whatever the other person says or does, you remain in control.

You don't have to be in control the way a prison guard is in control: you don't have to verbally beat the other person over the head with your Broken Record opinion. Indeed, if you must resort to this technique alone to assert your own opinion, chances are that you don't have that kind of leverage against the other person anyway. In my workshops I advise clients to combine the Broken Record technique with the Empathy Statement skill introduced in the previous chapter, as a way of softening the insistence. Instead of saying, "We have to do this my way," you say, repeatedly and calmly, "I see your point about this, but I think we have to go with 'plan B.' " And *give your reasons*. Anybody you're trying to influence deserves to know what they are.

This is assuming, of course, that you have *already* applied Reflective Listening—and that Reflective Listening is an integral part of your entire conversational style. To someone who energetically listens to others, Broken Record can be an invaluable assertion skill in situations where you are "sure you are right." To someone who doesn't listen to others, or who makes no distinction between his own good, fair, and lousy ideas, Broken Record can be merely an excuse for verbal bullying. As I'll explain in more detail in the chapters on Creative Problem Solving and Conflict Management, assertiveness is a contingent rather than absolute skill: if the Broken Record technique is used in isolation from Reflective Listening and consensus-building skills, it will almost certainly backfire, leaving you without an audience *or* a solution.

2. *Fogging.* The Oriental martial arts are frequently classified into "hard" and "soft" styles: hard styles, like most forms of karate, emphasize straight-line punching and kicking, while soft styles, like jiu-jitsu, emphasize "yielding" techniques that redirect an opponent's momentum so that in effect he defeats himself.

Fog is a lot like jiu-jitsu; its power is the power of yielding. Travelers who get lost in the fog are not pummelled into submission, but absorbed, enveloped, and confused. In the Fogging assertion technique, you make use of the yielding principle to create a kind of easily penetrable but ultimately invincible verbal fogbank that defuses an opponent's attack by *accepting* it. In using Fogging, you acknowledge the validity of criticism, and thus take the wind out of your attacker's sails. In effect you are saying to the critic, "You are entirely correct, and I don't care."

Fogging is *not* the same thing as simply "going along" with a criticism. I call it an assertive skill because its intention, as well as its effect, is entirely the *opposite* of simply admitting defeat. Fogging is not an admission of defeat. It is an acknowledgment that what the critic is saying—or, in some cases, *part* of what the critic is saying—may have some validity. And it is used not to end a discussion by crying "Uncle," but to carry the conversation forward, by validating the other person's view and thus making it easier for him or her to keep talking.

"Keeping the person talking" is a major benefit of Reflective Listening, too, and for this reason Fogging can be compared to the Reflective Listening skills, especially that of Rephrasing. (In fact, Fogging can often be used well in conjunction with Rephrased or Empathy statements.) Smith records a Fogging exercise which illustrates this double technique: A "Critic" and a "Learner" of the Fogging skill are discussing the Learner's nervousness about being faced with criticism.

Critic: You look nervous when I tell you things that you don't like.
Learner: I'm sure I do look nervous.
Critic: You shouldn't be nervous, I'm your friend.
Learner: That's true, I shouldn't be as nervous as I am.

Critic: I'm probably the only person who would tell you these things.
Learner: I'm sure you're right about that (sarcastically).
Critic: You were being sarcastic.
Learner: That's true, I was.

The discussion continues for two more pages, but you get the point. Fogging builds on the Zenlike truth that ultimately absorption is dispersion, victory is defeat, and that one of the best ways to take a punch is to "go with" the force of the impact. This may have little validity in the world of political antagonisms, but when the arena is personal and conversational, Fogging can be an effective tool, because it accomplishes something that toughing it out can never accomplish: it forces the antagonist to change tactics. Ironically, a common eventual result of using Fogging is that criticism *lessens* rather than increases.

This is a tricky and suspect point to people who are accustomed to viewing conversation as battle. I don't deny that Fogging can be a difficult technique. Few of us like to be criticized, and fewer still are comfortable in "welcoming" attacks on ourselves. But there is a profound difference between simply "taking the punch" and deflecting it as in Fogging. That difference, in terms of interactional dynamics, is simply that the Fogger is *in control.*

Look back at the passage I just quoted from Manuel Smith. In that passage the Critic is consistently on the attack, but if you read between the lines it's clear that the Learner is directing the exchange. Whatever tack the Critic takes, and no matter how personal or insulting he becomes, eventually he can make no headway, because everything he says is given credence. The moral is subtle and useful: aggression *depends* on resistance, and if there is no resistance, aggression may eventually be defused. This is an especially useful tactic in "one down" conflict situations, where you're trying to influence the Behavior of an aggressive, badgering superior.

3. *Negative Assertion.* The same point can be made about the third assertiveness technique: Negative Assertion. You use this technique in situations where you have "gone ahead" and later discovered you'd been wrong; perhaps you've reinforced someone at the wrong time or in the wrong way, or made some error of judgment in your department. It happens to the best of us. Negative Assertion can help you absorb the mistakes.

The trick in using this skill, as in using Fogging, is in maintaining an even, unemotional style while you are acknowledging something uncomfortable about yourself: It's really a matter of being able to isolate yourself from your actions or, as Catholic theologians have always pointed out, in separating the sinner from the sin. When you negatively assert that you have done something wrong, you are *not* saying, "I'm a miserable wretch and I ought to be drawn and quartered immediately." You're saying simply, "I made an error, I'm sorry, and I'll try not to do that again."

The difficulty in using this skill is that people are not accustomed to admitting *responsibility* for actions without feeling *guilty* about the mistake. Negative Assertion is a way for managers—who often feel they have to be right all the time—to acknowledge their own fallibility.

I can explain how Negative Assertion works by using an example from one of my company's recent seminars. It was a "communication improvement" seminar for managers in a steel-pressing plant, and one of the seminar participants was the assistant plant manager. One Friday afternoon, preoccupied with a rush order, he neglected to check a pressure gauge on a piece of machinery. As a result the machine malfunctioned, and was out of operation for two hours on Saturday morning. It was not a dangerous or serious mistake, but it did cost the company some time, and when the manager came in on Monday he was called on the carpet by his boss.

There were a number of traditional ways in which he could have reacted. He could have practiced the crablike art of trouble-avoidance by simply disclaiming responsibility—by shifting the blame to someone else or to the machine itself. Psychologists call this approach to criticism "denial." It's used all the time, of course, even though the results of using it are universally bad.

Faced with his error, the assistant manager could also have

responded with the fight or flight syndrome, either passively accepting blame and begging for forgiveness (flight) or standing up to his boss by dismissing the criticism as irrelevant (fight).

The manager in our seminar, since he had been trained in Assertiveness, did none of these things. He simply acknowledged his error, apologized for the oversight, and went back to doing his job. He didn't try to shift accountability somewhere else, or plead the unexpected rush order as an excuse, or whine about how overworked he was, or offer to commit hara-kiri. As a result, he told us, "My boss shrugged the whole thing off. Said I should be more careful in the future, and I agreed with him, and that was that. I know from past experience what his reaction would have been if I had weasled around it. He would have been on my case for a month."

So the real lesson of Negative Assertion, like that of Fogging, is that resistance to external attacks can sometimes merely intensify those attacks, while absorbing the punches and going on often seems to be the best way to come out a winner.

4. *Negative Inquiry.* The fourth assertion skill, Negative Inquiry, carries the usefulness of Negative Assertion one step farther, by asking the critic to *elaborate* on the complaint or reservation he has about you. In Negative Inquiry, you don't stop by saying, "Yeah, I really messed up." You press your critic for details: "You could be right about that. What is it particularly you don't like about the way I handled this job?"

Negative Inquiry, a particularly powerful way to consolidate your position by seeming to deny it, builds on many of the principles I've already introduced in this book. In asking the critic for details about your behavior, it is an example of the Pinpointing technique. In tacitly (or vocally) suggesting that you agree with the critic's point, it performs the validating function that is so important in Reflective Listening skills. And in asking for elaboration, it allows both Sender and Receiver, with the technique of Open-Ended Questioning, to clarify the overall situation and get closer to mutual solutions.

Mutual solutions. That means solutions where there is Involvement, and ownership, and respect among all the people concerned with the achievement of a common end. Those are the only solutions, as I've pointed out throughout this book, that have any chance of long-term survival. They're the only kind of solutions you can get your people up for. This point, of course, relates not just to Negative Inquiry, but to all four of the assertiveness skills, and to the Reflective Listening skills that I talked about in the previous chapter. I've spoken of good listening and good assertiveness as two "halves" of the same large interactional skill package. The final goal of these two halves is the same. It's to enhance communication, so that you can develop with everyone you talk to that condition of *active interchange* that is essential to all motivation and all performance.

Of course, a lot of what I've been saying in this and the previous chapter is as relevant in family life and general social life as it is in business settings. Making sure that you're "right" first by listening, and then "going ahead" by straightforward assertion—those two skills comprise a large part of good motivation in all these settings. Unfortunately, many people remain convinced—in spite of vast experience to the contrary—that the only way to get somebody to do what you want is to yell at him or threaten him into compliance. The lesson of the past two chapters is that a far more efficient way of motivating people into appropriate action is first to listen to what they have to tell you, and then to tell them what you want in a direct, nondefensive, nonthreatening manner. That doesn't guarantee you'll always get your way. But it does minimize the chances that you will spend countless hours of bitterness and recrimination going at each other like butting rams.

This is important anywhere, but it's especially crucial in team settings—as you'll see in the following section.

PART III

PUTTING IT ALL TOGETHER

EIGHT

BUILDING YOUR TEAM

> I want every one of my players to believe that he's the
> spark that keeps our team moving forward.
> —KNUTE ROCKNE

Two schools of thought prevail about how to effectively manage
a team. The older and more popular approach is the authoritarian one that sees the manager or coach as a cross between
Moses and Atilla the Hun—an all-wise, all-powerful father figure whose every word should be graven in stone—and that sees
the members of the team as underlings whose responsibility is
to listen to those words and obey.

Some great coaches have made headlines by subscribing to
the authoritarian model, not necessarily because it works but
because it makes for quotable observations. There's Pittsburgh
coach Fred Depasqua's comment that "Football is not a democracy. If the players want to debate, they can do it in political
science class." Or Ohio State basketball coach Fred Taylor's
snap at what he saw as the troublemaking players of the 1970s:
"You could put the brains of three of those guys in a hum-
mingbird and it would still fly backward." Or, for an all-time
high in managerial chutzpah, Vince Lombardi's supposed quip
to his wife when he got into bed and she complained, "God,
your feet are cold." As Lombardi's great running back Paul
Hornung tells the joke, the coach's response was, "Around the
house, dear, you can call me Vince."

But the authoritarian model is a going concern not just in sports. It's popular in every arena where groups of people are managed. You've heard the cliches a thousand times. "I pay him to do his job right, not to think." "It's my company and I'll run it any way I want." They're all spinoffs from the "enlightened despot" attitude of the nineteenth-century robber baron era. Whether you work for a company with ten or ten thousand employees, you've come across this attitude. There are still plenty of good old boys in the boardroom and the shop floor who think that being a manager means being 100 percent in charge.

The second school of thought about team management is the "democratic" or "participative" approach, where leadership is taken as the art of getting the best out of your people by encouraging them to talk, to give their opinions, to work solutions out in joint fashion. There aren't a hell of a lot of professional coaches who subscribe to this school of thought, at least publicly, partly because it doesn't make good copy, and partly because most coaches start out working with very young players, and get used to bossing them around. Most of us, after all, learn how to play sports in high school, and in high school, where there's an enormous gap in experience and maturity between coaches and players, it's not reasonable to expect the democratic approach to be effective. So everybody involved in the game starts by subscribing to the authoritarian model, and they carry it on into college and even into the pros, and it never gets reexamined.

The same is true in business. A kid's first job might be raking up leaves for a neighbor or delivering papers or wrapping hamburgers down at McDonald's. There's not a lot of opportunity in those situations for "participative management" or discussion, and I guess not a lot of need either. So the pattern gets set very early. As they say in the military, "You can't give orders until you've first learned to take them."

But does the popular, in fact nearly universal, authoritarian model *work*? Sure, it's comfortable, it's expected, it's the way things have always been arranged. But does it get the job done?

THE "BOSSMAN" STYLE: DOES IT WORK?

A lot of evidence says no. You can get team members to obey you by using a strictly dictatorial style, but to elicit real involvement, real motivation, and really top performance over a long period of time, you need something a little more sophisticated than "bossing."

In a revealing study done a few years ago, Hans Lenk, a German sports sociologist, showed what that something might be. In his book *Team Dynamics*, he investigated the relative effectiveness of the authoritarian and democratic coaching styles in European rowing teams. What he found overturns the common coaching wisdom that you've got to kick ass to get anything done on a sports team. Lenk admitted that authoritarian coaches tended to be more "task- and achievement-oriented" than democratic ones, but he failed to find that this orientation made an appreciable difference in the performance of the teams involved. In fact, just the opposite was the case. Teams controlled by a strong, boss-type leader and those that were run by collective leadership performed about the same at the beginning, but as time went on the "softer" style gradually began to get better results. In Lenk's description, this is how things developed over time:

The members were dissatisfied with the authoritarian leading; they reacted either aggressively against the leader and toward each other or with apathetic submission. In the case of strong control the performance was a little higher than with the "democratic" leading style. Then soon a decrease followed. The members who reacted apathetically did not show any motivation for performance and soon the decrease of motivation began.

That jibes pretty well with what I've observed on the playing field, and in dozens of businesses. The fact is that there's an upper limit to the effectiveness of any "hard" leadership style, a kind of "plateau effect" that sets in once players or workers have been consistently abused, and that invariably cuts down on motivation.

One reason that this plateau effect sets in is that even a so-called superhuman coach is still, when you come right down to it, only human. Even Vince Lombardi would have admitted that. And because the smartest and most authoritarian of leaders is only human, he can't ever be in two places at once, he can't always be on top of everything, he can't be *constantly* in control. Since he can't be constantly watching everything, at least *some* of the training and motivation on any team has to be left up to the group members themselves. And if they haven't been trained and reinforced for doing that, they're not going to do it well. Lenk describes this natural process:

Crews under authoritarian guidance . . . were often observed to start reserving their forces whenever the coach did not look. They did not really exhaust themselves if the coach was absent; they were not able to conduct a really full-scale training by themselves, without immediate guidance and control.

As a result, of course, whenever Big Daddy is "absent," performance is going to suffer, and bad habits will be formed.

There's an analogy here to the way you might raise a family. If you watch your kids at all times, do everything for them, and demand that they do everything your way, what are you going to get? A bunch of obedient clones, who will not be able to make any of their own decisions because you've never prepared them to do so. If you want to raise adults, you've got to give your kids *practice* in being adults: you've got to let them take risks, experiment and fail, participate in decisions that affect them even when you know their input isn't as "good" as yours.

This is pretty obvious to a parent. It's not so obvious to many coaches. And it's absolute heresy to a lot of company managers, who are comfortable behaving like Big Daddies and who don't really want their "kids" to grow up.

If you want some evidence of how "well" the Big Daddy approach to management works, take a look at our automobile industry. You can see the same gradual development there that

Lenk talks about in terms of rowing. He was talking about it, presumably, as something that happened over a fairly short period of time—a single season, probably. It's taken a lot longer for the process to happen in Detroit, because you're dealing there with large social forces, a huge work force, and much more complicated inter-group relationships than those on a rowing team. But it's still happened. We've seen the relationship between Big Daddy management and the "brainless," "child-like" workers go from one of simple obedience to one of apathy and rebellion—and for exactly the same reasons that this happened in Lenk's rowing teams.

The rebellion—in the form of angry bargaining sessions and protracted strikes—gets most of the press coverage, but the apathy can be just as damaging, and, in fact, is just the other side of the same coin. When critics of the "overpaid worker" talk about featherbedding, laziness, and the lack of pride in one's work that is supposed to characterize our big businesses today, they often forget that these problems arise *directly* from a management philosophy that says workers don't really *want* to work—that you have to force them to be involved, because they'll never pull the oar on their own.

The sports equivalent to laziness and featherbedding is what we call "sandbagging." The sandbagger is the guy who misses the block not because he lacks the necessary practice and training, but because his motivation is down—the guy who just doesn't care enough to give the play 100 percent. It happens. It happens on the best of teams. But it doesn't happen on teams where everybody is expected to perform to the best of his ability all the time, where everybody understands that it's in his own best interest to do so, and where there are clear-cut Consequences built in for letting your team members do your job. (I never heard about sandbagging, for example, on any team Dick Butkus played on. Butkus was tough, disciplined, and absolutely involved. He got everybody else involved, too. Not by believing they *couldn't* do better, but by believing they *could*—and demanding it, if they wanted to play with him.)

The lesson is simple. Unless you actively *involve* team members in the running of the team they belong to, it's ridiculous to expect them to be "loyal" to you when times get tough—or, for that matter, when times are good. A lot of people think Detroit's current problems can be traced to Japanese competition and recent economic downturns. That's bull. Detroit had the same problems in the 1950s and 1960s, when times were great. The difference was that, when the economy was booming, it was much easier to cover up the problems by offering huge pay packages and benefit programs to disgruntled employees—as if pay were the only issue that mattered. The covers came off in the downturn because that pure monetary reinforcement started to fall away, and suddenly workers who had always hated their jobs didn't even have the consolation of a thirty-dollar-an-hour slot any more. With that gone, all the old resentments flared up. And guess who they were directed against? Big Daddy in the front office, who had been telling his "children" for years that he knew all the answers, and that they should just take their bonuses and be quiet.

I saw a laid-off General Motors worker on a television talk show about a year ago, complaining about the raw deal he'd gotten. You know what he talked about? Not the huge managerial bonuses, or the fact that, after eighteen years of service, he had been let go on two days' notice. What really galled him, he said, was that, in all those years on the line (he was a frame assembly foreman) he had never once been asked for his *opinion* on productivity, efficiency, quality control, or anything else. "I'd *forgotten* more about that job than those front-office turkeys ever knew," he said. "I could have given them twenty tips on making my line run better. It never occurred to them to ask me."

And it doesn't happen only at the shop-floor level. I spoke recently to an executive at a multibillion-dollar company whose own salary was probably close to half a million a year, not counting perks. The guy had exactly the same complaint as the frame assembly foreman. "I just don't know what the hell anybody thinks of my work," he said. "The CEO just leaves me alone. I never get asked my opinion, I never get any feedback. It's scary."

What both these people were saying relates directly not just to Detroit's ongoing woes, but to what I said earlier about monetary reinforcement never being the principal ingredient in whether or not somebody's going to be motivated to improve. After eighteen years on the job, the foreman was making a bundle—and, of course, so was the executive. But it wasn't enough for them. They wanted to be involved.

INVOLVEMENT: THE TEAM MEETING

I've already spoken about the "participative huddle" approach I took to team leadership when I was quarterback of the Vikings. The principles we employed there work fine in business, too, and in this section I want to explain how you can get things you never dreamed of out of your people by creating participative "huddles" of your own. In the difficult, but rewarding, process of team-building, the team meeting, we've found, serves both as a solid structure to get things done and as a motivating model in its own right.

To use it effectively, though, you as the motivating manager have to keep a few guidelines in mind. The first, and most important, one defines the nature and function of your role as team leader.

Whether you're setting up a team meeting to improve assembly line productivity or to hash out a new marketing plan or to find out how well your sales force has penetrated a new market, you're always going to need a team leader. People will come together happily to solve mutual problems, but they expect *direction* from their own management in the mechanics of doing that. Without such direction, team meetings invariably dissolve into gripe sessions or exchanges of war stories.

One way of getting the role of team leader clear in your mind is to think of yourself not so much as a director or manager or "bossman," but as an educator or facilitator. I'm choosing these terms carefully. If you look up "educator" in a dictionary, you'll find that it derives from the Latin for "to lead out" or "to draw out." Education is the drawing out of inherent, but hidden, individual talent, and that's very much what good team leading is, too. It's a process of drawing out the best in all of your people. Or, as we often say, of "making it easy" for them to contribute. "Facilitator" means someone who makes it easy. We always like to think that the managers we train to be team leaders go back to their operating units with that idea burned into their brains.

One way of making things easier right at the outset is to lay out some basic ground rules under which the team meetings will be conducted. This should be done at the first team meeting, and the setting up of the ground rules should be accomplished in the same participatory manner that you want to have govern every meeting down the line.

You might start out the first meeting by acknowledging that you all have a limited amount of time, and that you want to get the most out of the time spent—so you will need some initial agreement on a "code of conduct" so you don't get bogged down later in parliamentary confusion. A line supervisor I know who has established effective team meeting formats in several different plants lays out that opening pitch, then offers a few suggestions for ground rules that have worked in the past. Things like this: "Start the meeting on time." "No interruptions or criticisms of other people's ideas." "Task assignment to be done on voluntary basis." And so on. Then, once he's thrown out these examples, he gathers other suggestions from his team members (Involvement, right at the start), and together they come to a consensus of what rules will be observed.

Having such a "code of conduct" set up at the outset of the meeting not only frees the team leader from having to improvise protocol and discipline; it also provides a "home base" that everybody can feel comfortable returning to. The team leader I'm speaking about here writes out the agreed upon rules on an easel sheet, and leaves them visible throughout every meeting. You'd be amazed at how much time that can save. If Linda interrupts Harry somewhere down the line, all the team leader has to do is point to Rule #3, comment, "Linda, we agreed not to interrupt; I'll get to you as soon as Harry finishes," and proceed with the business at hand. Very seldom will Linda buck that kind of advice, because, remember, she's had a hand in drawing up the code herself. And, as my company president Hank Conn likes to remind our clients, "People don't resist their own ideas."

Another thing you want to get settled early on is how often the team should meet. On the football field that decision was easy: we met after every down. You've got to come up with a team meeting schedule that works for your particular situation, depending on the nature of the problems you're going to discuss, on whether they're transient or chronic problems, and so on. Whatever you decide, however, be sure that the meetings are regular.

I emphasized regularity when I was talking about the Recording aspect of the P.R.I.C.E. scheme, and since team meetings are an important format in which to read and analyze your Recorded data, it follows that they have to happen every time— or at least every other time—the relevant data is posted.

If you've got a problem with the collection of marketing data, you can set up a one-time, ad hoc meeting to resolve the collection difficulty, and there may be situations in which this "hit and run" tactic is fine. But if you want to turn your seventeen marketing people into a team that sustains a high level of motivation over time, they've got to know that they'll be addressing the collection and other problems every Tuesday or once a month. Regularizing the team meeting is like regularizing a team practice in football. You only start to see real performance results in the second or third week of spring training. People get used to it, they come to the field knowing what to expect and what is going to be expected of them. They work at the practice, and they improve. The same thing goes in business. Involvement is a result of commitment to team process over time.

In addition to being regularly scheduled, the team meeting has got to be focused. That is, it has to be Pinpointed enough on real problems so that people know why they're attending, and will come to the meeting having thought about the agenda, rather than having it dumped in their laps when they arrive. This is especially important as you're starting up a team meeting structure. As you continue that structure, the set-up of future meetings becomes self-generating, because you can simply end the April 9 meeting by telling folks what to expect on the 16th. But at the outset, tell them what it's about. If you don't, I guarantee you're going to end up with at least one "team member" who thinks the meeting is a free-form bull session, and at least one other who thinks it's a grievance-airing opportunity. There are appropriate venues for bull sessions and for airing grievances in business, but the team meeting is not one of them.

Once you've set a regular time to tackle the ongoing data collection problem, and have advised team members what to expect, you're ready to start the first meeting. I'm going to lay out a simple format for you to do that, one that we follow in the managerial meetings we develop for our clients, and one that you'll be able to modify based on your individual needs. With those kinds of modifications, we've found this format to work very well at every level of organization. Supervisors, middle managers, and hourly workers alike have all profited from this basic "first team meeting" structure.

The format we advise people to follow has six sequential steps, each one corresponding to an objective that, you'll recognize, is an important feature of the P.R.I.C.E. system as well as of the team-building process. These six steps are to: Follow up, Review performance data, Reinforce, Problem solve, Plan actions, and Communicate.

1. *Follow up.* Every good team meeting ends with the team outlining a plan of actions that can be taken immediately to improve the performance picture. And every good meeting begins by finding out what progress has been made on the elements of that plan. This shouldn't be construed—and it shouldn't be described by a team leader—as a "checkup" or "score" of progress. Your goal in following up on the last meeting's business is neither to chide nor to praise, but simply to find out *where you are.*

It's a simple enough thing to do, and it's essential. Say at your last team meeting you discovered that one thing blocking the data collection process was that an external computer bank on which you relied was having maintenance difficulties. And let's say you had then decided that Joe Marks would look in to how they were doing. Obviously, one sensible way to start the current meeting would be to ask Joe to report his findings. What he tells you will affect any decisions you and your team can make now. So you always start the meeting by following up.

2. *Review performance data.* Next, you want to find out, together, how far and in what direction you've come since the last time you met. You do this by bringing in the Recording element of the P.R.I.C.E. plan, and by putting on overheads or easel sheets any relevant graphs or other performance measurements. Then you discuss the data together, looking not only for the progress or regress of individual workers or shifts, but also for long-range trends—the kind of cycles and patterns that I discussed in Chapter 5.

This step of the meeting is a way of getting everyone together to apply the Recording and the Evaluation elements of the system, by assessing where you're all moving, and by considering how to modify the feedback people have been getting to improve the performance results. A good performance data review is *not* simply a report on the weekly scores; it's a means of assessing those scores against a longer range business picture.

3. *Reinforce.* This is probably the most important single element of a good team meeting, and it's the one that's most frequently slighted. Once you've reviewed the data, you've *got* to provide reinforcement to those individuals and groups that have contributed to any improvement. Again I stress the value of providing positive Consequences for good Behavior, and of doing that in the 4:1 ratio that we've found to get the best results. A team format is particularly effective for this, since it allows your star performers to receive the well-deserved applause of their colleagues, and it motivates slower performers to better effort, so they can avoid looking bad by comparison.

You *can* also use negative reinforcement in a team setting, but it should be done sparingly, and only when there is no good alternative. Obviously if Joe Marks has not gotten the information your team needs to move on, it's appropriate to say you're disappointed. (And in this kind of a situation, you won't be the only one saying it.) But generally speaking, as the study by Lenk indicated, you're going to get much better results if you concentrate on positive reinforcement.

One thing you particularly want to reinforce is the idea of team cooperation itself. Sure, you want to thank Gene for the 15 percent cost savings his shift turned in last week. But you always want to phrase it in the context of teamwork as well. "Good job on the cost savings" is fine. But a better way of giving positive reinforcement would be to say, "It's great to see how well your guys are pulling together. They're showing us what good teamwork can do." Never be afraid to reinforce your team members for their specific business contributions and *also* for their contributions to your team and other teams. That way, you'll be reinforcing the very thing that has made them more productive in the first place.

4. *Problem solve.* The point of good reinforcement is not to make folks feel good, but to make them more productive *while* feeling good. Productivity is still the name of the game, and probably most of your team meeting time will be taken up with tackling ways to improve productivity and/or quality. In other words, it will be taken up with problem solving. If you've been motivating people properly throughout the meeting, this segment will not be the onerous chore it sometimes seems, but an opportunity for rich interaction, creativity, and plain fun. I'll go into this in detail in the following chapter, which is on Creative Problem Solving in the team setting.

5. *Plan actions.* After you've "solved" the problem—or laid out some tentative solutions, which is more likely—you take steps to get it under control. Those steps constitute an immediate action plan—your way of ensuring, very specifically, that you'll start up your next team meeting farther along toward a solution than you were at the beginning of this one.

By "action plan" here I simply mean a list of things that have to get done now, or by a certain designated time frame. Not things like "improve quality" or "speed up reports." Pinpointed tasks that can be assigned, on either a voluntary or a rotating basis, to one specific group member. Your action plan is essentially a list of Pinpointed personal objectives. "Joe Marks to inquire about Comex's maintenance problem by Friday." "Len to post new performance objectives by tomorrow." "Section 3 managers to supervise cleanup through next week." Each item on the action plan list should indicate *who* is going to do *what*, and by *when*.

A quick aside on task assignment. I say, "Either a voluntary or a rotating basis," but that's an ideal you're not always going to be able to achieve, at least not in the beginning. I suggest that, once your team has decided on what actions have to be taken by next week, you first ask for a volunteer to fulfill each action. If you get dead silence, you can try the "team within a team" approach, by asking for two or three people to work together to complete the necessary tasks. If that fails, too, you simply have to "volunteer" someone yourself, and you can lessen the dictatorial feature of doing that by asking rather than telling: "Would you be willing, Joan, to check into that late delivery report?" Most of the time, you'll get a yes. And the longer your team is in operation, the less frequently you'll have to resort to this method. As your team-building progresses— and that happens as an automatic side effect of the meeting format—you'll start getting the volunteers you need.

Your role as a facilitator of the *next* meeting requires that you remember accurately what the team has decided in the action plan, so take notes. These notes will be the springboard for the follow-up section of the next meeting.

6. *Communication.* We advise the managers we train to end every team meeting with a brief (four- or five-minute) segment on simple communication. I don't mean an encounter session— just the quick, direct exchange of information that can impact the group's current and future progress. This information-exchange segment need not have anything to do with the official "agenda" of the meeting, although of course it may raise issues for future agendas.

The information shared in this format could be as direct to the business involved as, "Mary Wright's going on maternity leave next month, so we have to make contingency plans for her department" or as distant from immediate concerns as, "Did you read the *Business Week* article on cost-cutting in billing procedures?" The value of such exchanges is twofold. First, it gives everybody the kind of information they need to make better informed decisions: in other words, it helps make everybody, not just the leader, a "better quarterback." Secondly, it reinforces the teamwork spirit without which no team can survive: it lets everybody know that you're working toward common goals, and that you're trying to get there together.

EAGLES AND MULES TOGETHER

Now, you may have problems generating and sustaining this kind of "common goal" spirit. I'm not going to be a Pollyanna about team spirit, and say that it's something anybody can develop anywhere. It can be a problem to get six or seven distinct individuals all pulling in the same direction at the same time, and the reason it's often a problem is that, in most organizations, even if you have a leader who sees himself as a facilitator and educator, you're still going to run into team members who see themselves as "better" or "worse" than the rest.

In addition to the manager/player split that I talked about with reference to Lenk's book, there's a second split that divides teammates—or people who *ought* to be teammates—into a bunch of superstars on the one hand, and a bunch of everyday, "ordinary" players on the other. The superstars, today, are often called "eagles." The rest of the folks are just "mules."

Some of this is inevitable. People do have different abilities. Some players do stand out. But it's easy to let the distinction between eagles and mules get out of hand, and when that happens the team always suffers. You see it all the time in big companies, where the eagles all wear coats and ties and the mules are the ones punching time clocks. The eagle-mule distinction takes on a debilitating class flavor in a lot of firms, which exacerbates tensions that already exist between "brain" people and "brawn" people, and which makes it only natural that management and workers see each other as enemies.

The terms "eagle" and "mule" come from a sports context, but actually I've seen very little "brain-brawn" or other "class" warfare in professional sports. The relevant question in pro ball is never "Where did you go to school?" or "What kind of car do you drive" or "Did your ancestors come over on the May-flower?" It's a much simpler one: "Can you play?" If the answer to that is yes, then come on board and prove it. If it's no, then I don't care how long your name has been on the social register, I don't want you on my team.

Actually, the term "mule" comes from the same Notre Dame team that spawned the name "Four Horsemen." In the news lingo of the day, what kept the famous backfield from getting sacked on every play was the world-class blocking of the Irish line: that seven-member battering ram known collectively as the Seven Mules. Pointman for the Mules was center Adam Walsh, himself an All-American, and it was Walsh who coined the term. "We are just the seven mules," he complained once with bittersweet humor. "We do all the work so that these four fellows can gallop into fame."

Coach Knute Rockne, aware of the linemen's sensitivity on this matter, periodically brought the flying horsemen down to earth and at the same time reinforced the importance of *team*, not just individual, motivation. When the Four Horsemen began to believe their press notices, Edwin Pope writes, "Rockne would casually remove the Seven Mules and let the horsemen stumble around behind scrub blocking. When they were ready to drop, he would reinsert [them] and taunt the backfield. 'Without the Mules, you Horsemen are just turtles.' "

It was true, too, and not just at Notre Dame. One of the reasons Rockne was such a great coach, and that his teams are still considered among the best of all time, is that he recognized the importance of collective motivation as a corrective to the all-too-human propensity for trying to outshine the group.

It's a sign of the maturity of professional sports that you don't see that tendency nearly as much today as you used to years ago. A case in point: Larry Bird, the Boston Celtics' phenomenal forward.

Larry Bird is a living demonstration of why aggressive, highly skilled players are often referred to as "eagles." With his energy and talent, Bird could spark even a mediocre group of basketball players to peak performance; working with players of the Celtics' caliber, it's not surprising that he consistently leads the team into close competition for the NBA playoffs. In a world of superstars, competitors like Bird stand out as among the most motivated performers of their time. But do you know *why* he's so motivated? Part of it is personal, of course. But part of it is the very fact that he is part of a winning organization. Bird, in fact, is one of the best team players you're ever going to see. He constantly displays that understanding of the link between personal and collective objectives that is characteristic of all true "eagles." Bird knows that the fundamental *point* of the game is not to show off to his friends or to get himself in the record books, but to have his team put the ball through the hoop more times than the other team. Like any successful player, he knows that the best way to accomplish that is to operate as part of a collective unit.

There's a certain subtle selfishness about this. Any eagle wants to fly, and any superstar wants to shine. But those who *remain* superstars do so by cooperating with the team. Ironically, they protect their own elevated status by appearing to downplay it. It's not charity that impels the court eagle to pass. It's a matter of collective, and therefore personal, survival.

This is something that few American workers are trained to understand, and as a result they often perform in a way that harms the team effort they should be helping. In other words, they behave like amateurs, not professionals. I can illustrate the difference with a story from amateur sports.

In his 1980 book *Competing*, psychologist Harvey Ruben tells the story of a childhood playmate named Toby who, in volleyball games, had no interest in setting up the combination returns on which successful volleyball depends: instead of passing off and setting up spikes, he simply smacked every ball hit to him directly back over the net, going for a winner every time. Although he was, according to Ruben, "the best all-round athlete I had ever encountered," Toby very soon became a liability to the team because the opposition came to understand that whenever the ball went to Toby, it would be returned from the same position. Ruben describes the outcome:

They soon learned to "use" Toby as their own best player. . . . They simply ganged up on him: all six of their players made all of their returns directly to him, and it wasn't long before he began to tire and make mistakes. We couldn't make him see that he was blowing the game for everybody, and we finally simply refused to play with him.

On a professional team, the situation would never even have gotten that far. With their own jobs and a great deal of money at stake, pro coaches get rid of hotdoggers like Toby before they even get on to the field. I sometimes think you could save a lot of grief in business if you hired some kind of corporate "coach" who would be free of hierarchical turmoil and whose sole job would be to point out to company employees—labor and management alike—that they were either hotdogging or sandbagging, and therefore hurting the team.

Realizing that you have to be a team player to survive is the first factor that undercuts interplayer rivalry in big-time sports. The other factor is related: it's that it simply *feels good* to be part of a winning organization—so good, in fact, that the feeling typically transcends all other potential feelings of personality clashes and "eagle-phobia." To achieve that feeling of well-being, accomplishment, and gratification that comes from having contributed to a winning effort, good players will sacrifice the "limelight" readily—for the very good reason that, by doing so, they ultimately gain more recognition, not less. It's a little like the Biblical proverb: He who exalts himself shall be humbled, and he who humbles himself shall be exalted.

I believe that the "exalted" feeling that comes from participating in a winning collective effort is a principal motivating factor in all group endeavors. It doesn't matter really whether the group under consideration is a basketball team, a management study group, or a family. Across the board, the groups that function best—that are eventually the most successful—understand a simple fact: every member of a winning team is just as important as every other member. Unless everybody pulls together and does the job assigned to him to the best of his ability, the team is not going to go anywhere. Every professional understands that. In fact, understanding it is what *makes* them professionals. They know they're only going to feel good if they do their best, and they know that the only way for anybody on a team to do his best is to subordinate his personal need to stand out to the general objective of winning.

There's an important corollary here which relates to altering the Consequences of Behaviors. It's that, when you assess how your team has performed in a given situation, you've got to make the distinction between those who have actually *contributed* to the joint effort and those who've just gone along for the ride.

DIFFERENTIAL REINFORCEMENT

This is true whether you're dealing with eagles, mules, or (as is always the case in reality) with a combination of the two. Too many managers seem to have the idea that, if the team brings in a victory, everybody deserves champagne—and, conversely, if the team loses, everybody should be sent to the doghouse. Anybody who's been on a sports team knows that's unfair in both cases.

You see this unfairness in practice every time a company adds up its quarterly earnings, discovers how the "team" has performed, and then gives out a general kudo, as if every worker and manager had been an equal partner in that performance. "We did terrific business this quarter," a general manager will announce. "You all did a wonderful job, and we congratulate you." Only thing is, some of the folks he's talking to *didn't* do a wonderful job. The record performance was achieved in spite of their presence, not because of it. *And they know it.* People know when they've been sandbagging, and when you tell them they've done a great job when they haven't, you send out all kinds of ultimately *demotivating* signals.

To the people who *have* contributed, it says, "You can get the same good Consequences next time if you only work half as hard." To the people who haven't, it says, "Don't worry about doing your best; your teammates will cover for you." This not only robs them of the chance to improve. It cheapens the rewards for the people who have performed well, and creates bitterness and confusion all around.

The same thing can happen in reverse, when a working group as a whole has not performed, and every member of the group is made to suffer as if it were his or her personal responsibility. "We fell 4 percentage points last month," the manager yells. "You've all been falling down on the job." Not true. Some people have been falling down, some have been doing "at least adequate" work, and some have been knocking themselves out in vain. Simple justice requires that, even when the overall figures are bad, the people who have put in extra effort get positive strokes for their work.

We call this *Differential Reinforcement*, which is just a more formal method of saying that you should give credit where credit is due. And nowhere else.

Donald Seibert, former Chief Executive Officer of the J. C. Penney Company, wrote a book called *The Ethical Executive* in which he makes some provocative comments about giving credit. Quoting his predecessor at the company, he says that "You can accomplish almost anything if you don't care who gets the credit." A wise observation, meant to demonstrate to the rising executive not that credit should be parcelled out indiscriminately, but that the leaders in a decision-making group should always remember the "nonleaders"—the hardworking mules of the team—when they're "passing psychological rewards around." And Seibert goes further. In speaking of his company's brainstorming sessions (a technique I'll get to later), he says:

In a typical freewheeling discussion in most companies, everybody throws out a certain number of thoughts and suggestions. A good boss will keep track of which idea came from which person, and then in his summary he'll compliment the various workers who made significant contributions.

That's Differential Reinforcement. It's involving every member of your team and then telling each one individually how he or she contributed. And rewarding them accordingly.

Obviously, Differential Reinforcement is not an abstract concept. It's a practical technique for improving performance that you can employ constantly on the job—and particularly in the team meeting settings that I've been talking about in this chapter. It's a great motivational tool for getting people to understand what is required of them as a unit.

Two caveats, though. In using Differential Reinforcement, you want to be alert to two possible misuses of the method, which can undermine the very thing you're trying to accomplish. The two biggest mistakes of the differentiating motivator is to come down too hard on the "mules" and to ignore the high-performing "eagles."

Actually, these two mistakes derive from the same misperception: the erroneous notion that the point of building a team is to get everybody performing *at the same level.* When you start off with that notion, it's easy to slight the eagles (because they're already doing well) and to hassle the mules right into quitting (because they're not performing as well as the eagles).

The truth is that you're never going to get everybody on a work team to perform at the same level of competence, ingenuity, or diligence. People don't have the same capacities, and if you try to cut them all to the same length, you're going to end up with what Procrustes ended up with: a bunch of dead workers. What you *can* do is to get all of them equally fired up, so that each of your team members does the very best *he* can do.

This means you've got to learn to read your people just as closely as you read the *Wall Street Journal.* Johnny Byers may be just another mule to you. He seems intimidated by the rest of the group, he seldom contributes, he's not giving it all he's got. Once in a while he comes up with a half-good idea, though—and that's when you want to pounce. That's when you want to praise the hell out of him, because he's done something that, for *him,* deserves that extra reinforcement. Ignoring the run-of-the-mill worker just because his contribution is not extraordinary is one of the worst misuses of the Differential

Reinforcement tool. It will get you nothing but an even more demotivated worker.

But it's just as dangerous to ignore the high flyers, and in my experience this is the most common error among managers who are trying to build teams. We're frightened, it seems, of superior achievement. We resent the people who stand out. As a result we suffocate the extraordinary energies that we have to work with in the first place, and end up with teams that are not teams at all—that are only collections of featherbedders trying just to get by.

If you want to raise the average motivation of your team members, if you want to transform a collection of individuals into a solid, forward-looking team, you've got to use your eagles, by reinforcing them constantly and publicly. If you want more Thomas Edisons and more Larry Birds, you've got to let them take risks—and constantly let them know that you appreciate the work they're doing. Doing that not only keeps that work coming. It also lets your hardworking, non-superstar mules know that doing your best on this team gets you noticed and rewarded. Whether your best is C− or A+, that's important to know.

There are always going to be some people who will resent the A+ performers. I don't know of any way to get rid of that kind of resentment, since it's been around since the days of Cain and Abel. Maybe the best you can hope to do, as a team builder, is to keep giving the Consequences that matter to your individual players, and let the personal gripes fall where they may. As long as they don't interfere with the work and productivity of your team, it's not your job anyway to deal with them. And if they do interfere, then you approach such personal antagonisms in the same way you would deal with any other difficulty in communication: you educate and facilitate, so that everybody, including the griper, gets to contribute to the team solution.

Differential Reinforcement, in other words, is a way of realizing Rockne's ideal of "sparking" each member of the team. I'll admit it. Sometimes the spark won't take. Sometimes you're going to find a dud. Sometimes, when that happens, you've got to scrap it and buy another plug. That's never a pleasant task, but sometimes it has to be done. Knowing when to do it is a matter of reading your people. Committing to doing it when it's obviously necessary is what makes the difference between the host of an encounter session and a manager who is building a team.

Don't fire the slacker yet, though. If you're faced with this kind of situation now, where one team member is slowing down the group by noninvolvement, you'll want to read the next chapter. It's about involving *everybody's* ideas—even the "idiot" ideas of the slackers—in forging a group identity and in reaching toward common goals.

NINE

CREATIVE PROBLEM SOLVING

> Vertical thinking is digging the same hole, only deeper.
> Lateral thinking is digging in another place.
> —EDWARD DE BONO

In the last chapter I said that good team management means coordinating the peculiar energies of your "eagles" and your "mules" so that they can come together in a unified, motivated effort toward common goals. In this chapter I'm going to discuss a specific, practical method of doing that in a team meeting format. It's a method my company uses all the time in our productivity seminars, and one which almost invariably shows the participating managers that participatory teamwork can give you not just better motivated players, but better plays—that is, better solutions to business problems—as well.

We call it Creative Problem Solving.

By "creative" we don't mean simply "intelligent" or "inventive"—although intelligence and inventiveness are certainly parts of the method. We mean "creative" in the original sense of "productive" or "generative." A creative method of problem solving is one that leads to unique and revolutionary solutions— solutions that could not be arrived at by simply "thinking hard" about the problem. Instead of asking managers to think harder, we ask them to think *differently*—with an entirely different mental *process* than most of them have been used to. That's creativity. And it gets results.

SET BREAKING

Creative Problem Solving, as we use it, is a definite, step-by-step process for attacking difficult business problems, and I'm going to walk you through that process in a moment. But Creative Problem Solving can also be seen as a mental *technique*, a *style* of attacking problems that leads, inevitably, to the process. We call this style or technique "set breaking," and using it over and over, until it becomes second nature, is one of the great secrets of success in every good motivator, and every good manager, I've ever known.

Although we use set breaking in a unique manner suited to the productivity problems we encounter, the idea behind it is not original with us. The idea of breaking a "set," or of approaching a problem from an unfamiliar, unconventional angle was first discussed extensively by the educator Edward de Bono about fifteen years ago. He developed his views on creativity in a popular book called *Lateral Thinking,* and we have borrowed several of his concepts because we have found them to make perfect sense in the problem areas we confront.

In de Bono's book, "lateral thinking" was a rich, creative type of mental process which led to quite different—and usually much better—solutions than the "vertical thinking" with which most of us are familiar. To summarize de Bono's findings about the difference between the two kinds of thinking:

- *Vertical thinking* is selective, unidirectional, and analytical. When you think vertically, you move from one point to another in a logical, predictable fashion, choosing the "right" solutions to intermediate problems at every step along the way, and rejecting those intermediate solutions that don't fit the pathway you have set out in your mind. You don't skip steps, you don't leave the beaten path, you follow the rules.
- *Lateral thinking,* on the other hand, is generative, multidirectional, and provocative. When you think laterally, you jump around in a completely "illogical," unpredictable

way. You allow yourself to be "wrong" if being wrong leads to a more interesting or more open set of possibilities. You don't assume you know where you are going, you don't have a map in your mind, and you don't impose a solution so much as you accept the solutions that the situation ultimately suggests to you.

It should be clear from this description that vertical thinking is the type of thinking that you generally practice: it's that time-honored way of getting at a problem that relies on such "logical" chestnuts as Aristotle's famous maxim "A cannot be not-A" and the technician's basic working proposition that Number 5 has got to come after Number 4, Number 6 after Number 5, and so on. Lateral thinking is the thinking of loonytunes and rule-breakers and folks who don't want to fit in. You know the kind of people I mean. Dopes like Christopher Columbus and Louis Pasteur.

What did Columbus and Pasteur have in common? They both went against the grain. They rejected the given wisdom of their time, which said that in order to solve a problem which had stumped thousands of other people, you had to follow the same path that had stopped them, only work at it a little harder. Given a certain mind-set because of the conditions of their times, they decided that progress toward a solution meant they had to discard, or "break" that set. And only after breaking the set did they get to where they wanted to go.

In Columbus's day, if you wanted to get from Europe to the spice-rich islands of the Orient, you headed east and started walking. Or you went around the Cape of Good Hope. Those were the only options. Many geographers and sailors knew the world was round, all right, but—good vertical thinkers that they were—they weren't about to act on the knowledge by sailing west. There were sea serpents out there, and incredibly violent storms, and just too damn much water to cross. You'd have to be crazy to sail west into the Great Ocean. Everybody knew that. It was the universally accepted, logical mind-set of the fifteenth century. Which nobody but a loonytune would want to break.

It was the same story with Pasteur. In the mid-nineteenth century, every educated person in Europe "knew" that milk spoiled in the summer because of spontaneous generation of minute organisms. There was nothing you could do about it. It was just the way the world was set up, and you were just wasting your time if you thought you could stop the growth of something that arose spontaneously, out of nothing. "What if the organisms didn't arise spontaneously?" Pasteur asked. "What if they arose out of *other* organisms? And what if you killed those other organisms? Wouldn't that keep the milk from spoiling?" Set breaking, again. Asking a question that nobody had thought of asking before, because it was off the beaten path, illogical—stupid. But Pasteur asked the question anyway, and as a result Europe got clean milk for the first time in history.

A few business examples. Remember the hula hoop? One of the toy industry's greatest marketing coups of all time. The hula hoop was constructed out of waste plastic tubing—excess material that a manufacturing company was going to throw out until some bright lateral thinker got the nutty idea of bending it into big circles.

How about Eli Whitney's mass production technique? It revolutionized American industry practically overnight, and it came from the crazy idea of making rifles out of interchangeable parts. Before Whitney's time, if you wanted *anything* constructed, you hired a single craftsman to do it all: to turn every piece, to fit it all together, to deliver a unique specimen that, incidentally, only he could properly repair. That was just the way it was done, until old Eli questioned the *fundamental assumptions* of the system—and came up with mass production.

And then there's the Post-it Note Pads that have been making 3M such a fortune in the past couple of years. Those are the pads that you can stick onto a sheet of paper, take off, and restick somewhere else. They were invented by a 3M employee named Art Fry who, like Whitney and Pasteur, asked a question everybody else "knew" was foolish.

Fry was a design engineer who—in accordance with 3M's liberal and far-sighted policy of letting employees do private projects on company time—had been trying to come up with a glue that would allow a sticker to be used more than once: the company legend says that he wanted something that would make a good page marker for his hymnal without tearing the pages when it was removed. None of the "good" glues worked, because by definition a "good" glue was one that kept two surfaces bonded tightly together and couldn't be pulled apart. So Fry asked a "stupid" question: What about using a bad glue? That is, what about using an adhesive that didn't do what it was *supposed* to do—that didn't meet company standards for quality? The rejected, "useless" glue turned out to be exactly what he needed to create the Post-it pad.

The moral of these stories is something that turns the conventional wisdom about "improvement" on its head. Sometimes the guy who makes a million bucks isn't the person who invents the proverbial "better mousetrap." Sometimes it's the person who figures out how to make stupid mice, or who uses the old, ineffective mousetrap as a clipboard, or doorstop, or windchime.

That's what set breaking is about. It's about digging the hole in a different place. But how do you apply it to motivation? How can you, as a manager interested in motivating your people toward better productivity and better quality, ensure that each one of them uses Creative Problem Solving as a tool toward those desirable ends?

The answer is that, in the team meetings I discussed in the last chapter, you create an atmosphere where set breaking is not only allowed, but *encouraged*. You motivate your people to be creative by giving them positive reinforcement in the team setting. Set breaking, lateral thinking, and creativity are not inherited characteristics that you either have or don't have. Just as you can learn to be more cooperative or more assertive, you can learn to be more creative, by practicing set breaking in a formalized context where creative Behavior leads to positive Consequences.

When we go into a company and teach managers how to run Creative Problem Solving sessions, we give them and their teams the necessary practice by running them through what we call Brainstorming exercises. Another term coined by de Bono, "brainstorming" is the first part of that lateral thinking *process* that I've said leads to such creative results in the companies we consult. It's the perfect way to get your eagles and mules together to come up with solutions that are better than those anybody could have come up with on his own.

BRAINSTORMING

We start the Brainstorming segment of our productivity training with a seemingly ridiculous proposition. We ask the participating managers to imagine that they have just been shipwrecked on a South Seas island with nothing in their possession but a size 38 leather belt with a conventional metal buckle. Their task is to come up with as many different uses for this object as they can in a ten-minute "brainstorm."

Try it yourself. Take ten minutes right now to list the uses you might make in that situation for a buckle and belt. Hold off glancing down at the list below, and just list whatever uses occur to you. I mean *any* uses. Not just your "good" ideas, or "inventive" ideas, or "appropriate" ideas, or the ideas that will get you off the island. List everything that comes to your mind.

All right. I'll assume that you've played fair at this little game, and have come up with a list of your own. Now look at the list below. It's a typical list created by managers like yourself from one of our recent seminars:

belt	picture-hanger
buckle	garter belt
signal mirror	bikini
flag	noose
slingshot	headband
knife	fishing line
food	clam digger
shovel	snare
clothesline	whip
notepad	meat hook
hatband	scarf
tie	noise maker

Now, I know what your reaction to some of these items is likely to be. You're probably going to be saying, "Even if you could hang pictures from a belt, there aren't any pictures on the island." Or, "Who needs a clothesline without any clothes?" We hear those kinds of reactions all the time in our seminars. They're natural, *logical* reactions. And, when we're running these Brainstorming sessions, we always tell the people who have these negative, critical responses that what they're saying is true, but irrelevant. Because Brainstorming is not an exercise in finding the best solutions; it's an exercise in *generating possibilities*. The more the better.

It's essential to remember this if you're running a Brainstorming session to attack a company problem. Let's say you've got ten or twelve people gathered together in a team meeting, and you're faced with the task of discovering a way of reducing spoilage in a given line operation. Consider two scenarios.

In Scenario One, you're a typical vertical-thinking leader, and you want to be sure that the ideas your people come up with are basically "on the right track." So when somebody comes up with an offbeat or "frivolous" suggestion, you just ignore it. Or, even worse, you tell him, "Let's get serious, Bobby." What reaction do you suppose that's going to elicit from Bobby? Most likely, he's going to stop giving you suggestions, because you will have *demotivated* him: you will have let him know that, unless he "follows the rules," the Consequences he can expect will be disapproval from you.

Scenario Two: You run an absolutely open, freewheeling Brainstorm. You sit your ten or twelve people around a table, bring out a chart and grease pencil, and say, "Let's roll. Whatever you say I'm going to write down." And when they start throwing out the ideas, you do just that. You don't judge and you don't stop writing for ten minutes. No matter how "ridiculous" the idea for reducing spoilage may seem to you, you put it down. What are you going to develop in that kind of a scenario? A lot of dumb ideas, sure, I don't dispute that. But you're also going to develop two things that you simply cannot develop if you second-guess your people as they go. If you nod positively to every suggestion, and encourage your people to keep coming with them, you are going to develop:

1. a much *longer* list of "possibles" than otherwise would be possible; and

2. a highly motivated atmosphere in which your team members *want* to keep talking

These two things work together, of course. And together they produce what you want: the generation of *new* ideas, not just the ideas you've all heard before, and rejected because they don't work.

In a Brainstorming session like the one I'm describing here, where a group of about a dozen managers addresses a problem, typically they generate sixty or seventy ideas in a ten- or fifteen-minute session! A lot of them are old, a lot are recycled, and some just tell them what they already "knew." But I'll tell you one thing. At the end of that session, they've got more going for them than just a list of solutions. They've got an energy going between them that no amount of good clean vertical thinking could ever generate. They've had some laughs and they've loosened up and they're up for solving that problem.

"Having some laughs" may not seem like your idea of a motivating experience, but don't you believe it. Never underestimate the power of humor to generate new ideas. A lot of times people will come into a problem-solving session tight-assed and tight-lipped, and the only thing that gets their creative juices flowing—the only thing that gets them up for thinking out a solution—is for somebody to crack a joke. Every after-dinner speaker knows the value of joke-cracking as a way of getting people's attention, and it's equally useful in a team meeting format.

The humor associated with "stupid" ideas, moreover, isn't just a way of *diverting* attention from the hard business at hand. Often it's a way of focusing that attention in a different, and creative, direction. Set breaking again. You don't expect Rachel's off-the-wall suggestion, but it gets you thinking about *another* suggestion that might not be so off-the-wall. Dumb ideas, in other words, just because they help you form new mental associations, can lead to good ideas.

In our seminars, we talk about "saving the good half" of a half-assed, or half-good, idea. No idea is *completely* idiotic, after all, and you can get good results by grafting the useful "half" of a mostly useless idea onto the useful half of another idea. An example from the Brainstorming list I gave above. You'll see that two of the items are "noose" and "meat hook." I remember how they came out in the team context. There was a crusty production manager involved who thought the whole idea of thinking up uses for a belt and buckle was pretty pointless, and he threw out "noose" to suggest that, if *he* ever got caught on a desert island, he'd end the game right away. The other managers in the group laughed, wrote down the "ridiculous" suggestion, and kept thinking. The very next suggestion thrown out was "meat hook"—a suggestion that had clear survival value. It came from an earnest young accountant who later told me, "You know, I don't do any hunting and I know I would never have thought of using a belt to hang game if it hadn't been for Larry's joke about the noose. I just thought, if you could hang *yourself* with a belt, what else could you hang?"

What had happened here was that the older manager's dumb idea had generated a line of thought in a team member that eventually led to a good idea. It happens all the time in team settings. When you utilize Brainstorming in a highly reinforcing atmosphere, you constantly find this kind of cross-fertilization happening, you constantly generate *hybrid* ideas (ideas that are two "good halves" put together) that are better than individual ideas. You constantly witness the Synergy Effect in action.

In order to get this kind of a productive effect, you as a manager have to observe that basic "no judgment" rule for as long as the ideas keep coming. You also have to be enough of a director of the interchange to be able to prevent *other* people from making judgments. To run an effective Brainstorming session, you should always start by laying out the ground rules, and those rules capsulize what I've been saying. Once you sit your people down and identify the problem you're going to be addressing, make these points crystal clear:

1. The point of this exercise is to generate as *many* ideas as possible.
2. Everyone should participate; we want to have everyone's contribution; no matter *what* it is.
3. *No judgments!*

If those ideas are understood and accepted by all your team members, I guarantee you you're going to have a session full of ideas. The key to keeping them coming is *momentum.* And the key to maintaining that momentum is for you, the team leader, to give immediate and positive Consequences—a nod, a "Thanks," a smile—to every person who says anything at any point along the way.

This goes back to what I said in the last chapter about the team leader's role as a "facilitator." In leading a Brainstorming session—as in leading any kind of team endeavor—you'll get the highest degree of drive and participation from your people if you refrain from "directing" them where you think they should go, and instead create the kind of consistently reinforcing atmosphere that makes it *easy* for them to problem solve. A "facilitator," remember, makes things easier: that's what your role should be. I don't mean you shouldn't contribute yourself. You should. But your judgment of where it's all going, at this point, should be confined to telling someone who has jumped on another person's idea, "We said *no* judgment, OK?"

From what I've said about the limitations of cash as a reward, you know that I'm not generally an advocate of a "more is better" philosophy in business. Except when it comes to Brainstorming. In this one formal exercise, the highest degree of motivation, and the highest level of good "possibles," always comes from an emphasis on *quantity.*

STEP TWO: CONSENSUS

Quantity isn't everything, though. If quantity was *all* you needed, the football team with the thickest playbook would take the Super Bowl every year, and the companies with the biggest R&D departments would be the consistent market leaders. That's not the way it goes down.

So, after you've enabled your team to generate as many ideas as they can in a given period of time, the next step is to narrow them down. In our productivity seminars, you do that by interaction that leads to Consensus.

The way we use the word, Consensus means "coming to general agreement." You don't get Consensus with a command type of decision-making, where the team leader says, "Here's how we're going to do it," or, "Thanks for your input; now here's how we're going to do it." You don't get it with the delegation type of decision-making, where the leader says, "Joe, you've heard what everybody has to say; now, you decide." And you don't get it by voting.

This last point deserves special emphasis because people frequently confuse Consensus with voting. That's natural in a democratic country, where "agreement" is usually taken to mean what the majority wants. In spite of the problems involved with this type of decision-making (such as what happens to the wishes of minorities), it still seems about the best way ever devised by human beings to run their political affairs. But it's no way to run a business, because it can bypass one of the most valuable aspects of Creative Problem Solving—the synergistic interchange of ideas that leads to solutions which are "better than the sum of their parts."

It's all right to use voting in the preliminary stages of a Consensus decision-making meeting to narrow down a long list of choices. Generally speaking, if you've Brainstormed twenty ways of solving your spoilage problem, people who are aware of the problem will be able without too much disagreement to focus in on the half-dozen or so reasons that most obviously impact the problem. If you can't do that—and if you can't do it in a quick straw ballot—then you probably haven't Pinpointed your problem clearly enough in the first place. But once you've gotten your "possibles" down to the top six or eight, it can be disastrous to choose a final solution by a show of hands. Not only will you be likely to ignore good ideas by doing this, but you'll also inevitably slight someone's contribution, creating ill will and a feeling that your call for "any ideas at all" was just an empty gesture.

The way to get people really Involved in the final solution, and the way to generate the most creative of solutions, is to insist that all of the six or eight "best choices" be reasonably considered and *discussed*, with reasons being given pro and con for why each one should be adopted. If Ryan's solution to your spoilage problem is the least popular of the top six, that doesn't necessarily mean it's the worst choice. In the Consensus part of your Creative Problem Solving meeting, you should ask Ryan to explain logically and fully the rationale for his solution, so that everyone can assess its relative value.

In other words, you're going to be asking Ryan (and the team) to think *vertically*. I'm not contradicting myself. Once the Brainstorming session is finished, you've got to start focusing on the most "logical" choices. You need vertical, "reasonable" assessment to do that properly. There's nothing *wrong* with vertical thinking; it's just limited as a generator of possibilities. When you're down to the best-of-five, vertical thinking is just fine.

So get Ryan to defend his views. And get people to *listen* to him. Remember that, in managing a Brainstorming session well, you want to "facilitate" the momentum of the team's thinking by reinforcing participation and demotivating those who make judgments. Facilitating in the Consensus stage is just as important. The goal is not to create a contest between possible solutions, but to get people to agree on a solution that is least offensive to each of them personally and most effective as a joint resolution.

The clients who attend our seminars find it useful, when they're trying to focus in on the best choices, to ask themselves two questions. Once you've got your list down to five or six, go through each one in turn, and ask yourselves as a group:

1. What's *urgent*, and can it be handled by this solution?
2. What's *possible* given our current resources?

In other words, you try to find out for each "possible" whether or not it can reasonably be expected to fulfill your *priority* needs right now.

There will be disagreement on this, of course. One technique we've found to be useful in clarifying the issues involved, and not getting tied up in personality dissension, is to make a simple "Pro and Con" chart for each of the solutions proposed. At a recent seminar where machine downtime was being addressed, for example, the managers came up with four possible solutions that could, and probably should, be implemented to tackle the problem. One of them was "repair of the aging armature assembly." Everybody agreed it should be done, but there was considerable resistance to having it done *now* because doing so would put the armature out of commission for at least three days. It was a classic Pro-Con problem, so we advised the managers to make up a two-column chart to help them visualize it better.

On the left-hand side of the chart, they listed the "Pros" of fixing the armature assembly immediately. These "Pros" included such items as "better production capability," "better quality," and "less aggravation among line workers." The right-hand column included only one item: "cost of immediate downtime." And so they were left with the question: Was the benefit of better production, better quality, and less aggravation worth the price of three days lost production? When it was set up that way—as a kind of cost-benefit ledger sheet—the problem seemed much more clear-cut, and the managers were able to address their dilemma in a much more Pinpointed manner.

Another advantage of using this kind of Pro-Con listing technique is that it enables you to compare choices that you might not have thought of comparing before. It enables you, in other words, to ask questions that might not otherwise have been asked. Here's set breaking again. Suppose a financial officer in your company, as a member of one of your team meetings, is strong for Choice #4 because the financial Pros of that choice are overwhelming. Nobody else likes that choice, because it would upset their departmental routines. Solution: look at the financial officer's Pro list and ask, "Are there any *other* choices we have identified that might fulfill Finance's Pro reasons for wanting Choice #4?" Saving the good half, again. Searching for the best course of action with the fewest of negative consequences.

Whether or not you can get Finance to abandon his favored position, you will at least get him to investigate the other choices again, with an eye to seeing whether or not something he never considered can satisfy his Pro reasons for Choice #4. Writing down and exchanging ideas on Pro-Con reason sheets is a valuable cross-fertilizing technique. It creates the attractive possibility that, once every team member seriously considers other people's choices, you may together come up with sound hybrid solutions.

Another advantage of having team members list reasons for preferring certain solutions and having them assessed in terms of Pro-Con balance sheets is that it helps you avoid what we have sometimes called the Influence-Accuracy Tangle.

THE INFLUENCE-ACCURACY TANGLE

American president Teddy Roosevelt defined a good executive as "one who has sense enough to pick good men to do what he wants done, and self-restraint enough to keep from meddling with them while they do it." That's a pretty good description of any good manager, and it gets right at the biggest problem you face when you handle a team in a participatory management style. The problem is seldom that of getting your team members to contribute their opinions; they'll always be willing to do that if you motivate them to do so by reinforcing them when they speak up. The problem is usually that of getting yourself to shut up—to take firm control, but from the back seat—so they can come forward in the first place. Roosevelt wasn't the first person to recognize that this takes a tremendous amount of self-restraint.

One reason this is so hard for managers to do is that we've been trained to believe that we know more than the team, and that we therefore have a right to influence the group's decisions more radically than the others do. And, since we're in positions of authority, we *do* tend to have more influence on how team meetings go. The only hitch is that "influence" does not equal "accuracy" or "intelligence" or "creativity"—no matter how much we wish it did. So, a strong, influential manager can sometimes find himself directing the course of a discussion to an entirely inappropriate conclusion. His team members will let him get away with this because, what the hell, he's the boss. And the whole team will end up in the cellar, because the boss and the members alike confused his influence on others' opinions with what they assumed to be wisdom.

You can run into this Influence-Accuracy Tangle even when the ostensible "leader" of a group is not the most influential member. In those cases—cases where an "expert" junior manager, say, will bring everyone else, including the leader, around to his way of thinking—it's not the boss who's doing the bossing, but the smart guy in the corner chair.

He might be a senior accountant who "knows" before it's ever employed that the government's new depreciation schedule is going to save (or cost) you money. Or a marketing veteran who doesn't want to waste her valuable time on an "obviously blue-sky" test marketing plan. Or a line supervisor who can "prove" to you by impeccable logic that his Quality Circle has to meet on Wednesdays or it will fall apart.

Whether the dominant voice in a team meeting is that of the leader or another resident "expert," though, the trouble and the tangle are the same. Unless you as the facilitator can fluidly, but firmly, direct the meeting by the rules I've outlined above, the consensual nod will often go not to the person with the best idea, but to the one with the appropriate reputation. He *might* have the best solution, but there is no guarantee of that. He might just as easily be aggravating your current problems by focusing on yesterday's answers.

We see this all the time when our client managers do the Arctic survival exercise that I talked about in the chapter on Involvement.

You'll remember that was the exercise where team members were supposed to imagine that they had just crashed in northern Canada with nothing between them and death but a pile of salvaged items: some sleeping bags, a knife, a bottle of rum, and so forth. They were to decide, first individually and then in a Consensus fashion, which of those items was most important, which was next, and so on down the line. The big lesson of that exercise was that, every time the exercise is done, the Accuracy of the group ranking of the items is better than the Accuracy of any individual member—no matter how "expert" that member may be. The danger is always that the supposed expert will, simply because he does know *something* more about the Arctic than the others, assume that his Influence ought to be absolute. In groups where the team members let the expert get away with that—where they defer to his wisdom—the overall Accuracy always goes down. Only in those groups where everybody's opinion—including that of the most Influential member—is subjected to rigorous questioning and analysis does the group really profit from expert advice, and shoot its Accuracy score up.

So, in group decision-making situations, you have the irony that the presence of a supposed expert can actually retard your progress, if the team leader or "facilitator" lets him take the reins. Your role as a facilitator, remember, is to get *everybody* to participate by appropriate reinforcement, and to see to it that everyone's expressed opinion receives the same open hearing and group judgment. That means you don't ignore someone's view simply because he or she is "unfamiliar" with the problem at hand. It also means you don't let the "eagles" in the group run over everybody else just because they've been "right" in the past.

There's obviously a need for balance here, and part of your role as a team facilitator is to achieve that balance. I don't mean that everybody's opinion is just as good as everybody else's. That's a dimwitted distortion of democracy, and it's not what team decision-making is about. I mean that, until *all* the opinions are in and until everybody has had a chance to discuss and assess them, you cannot *assume* that Joe's view is going to be better than Jane's, or vice versa.

There's a natural tendency for managers to forget this because they're impatient to get the problem solved, and they would like to believe that Joe, who has solved a similar problem five times, *must* have the answer to this one—so let's just let him call the shots and be done with it. The impatience here is an aspect of one common element of vertical thinking: the expectation that the best course of action is the one that looks and feels right at *every step* of the way.

BEING RIGHT AT THE END

Vertical thinking, I've pointed out, is sequential and logical. When you think vertically, you know you're on the right path because you're watching the landmarks along the way. You've been this way before, and you know where the road goes.

Because it's sequential, vertical thinking is very attractive and comforting to most people. That's why we continue to use it, even in situations where it's not working. We want immediate and constant feedback indicating progress, and so we look at the road signs outside the window and we see that they're the same road signs we've seen before, and we don't notice that the road we're traveling on is going nowhere. We get sucked in by the familiar, and wonder why we end up in a ditch.

What I'm suggesting you apply in your Creative Problem Solving sessions is an attitude not of "Great, I know this stretch of highway," but one of "Wait and see." I'm suggesting that, when somebody comes out with a strange idea, you suspend your judgment long enough to find out whether it's in fact (as you suspect) a dead end, or whether it might be a short cut. You need to do that because following the beaten path is a good idea only if nobody changes the road—and, in business today, the road is changing all the time.

People who are committed to the beaten path, who are continually suspicious of innovation and "quirky" ideas, are being run off the road more and more because they fail to acknowledge a basic truth. It's that you can be wrong every step of the way, and still be right in the end. That's not logical. It doesn't make "sense." But it's a fact.

The two kinds of thinking I'm talking about—the vertical

thinking that needs instant, constant reassurance that you're on the "right" path and the lateral thinking that allows for stops and "wrong way" turns—may be likened to two styles of football offense. The "vertical" style of offense is the kind that relies on the Big Play, the seventy-five-yard "bomb" pass, the quick fix that will make everything all right. The "lateral" kind of offense is the kind that doesn't mind losing a yard here or there, as long as you get where you're going in the end. I was always an advocate of the stop-and-start, "lateral thinking" type of offense. Not that I had anything against throwing a seventy-five-yard touchdown pass. But I found out from long experience that the Big Play—the Doug Flutie last-second miracle—is, most of the time, just wishful thinking. What wins football games is not that direct, all-or-nothing approach, but the hard, play-by-play work of a bunch of guys creating possibilities together. Trying #34 if #206 didn't work, and #67 if #34 falls through, and so on down the field. It's having not to make a TD on every play, but being satisfied if the final score shows you're ahead of the quick-fix artists.

I'll give you one specific football example, for which I'm better known that I ought to be. I've gotten a lot of credit over the years for revolutionizing the business of quarterbacking, because unlike previous quarterbacks, I "left the pocket" behind the center and scrambled all over the field. Very innovative, all the sports commentators said. Innovative, hell: I was just trying to save my ass. In eighteen years of professional football, I never did discover a way to put the ball in a receiver's hands when I was lying under two hundred and fifty pounds of defensive lineman. I started scrambling because I didn't want to get scrambled. Call it innovation if you want. I called it simple survival.

But it was a case of lateral thinking, and I adopted that approach to the game for the same reason that any good manager adopts a "lateral" approach to business problems. He sees that vertical thinking, even though it may mean he's right at every step of the way, is keeping him stuck in the pocket. It's not moving his team down the field. That's why you change quarterbacking styles. That's why you change business styles. That's how you develop Creative Problem Solving.

Of course, scrambling back and around a difficult situation takes more *time* than sticking to the pocket and going for the TD on every play. Just as it takes more time to discuss options with your team members and arrive at a Consensus rather than a majority vote. There's no denying that if you have to get to the solution *now*, Creative Problem Solving is not the best business approach.

But let's face it. If you think you have to get there now, chances are you're not going to get there at all anyway. Winning, I've often said, means being unafraid to lose. It means being willing to take a chance on a new, untried route and taking your lumps once in a while because you know that, over the long haul, you win more by taking calculated risks than by playing it safe.

You know the story about the guy who was lost in a thick fog and figured that if he just followed the taillights of the driver in front of him, eventually he'd find out where he was? This reasonable, logical plan was upset when the car in front stopped short and he plowed right into its rear end.

Getting out of his car, the driver who had been following behind started screaming at the person who had stopped. "What the hell did you pull up short like that for?"

"Why shouldn't I?" the other driver responded. "I'm in my own driveway."

A lot of people in business are like that guy in the car behind. They'd rather play Follow the Leader any day than come up with creative solutions, because Follow the Leader is "safe." In Follow the Leader, you know exactly how everything will turn out, right? As the anecdote illustrates, dead wrong.

I'm assuming you don't have to get there now, and I'm assuming that you're willing to take calculated risks—not the blind certainties of following the leaders—in order to get there. If these assumptions are correct, then the extra time I'm asking you to spend in developing mutual, creative solutions in team settings will be time well spent. I guarantee it. You might not see the results this quarter. But you will see them. In more fluid cooperation among your team members. In heightened synergy.

In off-the-wall solutions that wouldn't have occurred to you in a hundred seasons if you'd stuck with the "tried and true" methods of decision-making.

If you're in the game for the long run, then you should look at the extra time that Creative Problem Solving takes not so much as time *spent* as time *invested* in the future. No pain, no gain, like they say in a lot of sports situations. You want instant success or instant failure, fine: keep plugging away at the Big Play. Keep straightlining it all the way into the dirt. But if you want ongoing motivation and ongoing new ideas and ongoing productivity, you've got to think on your feet. Creative Problem Solving is the best way that I know of to keep that thinking light. Light as in "flexible," "easy to manage," and most of all "illuminating."

Yes, it takes more time. But it accomplishes something that the quick-fix, vertical styles of problem solving can never do. It gets you where you need to go.

TEN

CONFLICT MANAGEMENT

> If you burn down your neighbor's house, it doesn't make
> yours look better.
> —LOU HOLTZ

"If only I had a team full of clones," a successful line executive told me once, "I'd have a lot fewer problems. I'd only have to motivate one person, and everybody else would fall in line."

He was joking, of course, but his comment addresses a serious problem. If everybody on your team had essentially the same needs, goals, and reasons for being motivated or bored, your job as a motivating manager would be relatively simple. One of the major reasons it's often not simple is that people aren't clones of each other, or of their managers either. People are individuals with a natural tendency to go off in their own directions, even when that's at variance with the needs of their groups. As I've pointed out earlier in this book, they generally have to be persuaded to act with the team, by being continually reinforced for productive group action. And the lesson doesn't always take the first time. As a result, every time you sit down with your team, you face the possibility of conflict.

I don't want to gloss this over, and I know I couldn't get away with it even if I did want to, because with or without this book, you know enough about handling people to know that differences of opinion and needs are inevitable, no matter how tight-knit the team. When I say that teamwork is the answer to solving more and more business problems today, and when I say that

207

Involvement and mutual goal-setting and cooperation are essential to your survival in the marketplace, I'm not waving a magic wand that's going to dissolve every fly in the ointment. If all you needed to pull twenty different people into a single, motivated unit was the battle cry "We're the best team in the world," the Marines wouldn't constantly be searching for a few more good men: every kid who signed in to boot camp would eventually make it into dress blues.

The reason that the Marines don't get a 100 percent pass-through rate is the same reason that your company doesn't have a 100 percent attendance rate or a 100 percent no-defect record. It's that people are people, and they make mistakes. Sometimes they almost want to screw up, of course, because they've just not been properly reinforced to care more. More often than not, though, they really *want* to produce, but for a variety of personal reasons, they just don't contribute to the team effort in the way you would like them to. Somewhere there's a split between where the group needs to go and where the individual feels he needs to go. So you get dropouts, and bad attendance. And conflict.

Now, almost anybody can be a good manager when he doesn't have to deal with dissension. I don't know much about baseball, but I bet that if you gave me nine average players with no personalities—nine guys whose only interest was in furthering the interests of the team—I could get them to give Billy Martin a run for his money. Some managers might dream about that kind of a team; they might think it would be a surefire ticket to stardom to field a side called the Kansas City Clones or the Atlanta Automatons. But managers who have actually worked with humans before—in good times and in bad—know that the idea is ridiculous. They know the truth of Casey Stengel's remark about his own brilliant, but frequently bumpy, coaching career. Good managing, Casey said, is "keeping the five guys on the team who hate your guts away from the five who are undecided."

If you're working with human material, you're going to run into conflict. Always. Because human material, unlike steel or cotton or data bases, has an aggravating habit: it *thinks*. In the best-managed teams, sometimes it thinks in another direction from where you, and most of the team, want to go. Nothing I've said about the P.R.I.C.E. motivation system will make that "thinking in the wrong direction" go away. But it will help you manage it better.

Being able to manage conflict and internal team dissension, far from being an annoying side issue in our system, is really the system's acid test. Everything I've said up to now about reinforcement and feedback, about Pinpointing and Creative Problem Solving, about Assertiveness and Reflective Listening, comes together when you're faced with team conflict. If the principles in this book have any ultimate value at all, it's because they help the business manager resolve—sometimes only temporarily, but always effectively—the incidents of tension and disagreement he's constantly going to meet in team settings.

Notice I'm saying "resolve." Not "eliminate" or "avoid" or "combat." As long as people are involved, you're never going to eliminate conflict entirely. But you can bring it to a productive resolution, so that the motivation of the team is sustained and so that everything you want from that motivation—higher productivity, better work relations, better quality—keeps going where you want it to go.

The particular strategies you might want to use to resolve conflict vary, depending on the situation. But whatever strategy you resort to, there should always be the same goal that you want to get to at the end. That is, the techniques might differ, but they should lead to the same resolution.

That resolution is a situation in which everybody involved in the team setting is at least basically satisfied at the way things have turned out. I don't mean doing handstands. But not sulking in the corner either. You can come to a conflict resolution without every one of your team members feeling that he's come out on top; in fact, that's what's going to happen most of the time. But if *anybody* on the team comes out feeling he's on the bottom—feeling that he's "lost" because his input wasn't considered—then you haven't resolved the conflict. You've only deflected it, or crushed it. Crushed conflict is like crushed fruit. Stamp it into the dirt, and it's going to rise again.

In our productivity seminars, we tell our client managers to aim for a "9/9" conflict outcome. That's an outcome where both you and the person "causing" the conflict end up with nine of your ten possible "points" satisfied. We say aim for nine rather than the supposedly ideal ten because experience has taught us a bitter lesson: when everybody in a conflict situation is aiming for total victory (for that imaginary ten out of ten), inevitably you start to look for a score of ten to *nothing*: you start to aim for solutions that leave you feeling like a winner, and everybody else feeling like losers. The outcome of that is a paradox: everybody tries for the max, and everybody ends up with zero.

So we say aim for a realizable nine out of ten. Keeping that ideal in mind means you remember that nobody gets it all—nobody in any conflict situation is going to end up totally ahead of the pack. In fact, if that's where you want to find yourself, in business or in sports, you're soon going to be out of the game.

A lot of managers don't even get very close to the attainable ideal of "9/9." That's because they set their sights on the more commonly attained outcomes of "9/1," "1/9," and "5/5." And that's the best they ever achieve. I'll explain this jargon now, as I describe the most common ways that managers try to resolve conflict, show how each of them fails, and then tell you what you can do to transform each of these ineffective strategies into the "9/9" strategy that leads to real conflict resolution.

THE 1/9 STYLE: AVOIDANCE

The first, and by far the worst, of all conflict "management" styles is one that is frequently adopted by junior managers in the presence of intimidating superiors. It's the old yes-man style that editorial cartoonists are always ready to ridicule because it plays into the popular belief that every Big Business is composed of a dictatorial boss and a horde of minor toadies who want his job, and are willing to kiss ass for thirty years to get it.

Actually, this business-hating prejudice on the cartoonists'

210

part is not entirely off base—at least not with regard to middle management's readiness to go along with anything the Big Bad Boss says. You see this all the time in big companies.

Example: At a team meeting of investment counselors in a major international bank, top management seems unanimous on a new investment strategy. The bank will begin extending loans to various Third World countries who are already deeply in debt, on the expectation that future oil discoveries will enable the debtor nations to eventually pay back all principle and interest. The one conflicting opinion in this meeting is that of a young investment counselor who fears that one of the already debt-ridden nations is a bad risk. The vice-president for international investments asks for opinions all around the table. What does the doubting Thomas do?

If he's a practitioner of the 1/9 conflict management style, he simply avoids the potential flare-up. He looks down at the table and defers to the general wisdom. Or, if he's gutsy enough to test the waters but not dive in, he raises his hand meekly and says, "The debt repayment schedule seems a little optimistic to me, but I guess there's risk in everything." Translation: You fools are getting us in way over our heads, but I don't want to make waves, because I don't want you to think I'm a trouble-maker, and anyway you're older and wiser so maybe you do know best.

That's a pretty confusing message. But it's the best possible message you can deliver when you adopt the 1/9 style. We call it the 1/9 style because it leaves one party (in this case, the dissenting but intimidated manager) with one point out of ten, and leaves the other party or parties (in this case, the majority-opinion top managers) with an *apparent* nine out of ten. The numbers here refer not to any objective reality, but to the way the individuals involved feel about the encounter after it's over. Here the dissenter feels he's lost badly, because he never got to express his opinion, and the others feel they've won, because the team has "agreed" to do what they intended to do all along.

The advantages of the Avoidance style are immediate and very clear cut. When you back away from a potential flare-up, or when you express a modest, qualified dissension and then defer to "wiser" counsel, you achieve the immediate advantage of avoiding trouble. You preserve harmony, save time that might have been spent in fruitless discussion, and maintain an ostensibly good working relationship with the team, which might serve you well in future encounters. In addition, you avoid taking on responsibility for what might have happened if your weird idea had been adopted—and you get to *share* the responsibility for what will happen now with the other members of the group. You get to be seen as a nice guy, a team player. And what the hell, you might have been wrong. Maybe the problem you thought about will go away.

Comforting, isn't it? That's why Avoidance is practiced so often, especially in the lower management ranks. But it's a *deadly* tactic, built on the crackpot idea that conflict equals disaster, and that preserving harmony at all costs is a necessary function of team motivation and management. Here are the disadvantages of adopting a 1/9 style:

1. *No input.* The group is deprived of the benefit of hearing what might be a valuable opinion, and the 1/9 practitioner is himself deprived of the opportunity of contributing to the joint decision. Since the decision is reached minus one member's potentially valuable input, it is necessarily going to be less creative, less synergistic, than it would have been with that input. So everybody loses.

2. *No credibility.* The antibusiness press would have you believe that top executives like yes-men. Not true. I've never yet met a successful business person who wanted to be surrounded by characters without minds of their own—or by characters who were afraid to speak those minds. The first thing a 1/9 stylist hamstrings in situations like the one I've just described is his own credibility. And that's the one thing none of us can afford to lose. Gary Cooper got away with grunts and "Mmms" and head-nodding because his horse didn't really give a damn. Try that style in a business meeting and you're going to come off looking like a horse. Or part of one, anyway.

3. *Instability.* The 1/9 style might work once or twice. It might actually cut down on the aggravation that you're afraid of. But it's impossible to maintain it for more than a handful of meetings. Unless you're working with a roomful of clones, eventually somebody's going to say, "Jim, you agree with everything Mrs. Ryerson says. Do you have any ideas of your own?" Maybe the question won't come out as tartly as that, but I guarantee you it will come out. And you'll have grunted yourself right into a hole.

4. *Demotivation.* Again, unless you're a manager in a clone factory, you want the people you work with to speak up, to give you input, to get Involved in creative solutions so that your quality and productivity and all the rest of those good things go up. You can't expect them to do that if you don't do it yourself. With them, with your peers, *and* with your bosses. There's nothing more demotivating to team performance than a manager who "doesn't want trouble." Remember that people may be ignorant, but very few of them are downright stupid. You can blab all you want about Involvement, but if they see you zip your mouth shut every time your supervisor says boo, they're going to nod "Wimp" and zip their own.

Now, all of these problems will arise *even if* your "going along" strategy proves to be the right one in the individual instance. Even if the majority is proved right and you were right in shutting up, you're going to be wrong in the long run, for the reasons I've stated. If it turns out that your cockamamie minority idea was on target, you're going to be in the ludicrous position of thinking "I told you so" and not being able to say it!

You'll notice that the example I've been talking about here is hardly a hypothetical one. You know there have been meetings like this one, in every major international bank, and it stands to reason that some young manager somewhere must have thought, "This Brazil loan is for the birds." Why didn't he or she speak up? And if he did, and was shouted down because of an unpopular opinion, has the current debt crisis proved his wisdom, and is he now president of the bank? I doubt it. It's so much easier to just let things slide, so much easier to avoid than to confront—until you 1/9 yourself right into bankruptcy.

How do we change this common style? How do we fight the natural tendency to let others do the talking until we're all picking up unemployment insurance together? We do it by practicing those Assertiveness techniques that I talked about in Chapter 7. My advice for the manager who feels trapped in a 1/9 conflict management style is simple. It's to reread that chapter, and to focus especially on learning to identify your individual rights in a given situation, and on learning how to express your opinions even when—maybe *especially* when—they conflict with those of others in your working teams.

Assertiveness techniques do not make conflict go away, but they do help to move the conflict in a positive direction. If you are able to state your own differences of opinion in a calm, direct, and nonaggressive manner, you have a reasonable chance of transforming potential hostility into a discussion where Involvement really happens, and where Creative Problem Solving has a home. You also—and this is far from incidental—have a much better chance of getting others in your group to do the same. In fact, that's one of the major side benefits of using Assertiveness to modify a 1/9 style. It gets *other* people motivated to assert themselves, too—and the ultimate outcome of that benefit is the synergistic, 9/9 style that every good conflict manager wants to achieve.

THE 9/1 STYLE: CONTROL

Be reasonable, do it my way. That might be taken as the byword for practitioners of the 9/1 style. Just as the "one down" 1/9 style is common among subordinates dealing with superiors, so the "one up" 9/1 style is frequently adopted by superiors who are used to bossing rather than managing. To the 9/1 conflict manager, winning is everything, and he sees winning not so much as the achievement of valuable shared goals, but as the adoption of *his* particular idea or plan. His ultimate personal goal is to get his way, whatever the cost. As long as the score is 9 to 1, he's happy.

I guess this style has some value if you're a crowbar-munching football coach and the group with whom you're having conflict is the other team's defensive line. You want a manager to give no quarter when he strikes out against the competition. The trouble is that a lot of managers tend to see their *own* teams in the same light. You can get some good motivational results by treating the opposition as if they were dirt. Try that on your own people and one of two things will happen. Either you will get them so used to having your cleats in their back that you'll succeed in completely demotivating them from saying anything but "Yessir." In other words, you'll get the Punishment Effect— and a team of losers. Or they'll get tired of getting beaten up and they'll turn on you. In which case you'll get a face full of cleats, and be looking for another team. Either way, you lose.

The tough-guy managers who adopt a 9/1 conflict management style generally do so for one of two bad reasons. Either they, like their opposite numbers the 1/9 stylists, assume that conflict is always bad, and must be avoided at all costs. Or they actually *like* conflict, because it gives them an opportunity to demonstrate their superiority. Two diametrically opposed reasons, but the same lousy outcome: a team situation in which it is generally understood that success means doing it his way. And in which stating your opposing opinion means getting publicly humiliated for mouthing off.

The advantages of the 9/1 style are obvious, and obviously limited. By playing the Infallible Leader role, you get things done, and done quickly. You don't have to hold off on that new ad campaign for the next three weeks while the test market results come in, because you *know* what the results are going to be and, even if they're not what you think they'll be, you know better than the marketing department anyway, and so you can start the ad campaign now. There's no doubt about it. Making all the decisions yourself does save an awful lot of time.

In addition, the 9/1 stylist gets to have his own way, nearly all the time. That's immediately gratifying to anybody, and especially to those jellyfish in giants' clothing who need constant external reassurance that they really *are* in complete charge. I suspect there's a weak, nervous center at the heart of every tough-guy manager, and adopting the "I make the decisions" style makes it easy to disguise that center. It sets up a solid, impregnable image that convinces others—even if it doesn't convince the 9/1 practitioner himself—that he really is Somewhat More than Human.

Did you hear about the guy who dies and goes up to Heaven and is puzzled by the appearance of a bearded old man in a lab coat and surgical mask? The old guy is continually harrassing all the angels, ordering them about, telling them they've got to work faster, and so on. The new arrival asks an older resident about him, and is told, "Oh, don't pay any attention to him. That's just God. He thinks he's a doctor."

It's a story with a sobering point. Ask any hospital nurse to describe the average doctor's style of conflict management, or indeed his style of management in general. What you'll hear is an indirect description of the 9/1 style. The attitude among many physicians today is the same attitude that persists among some of the business community's older managers. It's the attitude that "I know best, so if you want to know what to do, just ask me." If you don't think that creates more conflict among team members—whether you're talking about hospital or factory teams—then you haven't been reading the papers.

The disadvantages of the 9/1 style overlap somewhat those of its "reverse," the 1/9 style. In both styles, the attempt to eliminate, rather than manage, conflict reduces the input of team members; creates resentment, timidity, and hostility; lowers general team morale; stifles creativity; inhibits cooperation; and, in general, sets up a thoroughly demotivating atmosphere where "teamwork" is seen, quite realistically, as a promise without any conviction. It should come as no surprise to any one that organizations where the Control style is common among managers have long been falling behind those where a more participatory management style is respected.

The solution? To get from a 9/1 style to the more productive, more motivated Synergy style that I've said is ideal, you need to practice the Reflective Listening skills that I discussed earlier. If you find yourself "playing God" or "pretending to be a doctor," I suggest you reread that material. Learning to listen reflectively is a critical component of any management style in which people's creativity and input is valued. Without it the only manager who is going to be right all the time is the one who has nothing to do, or who is bench coach of the Kansas City Clones. If you're dealing with real live people, you've got to learn how to *listen*.

Part of this, of course, is *reacting* to what you hear, and that too is part of Reflective Listening. Since reinforcement is such a major element of the P.R.I.C.E. motivation system, the manager plagued by a God/doctor complex would do well to review as well what I've said about positive Consequences, and about the need to give people "strokes" approximately four times as often as you give them "strikes" for poor Behaviors. First, open *your* ears. Then, fill *their* ears with what they want to hear, which is "Thanks for a job well done." Those are the basic, and critical steps in moving from a 9/1 style to the creative Involvement you need.

THE 5/5 STYLE: COMPROMISE

Compromise. It's such a chummy word. It sounds like the perfect solution to managing conflict. I give a little, you give a little, and we both come out OK.

The 5/5 style of conflict management, where we both end up "half winners," is a better way of dealing with dissidence than either the 1/9 or the 9/1 style. But it's far from ideal. Here's why.

The principal advantage of a bargaining, negotiation style of conflict management is that it reinforces one of the chief benefits of the entire P.R.I.C.E. motivation system: the sense of exchange, communication, and Involvement that is essential to good team solutions. You really can't entirely knock a style where people are committed to open relationships, to cooperation as a way of reducing conflict, and to a fair hearing for all views, however dissident. If the nations of the world could adopt that kind of conflict-resolution mode, we'd all be a lot better off.

But there are disadvantages, too. First, ironically, is the very fact that the 5/5 style, because it focuses so heavily on having everyone "win a little" so as not to "lose a lot," tends to reinforce agreement *itself* rather than agreement on the best or most creative solution. If I want to move a production schedule up by three months and you want to move it back three months, the best of all possible solutions might *not* be to leave it just where it is. That would be the ideal, mathematically "correct" compromise. But it might be very bad business.

Secondly, it's a commonly observed fact in the seminars I've visited that when people know in advance that their group is committed to compromise, they tend to *exaggerate* their own position because they know it will be cut back during the negotiation. There's a kind of haggling over price that goes on in many teams run with a 5/5 style. I may feel that the production schedule should ideally be set ahead two months, but I'll say in the meeting, "We've got to have a three-month advance." You may be satisfied with a one-month advance, but you won't come out and say that because you're afraid we'll have to negotiate it up to two. So, when you know that give-and-take is going to go on, nobody states his own best judgment—and as a result the best solutions can get lost.

Finally, in a compromise solution, nobody comes out feeling really satisfied, because there's an element of the conflict-as-combat model built in to all negotiating structures, and when you enter a combat hoping to win and fearing to lose, it's just as easy to see a middle solution as a defeat as it is to see it as a victory.

The basic problem with compromise is really one of attitude. We enter negotiation scenarios—whether they are collective bargaining meetings or investment counselors' strategy sessions—with an eye toward getting rid of the conflict that we know is going to arise, rather than with an eye toward finding the best solution for the problem or problems at hand. It's a subtle distinction, but an important one. If I know I'm sitting at a table to try to beat you back from your position so that we settle on something closer to mine, then the closer we come to my original position, the better I'm going to feel—even if the solution that gets us there still leaves us with incredible problems. And if we "settle" on a solution that more closely approximates your original position, then I'm going to feel that I've lost—again, even if the final solution is better than either of our original ones.

Getting beyond this simplistic balancing-act view of conflict management means starting to look at conflict not as an issue in itself, but as the inevitable spinoff of differences in the way we approach external problems. External problems. Not how we feel about each other or what you had for breakfast or how much I may resent the fact that you've got a "bossy" approach. If you start with the joint understanding that we're all in this business together, and that we're searching for the *best solutions*, the whole idea of "compromise" takes on a different meaning.

I've already mentioned that one real block to creative solutions is the deeply ingrained idea that, when something goes wrong with a production schedule or a sales quota, you've got to find somebody to *blame*. There's some of this same self-destructive tendency at work every time you aim for a merely "acceptable" compromise for a problem: what you're getting at, all too often, is a mock resolution where the game is over and all that's left is the whining. That is, you get to agree on the surface, but underneath you're pissed off at the person whose idea "beat" yours out, or he's pissed off at you, or you're both pissed off at each other because you've had to settle for less-than-the-best. The conflict is temporarily shelved, but the blaming goes on.

You solve that by getting beyond blame and beyond bargaining, to reach for mutual advantage. You stop asking, "Whose fault is this problem?" or, "How can *I* win in this situation?" but rather "How can *we* all *fix* this problem?" Is there a solution out there somewhere—maybe some eccentric solution in which *nobody* has a vested interest—that can make *all* of our lives easier?

Compromise, as it's now understood, is locked in to the same win-lose dichotomy that makes the Avoidance style and the Control style so unproductive. To get beyond that dichotomy, you need to modify your attitude toward "bargaining" and "negotiation" so that you search for a *mutual* bargain, so that you negotiate for something you *both* want.

You do that by turning the Compromise approach—which, after all, still leaves you all "5 down"—into a true synergistic approach, where everybody comes out a winner.

THE 9/9 STYLE: SYNERGY

I've said that the major difference between the 5/5 Compromise style and a true Synergy style is one of attitude. True. But there are also very specific, practical techniques you can, and should, employ as a team manager to raise the likelihood that your people will come out of a given encounter feeling that they've contributed to a satisfactory outcome rather than that they've been cheated.

First, you can identify the personal *interests* behind individual people's positions. That means both interests that relate to the job and those that extend beyond it. If Harry is adamantly opposed to the adoption of a new expense account protocol, you'll want to find out why. Maybe he's been fudging his vouchers for the past two years, and he doesn't want to have to justify his expenditures: that would be a personal interest that would clearly affect his judgment on the issue in question. Or maybe his department has been hassled by Finance for the past three quarters about expenses that are clearly justified, and he's tired of defending his turf when he knows he's right. That would be a job-related interest that you should know about before you— or the group—make any final disposition on the expense account matter.

Obviously, investigating people's personal interests in a given proposition means that you're going to have to *involve* yourself—just as you ask your people to involve themselves—in all the decisions being considered. This doesn't mean you've got to pry into people's personal lives. It does mean you should be aware—both as a manager and as a member of a team—of what extraneous, and internal, considerations are affecting your people's decisions.

You don't know what those factors are? Of course not. Who does before he asks? The point I'm getting at here is that managing conflict, just like managing anything else associated with human beings, means being sensitive to all the emotional issues that may be impacting the way people are reacting. Not just the business issues like "how long the line has been down" and "the increase in competition in Sector 4." You've got to pay attention as well to why Rachel Warren always seems a little down on Tuesdays—does she have a custody hearing Monday nights? You've got to be aware of why Will Roberts never has anything good to say about sales training programs—is it because he had a disastrous experience with a training program that nearly cost him his job?

You get my point. People are people. They're not simply their job descriptions. If you want to motivate them to better work, you've got to find out what makes them tick.

One of the ways to do this that I've already talked about is to ask them Empathy questions. In Chapter 6, on Reflective Listening, I talked about these kinds of questions, where you at the same time elicit further information from a person *and* reinforce what he or she has already said. This is particularly important when you're face to face with a person—it doesn't matter whether the person is your peer, your subordinate, or your boss—who clearly disagrees with what you're saying. In this kind of situation, asking an Empathy question is one of the best methods I know to move a potential $1/9$, $9/1$, or $5/5$ scenario to the healthier atmosphere of $9/9$.

Another way is to ask Open-Ended questions designed to find out the speaker's *reasons* for feeling the way he or she does. I don't mean just emotional reasons here; people are going to be reluctant to give you them anyway. I mean objective, business-related reasons—the kind of reasons any manager, and for that matter any fellow employee—always has a perfect right to ask, but that are seldom asked because it's easier to simply say, "Nonsense. That idea will never work."

I've been saying throughout this book that Involvement is an essential, that asking for everyone's opinions is not a luxury but a necessity, that every manager needs variant and even conflicting opinions because it helps him or her make more creative decisions. If any of that makes any sense, it's obvious that you have to keep asking *why* people support a given position even after you've decided it's "nonsense." If you don't do that, the best you can come up with is Compromise. Much more likely, you'll end up in mutual recrimination, hostility, misunderstanding, and the most noncreative of solutions.

A third way of transforming Compromise into Synergy is to focus on generating as many *alternative solutions* as you can in every team meeting where conflict arises. You'll recognize this as the Brainstorming technique that I described in the previous chapter. That technique has a value that transcends its importance as an aid to Creative Problem Solving. Since Compromise is at best a trade-off between two or more desirable alternatives, it stands to reason that your chances of reaching more than mere trade-off solutions is going to increase if we multiply the possible options. If I'm pushing for the three-month production schedule extension and you're committed to the one-month schedule, the best we may be able to come up with is a mutually unsatisfying two-month Compromise. But if we open out the discussion to everybody else involved in production, who knows what we might come up with? We might find somebody to show us a way that we can get the same productive capacity that I want with a one-month extension. Or somebody who introduces a marketing projection that makes the three-month design irrelevant. You don't know until you try. And the only way to try is to commit yourself, as a team, to "whatever the best choice might be" *before* you find out what it is.

Commitment to that kind of optimum solution, my company has found, tracks really well with the Involvement and teamwork models that I've been talking about in this book. And it opens out the possibility that what you all come up with together is going to be more satisfying than a 5/5 solution.

A final note on moving from a Compromise solution to a fuller Synergy result. I *know* that working toward the "best" solution when a workable Compromise is in sight can be a trying and frustrating process. It takes a hell of a lot more time than "settling." And it's psychologically risky. Working toward Synergy drains you of energy as well as time. It means you have to believe even when you don't believe. It means you have to have faith in the eventual motivational energies of your team even when you don't feel up for the game yourself. Finally, it means you've got to know that, in the *long* run, you and your people can accomplish more than you can, or they can, all alone. This is the land of the free and the home of the brave and the residence of the rugged individual. So it's not going to be easy.

But it can be done. And when it is done, it creates solutions that are not only better formed, better imagined, better created, than other solutions; it creates solutions that everybody can *own*. And ownership is essential. If you want the decisions you reach to be ongoing, continually productive decisions, you've got to involve everybody in their making. You can do that only half way (only 5/5) in a Compromise style. If you want everybody to continue producing, continue introducing input, continue creating team solutions, you've got to give them more than a 5. You've got to give them the same 9 that you would want for yourself. You do that by generating Synergy.

BEYOND THE ZERO-SUM GAME

To a mathematician, everything I've been saying might come as a big surprise. If you're used to making business decisions based on how well the numbers add up, you may take it as a surprise, too. But it shouldn't really be surprising. It's only in "pure" mathematics that nine plus nine has to equal eighteen. In applied mathematics, in real-world physics, and in the human versions of real-world physics, where you're dealing with human "quantities" and not integers, nine plus nine can equal anything you want it to equal. Put nine apples and nine apples together, and you're always going to get eighteen apples. Put nine people and nine people together, and you don't know what you're going to get. You might end up with a crackerjack advertising team that pushes your company from 12 percent of a hardball market into 31 percent in three months. You might end up with a skunk-works that produces nothing but stink.

The outcome in human "addition" like this is determined by more than the numbers. It's determined by what you do with the human potential you've got. You can start with the average side of nine and motivate them—with proper reinforcement—into the next World Series. Or you can start with the last Super Bowl team and demotivate them—by ignoring motivational principles—right into the next season's cellar.

A lot of business experts today like to talk about the "zero sum" model, where there is just so much natural resources, just so much capital expenditure, just so much revenue draw, and just so much human possibility that can be put into the overall social and industrial mix. When you strain the limits of that "just so much," these analysts say, you press the system beyond its limits, and something's got to give somewhere. Ask too much from revenue expansion, and the corporate sector has got to contract. And so on.

It's a neat enough picture, I guess, but it badly distorts one element. That element is human potential. What the dollars and cents boys and the revenue chart analysts and the rest of the zero-sum experts don't consider is the tremendous untapped potential in the human beings who do the work of this economy. I believe that our capacity for invention and synergistic production has up to now barely been touched, and that if we can get our human material *more* Involved, *more* committed to teamwork, *more* focused on creativity, we will discover a mathematical miracle. I'm convinced we will discover that nine plus nine equals twenty-one. Or forty-two. Or God knows what "imaginary" number.

The trouble with all the approaches to managing conflict that do not recognize synergy is that they assume, implicitly or explicitly, that nine plus nine equals eighteen. And they assume as well that, in the workplace, and political environment, and every place else where human beings come together, there have got to be losers and winners. There have got to be those who achieve and those who fall by the wayside. There have got to be the eagles and the mules. Therefore (they assume), there's no such thing as a 9/9 solution; that goes against the laws of logic.

This reasoning is OK as long as you're talking about you versus the competition. The problem is that many people in business say on the one hand that they want to motivate their people to beat the competition, and on the other hand that the best way to accomplish that is to beat *them* into submission. One episode of the coyote and the road runner can tell you that this ain't the way it goes down. You want to beat the bad guys, you've got to focus your hostile energies outward, and your productive, motivational energies inward. If you can't do that, you might as well be working *for* the competition.

Beat the competition? Fine. I don't have anything against honest, hard competition. What quarterback would have? But competitive energies are valuable only in so far as you know how to control and direct them. The drive to win is powerful as hell. It's easy to let it get out of hand. It's easy to let it take you over, convince you that it's an absolute, rather than a contingent, value. When that happens, you start to look at everything—including your teammates—as the competition. It should be obvious what happens then. You start to play *against* the very group that should be contributing to your success. You start to act as if conflict is not just an inevitable, energizing factor, but as if it's the reason for your being here. You start to think that *competing*, and *winning*, and beating the hell out of the other guy, are the reasons you've been playing the game. When you start to believe that, you're trying to be saved on other people's sins—and you're going to fail, because you're pitting yourself against the very people you're supposed to be working *with*.

So ultimately the management of conflict means directing the energies of conflict—those disruptive but potentially creative energies—where they will do the most good: toward the discovery of better solutions that can satisfy everybody on your team. The danger is in seeing *internal* conflict in the same way that you see conflict from the outside: as a threat to your company, your person, your entire way of doing things. The experience of the most productive, most motivated, and most *motivating* team members gives the lie to that every day.

MOTIVATING TO WIN

> If it's worth playing, it's worth paying the price to win.
> —PAUL "BEAR" BRYANT

There's a medium-sized Midwest bank that is now in desperate financial trouble because, several years ago, its management invested about a quarter of a billion dollars in a sure thing.

The sure thing was the ill-fated Penn Square project, a badly planned and quickly overextended real estate scheme that sent banking lions like Continental of Illinois whimpering off into the Wall Street jungle like terrified mice. The small bank I'm talking about made a classic error with regard to this scheme. Instead of sizing up the project for themselves—instead of asking for financial statements and running risk analyses—the managers simply followed the herd, assuming that, if the big guys were in on the deal, it was just naturally going to be a fountain of gold. Ignoring the principles of Pinpointing and Recording and Evaluation, they let the bank industry leaders do their "thinking" for them—and followed those leaders down the tubes.

I call this a classic error because it illustrates with gruesome clarity a kind of thinking that is extremely widespread in business circles today, and that always gets managers into hot water. There are two, related bonehead notions tied up with this kind of thinking. First, you *can* get something for nothing—that is, there is a free lunch after all. And second, the people who are now out in front know where that free lunch is. The conclusion to be drawn is simple: If you want to succeed in what you're doing, let other people tell you what works.

The bank managers I'm talking about didn't fall into this self-destructive mode of "analysis" all by themselves. The path to their investment bungling was laid out for them long ago, by generations and generations of managers whose watchwords were "Don't rock the boat" and "I can get it for you wholesale," and—most disastrous of all—"Follow the leader, he knows where he's going."

It's one of the most distressing features of modern business life that adherence to cliches like these are actually built in to the way managers think. We are amazingly adept at reinforcing the status quo. A young guy comes on board eager to learn and all fired up to perform, and he quickly gets the message from top management that he hasn't been hired to shake things up, he's been hired to keep them in place. Just follow orders. Do it my way. Observe the chain of command. Play it safe. *But*—and here's the joke of it all—at the same time *get your people to perform.*

That's as confounding a mixed message as you're ever likely to hear. On the one hand the manager is told that he's supposed to play by the rules, and on the other he's told to get out of his people something that can only be achieved by *breaking* the rules. We ask our managers to be winners, and we expect them to develop winning teams. But we *train* them, all along the way, to be wimps. And then we wonder why the quarterly report shows a drop in production or a rise in absenteeism. We wonder why this guy, whom we're training to be a good follower, isn't acting like a leader.

I really believe that the worst thing we do in American business is to manage managers—that is, to train managers to manage people, rather than juggle inventory and overhead. We have lost sight of the one truth that can turn a group of individuals into a winning team—the fact that they *are* individuals, and need to be motivated as such. We've forgotten Robert Half's wise observation that companies cannot create productivity; only people can. As a result, we're continuing to motivate people to do exactly what we *don't* want them to do: to feel and behave like followers. In other words, like losers.

Ironically, we are doing this precisely because we are *afraid* of losing. We're so afraid of missing out, of being left behind, of making a mistake and being found out for it, that we have built up a whole business culture that is built on the philosophy of "CYA." You know what that stands for. Cover Your Ass. First, last, and always, be sure that if something goes wrong, somebody else gets the blame. Worry about fixing it later. Much later. Your first order of business—whether you're on the assembly line or in the office next to the president's—is to keep a low enough profile so that no one will know you've screwed up. That's the way to succeed.

Crazy, isn't it? But it's part of the culture, all over the place. Anybody who's been in business for more than two weeks knows it.

This attitude of being afraid to lose is responsible for more losses, I believe, than anything else in business. It's a profoundly demotivating attitude which gets the minimum level of concentration, and initiative, and innovation out of people, and what you get out of that level is exactly what you should expect. "The employer gets the employees he deserves." Walter Gilbey said that back in 1901, and it's just as true today as it was then. You want to train your people not to take chances, fine. But pretty soon you're not going to have any chances to take.

The solution to this sorry state of affairs lies in allowing people to take *risks* even if they don't always bring home the bacon. When I talked about Creative Problem Solving, I said that good ideas often come as hybrids of "bad" ideas, and that if you want your people to be creative and involved in your operation, you've got to motivate them to be so. The point applies to every business I've ever seen. If you want progressive, nimble people on your team, you've got to reinforce the risk-taker, not the stick-in-the-mud whose career goal is to follow your lead.

If you do this, I'll tell you what's going to happen. Sometimes you're going to win, and sometimes you're going to lose. That's a fact. I don't care how good your team is, or how religiously you follow the motivational principles I've been laying out in this book, sometimes you're still going to lose. Sometimes the person you reinforced for being inventive is going to invent another Edsel, and you're going to lose time and money.

And that's where your real test comes in. That's when you've got to say, "OK, we blew it here. Let's find out why. Let's use a little Pinpointing, and Recording, and Evaluation and see what happened, and what we can do to fix it." Rather than saying, "Oh God, we just went out on a limb and it got cut off. Let's never go out on a limb again."

It always bears repeating: *Winning means being unafraid to lose.* I mean being unafraid not because you don't give a damn or because the game doesn't really matter all that much, or because you like the thrill of being #2. I mean being unafraid because you know the long-term figures. You know that, if you're in the game for the *whole* game, and the whole season, and the whole life of your company, you can afford a mistake now and then, because in the long run allowing those mistakes creates a more motivated and more productive team than firing every fumbler on the spot.

You know what happens to a football team that is terrified of losing? It loses. Period. It gets so psyched up worrying about the coming defeat that it creates its own self-fulfilling prophecy; the people on the team spend so much time thinking about the Final Outcome that they screw up all the little things they have to do well to make that outcome rosy. And they end up with weeds instead. That's what happened to the bankers who went running for the Penn Square bonanza. They were so afraid of losing out to the big guys that they followed them right into the hole.

The fact is that, in business as well as in sports, you only need to be right 60 or 70 percent of the time to come out with a championship season. That may not sound like much, but think of how you would feel if your company was producing 60–70 percent of the output in your particular industry. Or had a 60–70 percent share of an ad market. I'd say that deserved champagne, not tears.

The real winners know this is true. For example, consider this comment: "Every man's got to figure to get beat sometime." Sound like a loser? Sound like some wimpy, nonmotivated plodder who just doesn't want to give 100 percent? That comment was made by Joe Louis, the fabled Brown Bomber of the 1930s who held the heavyweight crown for longer than anyone else in history and who retired for good in the 1950s with a 68–3 record. Unafraid to lose. A winner.

Or take one of football's all-time winners: the Green Bay Packers' Vince Lombardi. Lombardi is constantly quoted as saying, "Winning isn't everything, it's the only thing." What he actually said is subtly different. In his 1973 memoir *Vince Lombardi on Football*, he wrote, "What I said is that 'Winning is not everything—but making the *effort* to win is.' " Like every other winner and every great motivating manager, Lombardi knew that the Perfect Season idea was far more legend than reality. He knew nobody could ever take home all the trophies. And he knew that putting in your best effort—giving the game all your drive and concentration and involvement—was what really made you a winner.

Doing that, of course, means taking risks. Not crazy, off-the-wall gambles. I'm not advising anybody to shoot popguns off in the dark. As you know from the P.R.I.C.E. system I've described, I'm a strong believer in careful assessment and reassessment and re-reassessment. But that is a lot different from saying, "We have always done it this way, and it's the safest way, and we will continue to do it this way." Intelligent management is the art of balancing the "eagle" and the "mule" in every player. It is the skill of motivating each person to realize his or her highest potential—even when doing that means running the risk of losing yardage.

Losing yardage, of course, is *always* a risk. But that doesn't mean you shouldn't play. A lot of savvy coaches will tell you, "When you pass the football, three things can happen, and two of them are bad." The two bad things are an incompletion and an interception, but just because the odds are two-to-one doesn't mean you shouldn't ever pass. Even with the odds against you, if you're going to win any ball game, you'd *better* be able to pass. Yes, you'll lose yardage. But that's part of the price you pay for winning, and taking calculated risks is part of every good manager's way of dealing with his people.

In the end it comes down to that—to people. We're great at getting managers to deal with machines and numbers and flow-charts and cost-benefit projections. We're not nearly so good at getting them to deal with the human material that makes all of those other things happen. The managers who are going to lead things for the rest of this century and beyond will be the ones who understand their people, who understand that what folks want—and what they need in order to give their best—goes way beyond a paycheck. The leaders will be those who understand that every member of their team needs to know exactly what's expected of him, needs to have access to a score-keeping system that lets him know how he's doing, needs to feel that he's contributing to the team, needs to get constantly and consistently reinforced for that participation, and needs to have access to feedback on how the team is doing.

You'll probably recognize this litany as a restatement of the P.R.I.C.E. system. That's no accident. I really believe that the secret to managerial success today lies in applying the five principles of that system—Pinpointing, Recording, Involvement, Consequences, and Evaluation—to each and every human situation. That's the way to get the best out of your people. And the reason it works is very simple: it's that paying this "P.R.I.C.E." for success recognizes that your people are people, and not just machines with opposing thumbs.

In the end, the most successful managers will be those who can motivate to win because they understand what turns people on. I hope the principles I've laid out in this book will help you do that more effectively. I hope they will help you nurture and reinforce the most creative and flexible and, yes, risky aspects of your business environment. And I hope you will come to understand that taking a chance on your teammates always, in the long run, pays off. Not just in bottom-line results like better productivity and better quality, but in better people results too.

For me, that's always been the best thing about putting a P.R.I.C.E. system into place. It's great taking the tangible results to the bank. But it's even better watching employees grow:

watching them develop into real team members. People with real team spirit, and real involvement, and a real commitment to putting in 100 percent, all the time.

People with the old ziperoo.

INDEX

ABC Model, 7
  Evaluation and, 101–4
Acceptance, Empathy
    Statements and, 136
Accuracy, 201, 202. *See also*
    Influence-Accuracy Tangle
Achievement
  fear and resentment of, 185
  as motivator, 94
Action plans in team meetings,
    176–77
Adaptation, 113–15
Aggressiveness, 142, 144–47
  Punishment Effect and, 147
  resistance and, 158
Alberti, Robert, 143
Allen, Fred, 70
Ambiguity of language, 123–24
Antecedents, 7–8, 79
  definition of, 102
  of punishment, 84
Appropriateness of
    Consequences, 85–86, 110–
    11
Arctic survival exercise, 75–77,
    201–2
Assertion Scale, 148–54

Assertiveness, 142–61
  Broken Record technique,
    155–56
  in conflict management, 214
  definition of, 144
  Empathy Statements and, 156
  "fight or flight" response and,
    144–48
  Fogging, 157–58
  Involvement and, 146
  Negative, 158–60
  Negative Inquiry, 160–61
  Reflective Listening and, 156,
    157
  scale for Recording, 148–54
Attention, 124
Attitudes, 9–10
  toward authority, 63–64
  Behaviors vs., 28
  Pinpointing objectives and,
    32–33
  toward work, 64
Authoritarianism, 165–71
  drawbacks of, 167–71
Authority, attitudes toward, 63–
    64

Avoidance in conflict
    management, 210–14
Assertiveness and, 214
drawbacks of, 212–13

Bargaining in conflict
    management, 217–20
drawbacks of, 217–19
Synergy and, 220, 222–23
Baseline, 54–56
on Assertion Scale, 154
Behaviorist school of
    psychology, 6–9
Behaviors, 7–12
attitudes vs., 28
definition of, 8
motivation and, 11–12
outcomes vs., 27
as performance variables, 54
Pinpointing. See Pinpointing
    Behaviors
positive reinforcement of
    changes in, 88
punishment and changes in,
    87–88
Berra, Yogi, 100
Big Daddy management. See
    Authoritarianism
Bird, Larry, 179–80
Body grammar, 130
Bossman style of management.
    See Authoritarianism
Bottom up method of
    Pinpointing objectives, 31,
    33–35
"Brain-brawn" distinctions, 178–
    79
Brainstorming, 191–96
in conflict management, 222
facilitating, 196, 198
rules for, 195–96
set breaking and, 194–95
Synergy Effect in, 195

Broken Record technique, 155–
    56
Bryant, Bear, 52, 115
Butkus, Dick, 169

Carroll, Archie, 119
Clarification in Reflective
    Listening, 132, 134–35, 140
Class distinctions, 178–79
Close-Ended Questions, 128–31
leading, 131
Rephrasing as, 134
rhetorical, 129
Coding Process, 122–25
Columbus, Christopher, 189
Communication, 120, 142–44,
    148. See also Assertiveness;
    Reflective Listening
in team meetings, 177–78
Competing (Ruben), 180–81
Competition, conflict
    management and, 224–25
Compromise in conflict
    management, 217–20
drawbacks of, 217–19
Synergy and, 220, 222–23
Conflict management, 207–25
competition and, 224–25
Consequences in, 217
5/5 style, 217–20
individuality and, 207–9
Involvement in, 213, 217, 221–
    22
9/9 style, 210, 220–25
9/1 style, 214–17
1/9 style, 210–14
zero-sum game and beyond,
    223–25
Conn, Hank, 173
Consensus, 196–200
definition of, 197
facilitating, 198–200
set breaking and, 199–200

Consequences, 7–17, 78–99. *See also* Negative reinforcement; Positive reinforcement; Punishment; Reinforcement
  appropriateness of, 85–86, 110–11
  in conflict management, 217
  consistency of, 86, 111–12
  definition of, 8, 102
  demotivation, 11–13, 182–83, 193, 213
  Extinction Effect, 17–18, 79–81, 83–84, 93, 97
  fine-tuning the system and, 109–12
  4:1 Syndrome and, 14–16
  justice of, 85–86, 111
  manipulation of, 8–9, 13–14, 16–18
  of Recording, 49–51
  Satiation Principle, 112
  in team building, 175–76
  timeliness of, 84–85, 97, 109–10
Consistency of Consequences, 86, 111–12
Constructive criticism, 82
Contingent (naturally occurring) reinforcement, 90–92
Control in conflict management, 214–17
  drawbacks of, 216
  Reflective Listening in, 216–17
Cooperation in team meetings, 176
Copies of Reinforcing Memos, 97
Cover Your Ass philosophy, 228
Creative Problem Solving, 187–206
  brainstorming, 191–96, 198, 222
  consensus in, 196–200

Creative Problem Solving (*cont.*)
  definition of, 187
  demotivation in, 193
  humor in, 194–95
  Influence-Accuracy Tangle, 200–3
  Involvement in, 198
  set breaking, 188–92, 194–95, 199–200
Credibility in conflict management, 212
Criticism
  constructive, 82
  Fogging during, 157–58
Cycles, 106

de Bono, Edward, 188, 191
Decision-making
  group. *See* Creative Problem Solving
  worker participation in, 64. *See also* Participative management
Decoding Process, 122–25
Defensiveness, 139
Degree of Discomfort, 149–52
Demanding, 143
Democratic management. *See* Participative management
Demotivation, 11–13
  in conflict management, 213
  in Creative Problem Solving, 193
  team building and, 182–83
Denial, 159
Depasqua, Fred, 165
Differential reinforcement, 90, 112
  errors in using, 184–85
  team building and, 182–86
Discomfort, Degree of, 149–52
Discounting, 139–40
Drucker, Peter, 4, 86

Eagles and mules, 178–82
  differential reinforcement for, 184
Education, 171–72
Efficiency experts, 49
Emmons, Michael, 143
Emotions, 137. *See also* Feelings
Empathy Statements, 135–40
  acceptance and, 136
  Assertiveness and, 156
  in conflict management, 221
  misuse of, 139
Enjoyment of work, productivity and, 59–60
Ethical Executive, The (Seibert), 183
Evaluation, 100–15
  ABC Model and, 101–4
  evolution and, 112–15
  fine-tuning the system, 107–12
  graphing in, 102–6
  in team building, 175
Evolution, Evaluation and, 112–15
Extinction Effect, 17–18, 79–81
  definition of, 17
  positive reinforcement vs., 93
  punishment and, 83–84
  timeliness of reinforcement and, 97
Extrinsic positive reinforcement, 89–90

Facilitating, 171–72
  in brainstorming sessions, 196
  consensus and, 198–200
  Influence-Accuracy Tangle and, 201–3
Featherbedding, 169
Feedback, 102. *See also* Evaluation in Reflective Listening, 125, 127

Feelings, Empathy Statements and, 135–40
55 mile-per-hour ratchet, 80–81
"Fight or flight" response, 144–48, 160
  examples of, 146–48
  Wind-Testing, 145
  Standing Ground, 145–46
Financial reward as motivator, 94, 170–71
Fine-tuning the system, 107–12
  Consequences and, 109–12
  Involvement and, 108–9
  Pinpointing and, 107–8
  Recording and, 108
5/5 style of conflict management, 217–20
  drawbacks of, 217–19
  Synergy and, 220, 222–23
Fogging, 157–58
Followers, 226–27
Follow up in team meetings, 174–75
Four Horsemen, 179
4:1 Syndrome, 13–16, 98–99
  Consequences and, 14–16
  definition of, 14
  punishment and, 88–89
Fry, Art, 190–91
Fun
  in Creative Problem Solving, 194–95
  productivity and, 59–60

General Motors, 114
Gilbey, Walter, 228
Gilliam, John, 93
Goal line, 56–57
Grant, Bud, 1–3, 93, 128, 143
  on punishment, 85
Graphing, 52–57
  of baseline average, 54–56

Graphing (cont.)
  in Evaluation, 102–6
  goal line in, 56–57
  of performance variables, 52–53
Group decision-making. See
    Creative Problem Solving

Halas, George, 4
Half, Robert, 227
"Hawthorne effect," 58–59
Hennion, Donald R., 71–74
Hewlett, William, 19, 65, 67
Hewlett-Packard, 19
Hornung, Paul, 165
"Human management," failure
    of, 18
Humor in Creative Problem
    Solving, 194–95
Hybrid ideas, 195

Ideas
  brainstorming and, 191–96,
    198, 222
  hybrid, 195
  inventing and, 190–91
  set breaking and, 188–92, 194–95, 199–200
Inattention, 124, 138, 141
Individuality, conflict
    management and, 207–9
Inertia, 148
Infallible Leader role, 215–16
Influence, 201
Influence-Accuracy Tangle,
    200–3
  facilitating and, 201–3
Information as a business asset,
    45–46. See also Recording
Input in conflict management,
    212
Insecurity, 143

Instability in conflict
    management, 212–13
Interrupting, 139
Intimidation, 129
Intrinsic positive reinforcement,
    89–92
Inventing, 190–91. See also Set
    breaking
Inverted pyramid organization,
    33–35
Involvement, 62–77
  Assertiveness and, 146
  benefits of, 68–74
  in conflict management, 213,
    217, 221–22
  in Creative Problem Solving,
    198
  fine-tuning the system and,
    108–9
  participative management, 18,
    22, 65–74
  productivity and, 65
  in questioning, 129
  Reflective Listening and, 137
  resistance to, 66–68
  Synergy Effect and, 74–77
  team building and, 169–71

Joiner, Tom, 135
Jones, Bobby, 115
Judging, 140
  avoidance of, in
    brainstorming, 195–96
Justice of Consequences, 85–86,
    111

Labor
  in inverted pyramid
    organization, 33–35
  participation of, in decision-
    making, 64
  Recording and, 47–51

Labor (cont.)
  in Self-Managed Work Teams, 72
Lance, Bert, 100
Language, ambiguity of, 123–24
Lasorda, Tommy, 86
Lateral thinking, 188–89
Lateral Thinking (de Bono), 188–89
Laziness, 169
Leaders, 226–27
  Infallible Leader role, 215–16
Leading questions, 131
Lenk, Hans, 167–69
Listening, 121. See also Reflective Listening
Lombardi, Vince, 4, 165, 230
Losing, 226–30
  fear of, 228–30
Louis, Joe, 230
Louis, Joe E., 44

"Made in America" (Montgomery), 51–52
Management
  authoritarian model, 165–71
  Conflict. See Conflict Management
  in inverted pyramid organization, 33–35
  motivation and, 3–4
  participative, 18, 22, 65–74
  Recording and, 47–51
Manipulation of Consequences, 8–9, 13–14, 16–18
  definition of, 13
  reluctance to use, 13–14
Mara, Wellington, 15–16
Marinaro, Ed, 93
Mayo, Elton, 58–59
Meaningful objectives, 38–39
Measuring objectives, 36–37
Meetings. See Team meetings

Memos, Reinforcing, 94–99
Mencken, H. L., 59
Messages, 123–24
  mixed, 119
Millikan, Roger, 98
Mixed messages, 119
Money as motivator, 94, 170–71
Montgomery, M. R., 51–52
Motivation
  definition of, 6
  demotivation vs., 11–13
  importance of, 4–7
  management and, 3–4
Motivators
  achievement, 94
  financial reward, 94, 170–71
  recognition, 94
"Muddle in the Middle," 81
Mules and eagles, 178–82
  differential reinforcement for, 184
Mutual solutions, 160–61

Naturally occurring (contingent) reinforcement, 90–92
Negative Assertion, 158–60
Negative Inquiry (negative questions), 131–32, 160–61
Negative reinforcement, 12, 17, 78. See also Constructive criticism; Demotivation; Punishment
  appropriateness of, 110–11
  Consequences of, 17
  in team building, 175–76
Neutral reinforcement, 17, 78–81
Nicklaus, Jack, 115
9/9 style of conflict management, 210, 220–25
  drawbacks of, 222–23
  zero-sum game and beyond, 223–25

9/1 style of conflict
   management, 214–17
   drawbacks of, 216
   Reflective Listening in, 216–17
Nonverbal Messages, 123–24
Nonverbal prompts, 128

Objectives
   meaningful, 38–39
   measuring, 36–37
   owning (setting), 40–42, 108,
     146, 223
   Pinpointing. See Pinpointing
     objectives
1/9 style of conflict
   management, 210–14
   Assertiveness and, 214
   drawbacks of, 212–13
Open-Ended questions, 128–32
   in conflict management, 221
   Negative Inquiry as, 160
   positive and negative, 131–32
   Rephrasing and, 134
Outcomes
   Behaviors vs., 27
   Pinpointing, 26, 27
Owning (setting) objectives, 40–
   42
   Assertiveness and, 146
   in conflict management, 223
   fine-tuning the system and,
     108
   supervisor approval and, 41–
     42

Participative huddle, 68–69
   team meetings as, 171
Participative management, 18,
   22, 65–74
   benefits of, 68–74
   resistance to, 66–68
Passiveness, 144–47
   in listening, 121

Pasteur, Louis, 189–90
Pegler, Westbrook, 44
People, productivity through,
   18–22
Performance variables, 52–54
   Behaviors as, 54
   choosing, 53–54
   graphing of, 52–53
Personal interests in conflict
   management, 220–21
Pinpointing Behaviors, 26–29
   fine-tuning the system and,
     107, 108
   Negative Inquiry in, 160
   quantifiability in, 29
   in Recording, 54
   specificity in, 28–29
   in Super Bowl IX (1975), 32–33
Pinpointing objectives, 26, 29–42
   attitude and, 32–33
   "bottom up" method of, 31,
     33–35
   at every level of organization,
     34–35, 41–42
   fine-tuning the system and,
     107–8
   meaningful, 38–39
   measuring, 36–37
   owning (setting), 40–42, 108,
     146, 223
   realistic, 37–38
   simple, 39–40
   in Superbowl IX (1975), 31–33
   in team meetings, 176–77
   "top down" approach to, 30,
     33–35
Pinpointing outcomes, 26, 27
Pitney Bowes, 70
Planning actions in team
   meetings, 176–77
Pope, Edwin, 179
Positive questions, 131–32

Positive reinforcement, 12, 14,
    78, 89–94
  appropriateness of, 110–11
  of changed Behavior, 88
  in conflict management, 217
  Consequences of, 16–17
  differential, 90, 112, 182–86
  errors in use of, 97–98
  Extinction Effect vs., 93
  extrinsic, 89–90
  fallacies regarding, 92–93
  intrinsic, 89–92
  in team building, 175–76
  timeliness of, 97, 109–10
Precision in Reinforcing Memos,
    96
Pre-emptive queries, 131
P.R.I.C.E. Motivation System,
    definition of, 22
Problem Solving, 140. See also
    Creative Problem Solving
  in team meetings, 176
Pro-Con charts, 199–200
Productivity
  enjoyment of work and, 59–60
  "Hawthorne effect" and, 58–
    59
  Involvement and, 65
  through people, 18–22
Prompting, 127–28
Psychological Services of
    Pittsburgh, 94
Punishment, 82–89
  Antecedents of, 84
  appropriateness of, 85–86,
    110–11
  Behavior-correcting, 87–88
  consistency in, 86
  Extinction Effect and, 83–84
  4:1 Syndrome and, 88–89
  timeliness of, 84–85
  warning before, 84, 85

Punishment Effect, 82–83
  aggressive Behavior and, 147
  in conflict management, 215
  definition of, 82

Quantifiability
  in Pinpointing Behaviors, 29
  in Recording, 53
Questions
  Close-Ended, 128–31, 134
  Involvement and, 129
  leading, 131
  negative (Negative Inquiry),
    131–32, 160–61
  Open-Ended, 128–32, 134, 160,
    221
  positive, 131–32
  pre-emptive, 131
  rhetorical, 129

Range, 104–5
  definition of, 104
Rashad, Ahmad, 68
Realistic objectives, 37–38
Receivers, 122
Recognition as motivator, 94
Recording, 43–61
  Assertion Scale, 148–54
  benefits of, 57–61
  Consequences of, 49–51
  failure of businesses to do, 45–
    52
  fine-tuning the system and,
    108
  graphing in, 52–57
  management and, 47–51
  Pinpointing Behaviors in, 54
  quantifiability in, 53
  specificity in, 53–54
  in team building, 175
  in team meetings, 175–76
  workers and, 47–51

Reflective Listening, 119–41
  Assertiveness and, 156, 157
  benefits of, 127
  clarification in, 132, 134–35,
    140
  Coding and Decoding, 122–25
  in conflict management 216–
    17, 221
  definition of, 124–25
  Empathy Statements, 135–40,
    156
  feedback in, 125, 127
  Involvement and, 137
  Negative Inquiry in, 160
  objections to, 126–27
  Open-Ended Questions, 128–
    32, 134, 160
  Prompting, 127–28
  reinforcement in, 132, 135
  Rephrasing, 125, 132–35
  seven Don'ts of, 138–40
Regularity of team meetings, 173
Rehearsing in Reflective
    Listening, 138
Reinforcement, 140
  contingent (naturally
    occurring), 90–92
  of cooperation, in team
    meetings, 176
  differential, 90, 112, 182–86
  negative. See Negative
    reinforcement
  neutral, 17, 78–81
  positive. See Positive
    reinforcement
  in Reflective Listening, 127,
    132, 135
Reinforcing Memos, 94–99
  checklist for writing, 96–97
  errors in use of, 97–98
  Synergy Effect in, 97

Rephrasing, 125, 132–35
  Close- and Open-Ended
    Questions and, 134
  Empathy Statements, 135–40
Resistance
  aggression and, 158
  to Involvement, 66–68
  to participative management,
    66–68
Resolving conflict, 209. See also
    Conflict management
Response Probability, 149–52
Reviewing performance data in
    team meetings, 175
Rhetorical questions, 129
Risk-taking, winning and, 228–
    31
Rockefeller, John D., 3, 81
Rockne, Knute, 11
  team building by, 179
Roosevelt, Theodore, 200
Rosow, Jerome, 63–64
Royal, Darrell, 26
Ruben, Harvey, 180–81

Sandbagging, 169
Satiation Principle, 112
Scorekeeping. See Recording
Seibert, Donald, 183
Self-concept, 143
Self-Managed Work Teams, 72
Senders, 122
Set breaking, 188–92
  brainstorming and, 194–95
  consensus and, 199–200
  encouragement of, 191
Setting (owning) objectives, 40–
    42
  Assertiveness and, 146
  in conflict management, 223
  fine-tuning the system and,
    108

Setting (owning) objectives
(cont.)
supervisor approval and, 41–
42
Simplicity of objectives, 39–40
Skinner, B. F., 6, 8
Smith, Manuel, 155–60
Solutions, mutual, 160–61
Specificity
in Pinpointing Behaviors, 28–
29
in Recording, 53–54
in Reflective Listening, 133
Stability in conflict
management, 212–13
Standing Ground, 145–46
Stengel, Casey, 208
Super Bowl IX (1975), 31–33
Pinpointing Behaviors in, 32–
33
Pinpointing objectives in, 31–
33
positive reinforcement in,
109–10
Supervisor approval and
ownership of objectives, 41–
42
Synergy Effect, 74–77
in brainstorming, 195
exercise for illustrating, 75–77
Involvement and, 74–77
in Reinforcing Memos, 97
Synergy in conflict management,
220–25
beyond zero-sum game, 223–
25
drawbacks of, 222–23

Talking, 142
Task assignment in team
meetings, 177
Taylor, Fred, 165

Team building, 165–86
authoritarianism and, 167–71
Consequences in, 175–76,
182–83
differential reinforcement and,
182–86
eagles and mules, 178–82, 184
Evaluation in, 175
Involvement in, 169–71
meetings for. See Team
meetings
Recording in, 175
winning and, 231–32
Team decision-making. See
Creative Problem Solving
Team Dynamics (Lenk), 167–69
Team meetings, 171–78
brainstorming in, 191–96
communication in, 177–78
consensus in, 196–200
facilitating, 171–72, 196, 198–
203
Follow up in, 174–75
Influence-Accuracy Tangle in,
201–3
Pinpointing objectives in, 176–
77
planning actions in, 176–77
Problem Solving in, 176
reinforcing in, 175–76
reviewing in, 175
rules for, 172–73
task assignment in, 177
Thinking
lateral, 188–89
vertical, 188, 198
"Time and motion" studies, 49–
50
Timeliness of Consequences, 84–
85, 97, 109–10
Extinction Effect and, 97
Tinglehoff, Mick, 68

Top down approach to
Pinpointing objectives, 30,
33–35
Trends, 104–5
Truman, Harry, 153
Twain, Mark, 44

Understanding, Empathy
Statements and, 136

Validating in Reflective
Listening, 127
Verbal Messages, 123–24
Verbal prompts, 127–28
Vertical thinking, 188
consensus and, 198
Voting, 197–98

Walsh, Adam, 179
Warnings before punishment,
84, 85
Watson, John, 6
When I Say No, I Feel Guilty
(Smith), 155–60

White, Ed, 68
Whitney, Eli, 190
Wind-Testing, 145
Winning, 226–32
fear of losing and, 228–30
risk-taking and, 228–31
team building and, 231–32
Winter, Max, 93–94
Work, attitudes toward, 64
Workers
in inverted pyramid
organization, 33–35
participation of, in decision-
making, 64
Recording and, 47–51
in Self-Managed Work Teams,
72
Work in America Institute, 63–
64

Zero-sum game, 223–25
going beyond, in conflict
management, 224–25